D0820679

THE
Ayub Khan Era
POLITICS IN PAKISTAN

ZIRING, Lawrence. **The Ayub Khan era; politics in Pakistan, 1958–1969. Syracuse, 1971. 234p map tab bibl 78-134394. 10.00. SBN 8156-0075-5**

Tightly written, well organized, and documented account by an American political scientist directly familiar with Pakistan's internal scene. He poses the theme that the Ayub era may best be classified as one of lost opportunity. Appearing on scene at the right moment, Ayub unfortunately was not the man for the job. He failed to accomplish national integration, to ease the disparity between East and West Pakistan, to close the gap between landlords, peasants, and bureacrats, or to satisfy the urban sophisticates. The Ayub legacy bequeathed a poorly conceived system for political stability, economic progress for the few, and social stagnation for the many. Ziring warns that radical innovations are essential if Pakistan is to survive and develop as Ayub critics have warned for years. Study has marginal value for Pakistani experts, being suited for undergraduates who should read it in connection with Sayeed, *Political system of Pakistan* (CHOICE, Nov. 1967), Von Vorys, *Political development in Pakistan* (CHOICE, Feb. 1966), Braibanti, *Research on the bureaucracy of Pakistan* (CHOICE, Dec.

1966). and others, for the tone and content of the book lacks overall balance. Especially disappointing are the discussions of Pakistan's foreign policy, an inadequate analysis of the 1965 election, and the impact of American aid programs. Index.

CHOICE   *MAY '71*

History, Geography & Travel

Asia & Oceania

DS
38.4
Z81

Asia & Oceania

LAWRENCE ZIRING

THE

Ayub Khan Era

POLITICS IN PAKISTAN

1958–1969

SYRACUSE UNIVERSITY PRESS

Copyright © 1971
by Syracuse University Press
Syracuse, New York

ALL RIGHTS RESERVED

First Edition

LIBRARY
APR 22 1971
UNIVERSITY OF THE PACIFIC

233505

Library of Congress
Catalog Card Number: 78-135394

Standard Book Number 8156-0075-5

Manufactured in the United States of America

For My Mother and Father

GLOSSARY

Anna: Small coin.

Ansar: Civil armed guards.

Babu: Gentleman, father in Hindi, but when used disparagingly by Muslims connotes cunning merchant or moneylender.

Baradari: Families extending from a common ancestor.

Badshah: King.

Begum: Title for a married woman (Mrs.).

Charpoy: Simple bed of woven string on a wooden frame.

Chowkidar: Watchman.

Eid: Muslim festival day.

Hindu Mahasabha: Militant Hindu organization in India.

Hookah: water-cooled pipe.

Inshallah: "If God wills it."

Izzat: Tradition of respect, honor.

Jagirdari: Landed estate (form of land tenure common under the Moghuls).

Jan Sanghis: Members of a Hindu political party in India.

Kammi: Artisan or simple laboring castes.

Kumara: Community assistance in West Pakistan (usually under government supervision).

Lathi: Long, steel-tipped club usually carried by police on riot duty.

Maang: Voluntary help. (Also maangali, blandoror, hashari.)

Maulana: Religious title, but not necessarily a religious personage. (Also maulvi.)

Mohalla: Street or neighborhood in a town.

Mujahid: Defender of the Faith (from Jihad, Holy War).

Panchayat: Local or village assembly and court.

Patwari: Government servant at the village level who maintains land revenue records. (Also lambardar.)

Pucca: Finished item, proper, complete, ripe, etc.

Qaid-i-Azam: The Great Leader. (Title bestowed on Mohammad Ali Jinnah.)

Ramadan: Month of Fasting.

Sardar: Tribal chief.

Sarkar: The government.

Taluka: District revenue subdivision in Sind.

Tehsil: Similar subdivision in West Pakistan.

Thana: Subdivision of a district in East Pakistan. (Also a police station in West Pakistan.)

Ulema: Men of religious learning.

Waqf: Charitable endowment, usually land.

Zamindar: Landowner, landlord.

FOREWORD

EVENTS in Pakistan have come full circle. In March 1969, as in October 1958, the military declared martial law. Once again a general has taken up the reins of government. Now, as then, a prevailing constitution has been abrogated. Now, as then, there are intentions to write a new constitution, reconstitute the political system, purge the corrupt bureaucrats and resolve socioeconomic inequities. Now, as then, there is the ubiquitous promotion of modernization schemes.

It is all so familiar, it seems strange that there should be so much talk about a new beginning—or is it a return to an old beginning?

It is perhaps necessary to recall that Ayub Khan came to power amidst turmoil and apprehension. The nine-year battle over constitution-making (1947–56) had taken its toll. When the document was finally presented to the nation the political situation had so deteriorated that legal instruments were of little consequence. Within two years of the Constitution's promulgation, and before general elections could be held, the Army put an end to the political experiment that it envisaged. Pakistani politicians, schooled in a version of British parliamentarianism, cried foul, but their vision of democracy faded in the aftermath of the declaration of martial law.

Despite forty-four months of martial law, Ayub Khan persistently stressed his intention to restore representative government to Pakistan. However, he always qualified this objective with the view that it must be intelligible to those not sharing the sophistication of erstwhile political elites. Moreover, Pakistan's peasant masses were not only to be familiar with, they also were called upon to help operate the new system which Ayub naively but deliberately called Basic Democracies. These Basic Democracies were an insult to the intelligence of the politically conscious and, coupled with the severe restrictions imposed on the more prominent politicians, quickly brought Ayub the opprobrium of the attentive public. Furthermore, with the nationalized "steel frame" of colonial government dominating the country's political and economic life, Ayub's statements about building democracy were treated with outright contempt.

Ayub Khan had a standard reply for those who questioned his sociopolitical engineering. He would chide his interrogators with the comment that he had read the book of Pakistan, that his policies were designed to fit the genius of his people rather than the genius of former conquerors. But there was a paradox in this conception. The bureaucratic system which Ayub substituted for the parliamentary institution was also an alien contrivance. True, the British structured their colonial administration over a Moghul foundation, but the fact remains that bureaucracy more than parliamentary government was identified with distant foreign dominance. Hence, the subordination of the Basic Democracies to the higher bureaucracy was perceived as reinforcing the rule of privileged elites rather than promoting general participation.

With the new 1962 Ayub Constitution in force, the President was unable to resist the demand that political parties be reinstated. And although uncomfortable with the arrangement, he was compelled to organize and lead his own party. Nevertheless, Ayub's performance made political parties anachronistic and, just as the opposition was handicapped by the bureaucratized governmental structure, so the President's party was handicapped by its failure to develop coherence.

Ayub was shielded from the realities that moved his country and, because he leaned so heavily on the bureaucrats, political institutions were allowed to atrophy. The bureaucracy sustained Ayub in the 1964–65 election campaign. They gave yeoman service during and after the brief Indo-Pakistani war and the popularly distasteful Tashkent Agreement. When illness incapacitated the President in the early months of 1968, the bureaucracy filled the vacancy with alacrity and dedication. Thus, when Ayub was finally pressured into passing his authority to General Yahya Khan in March 1969, it was not surprising that the higher bureaucracy remained omnipresent or that the new regime should perpetuate the administrative state. It can be argued that martial law is merely an extreme manifestation of the administrative state, a form of crisis management given the peculiarities of the system. Hence General Yahya Khan's decisions to revive political activity, to hold the long-postponed general elections, to order that a newly elected national assembly draft still another constitution (once more along parliamentary lines), must be seen against a background of political impotence and administrative dominance.

The author has benefited from a reasonably long acquaintance with Pakistan, Pakistanis, and persons genuinely interested in this South Asian country. I was first exposed to Pakistan while a graduate student at Columbia University where I had the privilege of studying with Dr. Ishtiaq Husain Qureshi. Dr. Qureshi had served as Pakistan's Minister

for Education until 1954. He is credited with the authorship of the
Objectives Resolution which was to guide the early constitution-makers
in preparing a document which would be parliamentary in structure but
Islamic in spirit. I am grateful to him and Columbia University for send-
ing me to Pakistan in 1957 and 1959–60. I am indebted to Mohammad
Vardag Khan, Latif Sherwani, and Azizur Rahman for introducing me
to the people of Pakistan in those first trying days. I am also appreciative
to Dr. K. J. Newman, who as chairman of the Department of Political
Science at Dacca University invited me to join his department as a
visiting lecturer in 1959–60. It was during this stay in Pakistan that I
conducted my doctoral research. My dissertation, which focused on East
Pakistan's relations with the Central Government from 1947 to 1958,
provided me with a solid platform from which to launch the study contained in these pages.

Later, Syracuse University was to send me to Pakistan, this time as
an adviser to the Pakistan Administrative Staff College situated in
Lahore. I remained in Pakistan from 1964 through 1966, lecturing,
studying, and writing. This book took shape during this period.

The first draft of the manuscript was completed prior to Ayub's fall
from power. Initially, my purpose was to weigh the Ayub administration's failures alongside its reputed accomplishments. In its present form
the book highlights the bureaucratic regime's seeming inability-cum-
reluctance to cope with fundamental issues, Ayub's relative insensitivity
and misperceptions, and the complacent arrogance of privileged elites.
Ayub wanted the affection of his people but failed to ingratiate himself
with them. He was never a popular leader. Insulated from the real world
by a bureaucratic apparatus, surrounded by experts and advisers, foreign
as well as domestic, he could not touch his people, nor they be thrilled
by him. How well the author recalls the many times Ayub came to
Lahore and how indifferent the population was to his comings and go-
ings. The huge crowds and the outpouring of spontaneous sentiment
for the visiting Chinese Communist leaders in 1966 will always stand in
vivid contrast.

The Ayub Era, with the passage of time, eventually may be known
as an interregnum in Pakistan's history or, more likely, a lost opportunity.
It is the author's opinion that Ayub came upon the scene at the right
moment but unfortunately was not the man for the job. To paraphrase
Nasser, the role continues to search for a leader. Future Pakistani authorities undoubtedly can learn something from Ayub's accomplishments and shortcomings. It is hoped that studies like the present volume
can assist in this effort.

For purposes of explication and clarity the book has been divided into two parts. Part I is presented in the form of a political survey. The quasi-chronological approach should enable even the uninitiated reader to identify the important personalities, their relationships, and the subsequent events which set the dynamics for the Ayub Era. The section avoids pure description, however. I have sought to weave into the scenario situations and interpretations that may enhance understanding and enliven the narrative.

Part II aims at linking the foregoing political experience with aspects of the traditional political environment that transcend periodic explanation. In this sociopolitical section special emphasis is given to analyzing the bureaucratic legacy, the rural power structure, and the somewhat disconnected and hence incoherent urban intelligentsia. Intelligent Pakistanis seem always to suggest that the real difficulty in evolving a viable democratic system lies in their preference for a multiplicity of political organizations. As the lament goes: "If only Pakistanis were capable of establishing and operating two or three political parties. Then responsive and responsible civilian government would be assured." Such statements may be sincere, but nevertheless betray a myopic awareness of the institutional setting conditioning Pakistan's political culture.

The bureaucratic–rural–urban triangle shapes political events, and thus far has been largely unaltered by episodic changes in the country's political elites. In the parliamentary period, as during the presidential decade, identical compelling forces fixed the operative patterns and therefore the limits of systemic development. The future would appear to be confined to the same configuration, and this is briefly touched upon in the Epilogue.

I want to take this opportunity to thank collectively those anonymous persons who encouraged and assisted me in producing this study. I would like to show my appreciation to Professor Wayne A. Wilcox of Columbia University and Professor Walter D. Jacobs of Maryland University for their reading of the early draft. I would also wish to recognize my association with Professors Irving Swerdlow and Guthrie Birkhead of Syracuse University. They might be interested to learn that their support provided the impetus for this study. Finally, I must express a debt of gratitude to my wife, Raye, without whose help this book would never have materialized. Her dedication and unfailing industry will never be forgotten. At the same time it must be stated that errors of fact or interpretation are my responsibility alone.

Western Michigan University   L. Z.
15 April 1970

CONTENTS

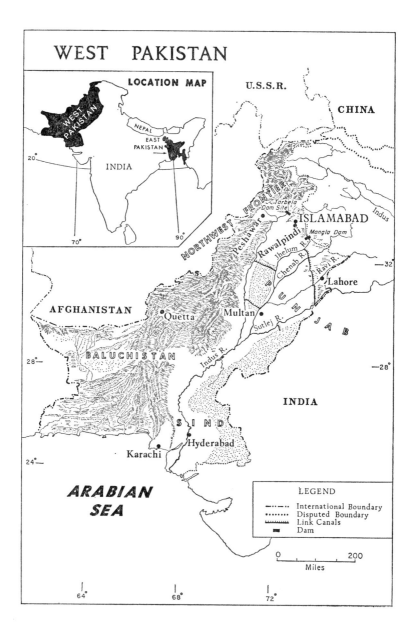

WEST PAKISTAN

LOCATION MAP

U.S.S.R.

CHINA

WEST PAKISTAN

NEPAL

EAST PAKISTAN

INDIA

20°

70°

90°

NORTHWEST FRONTIER

Tarbela Dam Site

ISLAMABAD

Indus

Peshawar

Rawalpindi

Mangla Dam

Jhelum R.

32°

Chenab R.

Ravi R.

P U N J A B

Lahore

AFGHANISTAN

Quetta

Multan

Sutlej R.

BALUCHISTAN

Indus R.

28°

28°

INDIA

S I N D

Hyderabad

Karachi

24°

ARABIAN
SEA

LEGEND

———·—·— International Boundary
············ Disputed Boundary
� Link Canals
▬ Dam

0   200
Miles

64°   68°   72°

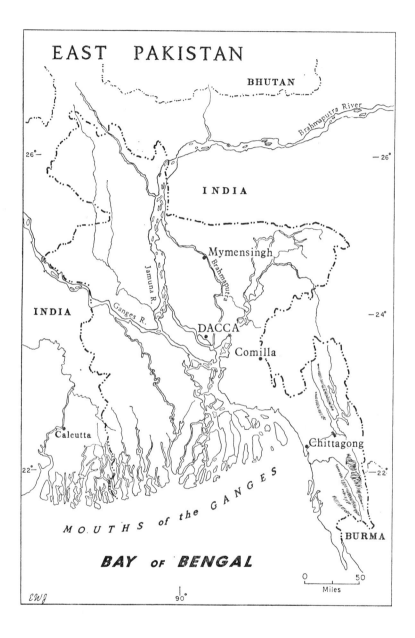

EAST PAKISTAN

BHUTAN

Brahmaputra River

26°

INDIA

Mymensingh

Jamuna R.

Brahmaputra

Ganges R.

DACCA

Comilla

24°

INDIA

Calcutta

Chittagong

22°

22°

MOUTHS of the GANGES

BURMA

BAY OF BENGAL

0   50
Miles

EWJ

90°

Chapter 1

Ayub Khan: Genesis, Philosophy, and Reforms

MANY still insist Ayub Khan was a dictator. Less critical observers charcterized his rule as benign but firm. Still others saw his leadership as beneficent or enlightened. Doubtless the same could be remarked about any leader. But what more can be said of this particular personality? He practiced none of Sukarno's flamboyance. He gave the impression of being more rational than Nasser. While possessing neither the charisma of an Ataturk nor the brooding introspection of a Nehru, he could still be described as a visionary. Unlike Nkrumah, however, he was indifferent to grand designs. Ayub clung to power for more than ten years but was never absolutely powerful. Perhaps this should be his epitaph.

A source for new ideas, a reformer of sorts, he sought institutional devices for changing the Pakistani life-style, but in the last analysis he failed in most of his political undertakings. Ayub tried but could not construct an operative political organization. He neglected to enlist the support of the public and leaned too heavily on the conventional bureaucracy. He persisted in widening the gulf which lay between his government and the nation's youth. Paradoxically, while his attention focused on the mechanics of social mobilization, his policies stimulated fragmentation and alienation. He dreamed of a new Pakistan but remained a prisoner of his own and his country's historic legacy.

Ayub could not be effective without popular support. For the same reason his regime's legitimacy suffered. His inability to build a political base, his thinking that government meant administration and that politics was to be eliminated rather than understood, all contributed to his downfall. Pakistan is yet to experience a genuine revolution, but Ayub Khan's personal decline resulted from nothing less than popular revolt.

Ayub's philosophy of government meshed with Pakistan's vice-regal tradition. In a society accustomed to paternalism the great-leader syndrome is unavoidable. Even an astute scholar like Samuel Huntington could write: "More than any other political leader in a modernizing

1

country after World War II, Ayub Khan came close to filling the role of a Solon or Lycurgus or 'Great Legislator' on the Platonic or Rousseauian model." [1] Infallibility in an era of increasing sophistication, however, is becoming less palatable. Newly independent countries display a need for strong, decisive leadership but they also shelter persons who are just as concerned with limiting the uses of arbitrary power. Whereas for some, stability is a *sine qua non*—the first purpose of government—for others human fulfillment is given priority status. A man with the lifestyle of Ayub Khan would neither be able to see nor, if he could, understand this.

Nonetheless, Ayub was no simple personality. Even as President of Pakistan he craved solitude. Even while in the thick of public activity he appeared somewhat distant and remote. He was not adept at communicating his policies, and his personal habits complicated his task with all strata of society. Perhaps this partially explains his unpopularity and his own determined aloofness. It is difficult to say even of those men who worked with him on an intimate basis that they shared a common bond of affection. That he enjoyed their obedience and secured their loyalty is another matter. Generals Azam, Sheikh, Musa, and Yahya Khan and bureaucrats like Akhter Husain, G Mueenuddin, S. M. Yusuf, Fida Hasan, and Altaf Gauhar served him dutifully. On the political side he called upon such disparate figures as Malik Amir Mohammed Khan, Abdul Monem Khan, and Zulfikar Ali Bhutto to buttress his authority. Their remarkable service spread over a major segment of the Ayub Era. The professions also responded, with intellectuals like Manzur Qadir, I. H. Qureshi, S. M. Zafar, and Z. A. Suleri playing significant roles.

Personalities like these influenced Ayub's decisions. They advised him, and often he acted in accordance with their advice, but only in rare circumstances and for brief periods did they ever sway him.

Although relative political stability was achieved up to the rioting in late 1968, the changing complexion of the Ayub regime deserves attention. There were at least five different cabinets. The first was formed after the exiling of President Iskander Mirza in the period of martial law; the second evolved under the Presidential (Election and Constitution) Order of 1960; the third was made necessary by the promulgation of the new constitution in 1962; the fourth was a natural outcome of the presidential election of January 1965; and the fifth developed with the "resignations" of Zulfikar Ali Bhutto and the Governor of West Pakistan, Malik Amir Mohammad Khan, in the summer and autumn of 1966, respectively.[2] The following illustrates this:

GOVERNORS

EAST PAKISTAN

October 1958	Zakir Husain	April 1960
April 1960	Lt. Gen. Mohammad Azam Khan	May 1962
May 1962	Ghulam Faruque	October 1962
October 1962	Abdul Monem Khan	March 1969
March 1969	M. N. Huda	March 1969

WEST PAKISTAN

October 1958	Akhter Husain	April 1960
April 1960	Malik Amir Mohammad Khan	September 1966
September 1966	General Mohammad Musa	March 1969
March 1969	Yusuf Haroon	March 1969

PRESIDENTIAL CABINETS

1. OCTOBER 28, 1958—FEBRUARY 17, 1960:

Lt. Gen. Mohammad Azam Khan	Mohammad Shoaib
Lt. Gen. W. A. Burki	Abul Kasem Khan
Manzur Qadir	Habibur Rahman
Mohammad Ibrahim	Zulfikar Ali Bhutto
Lt. Gen. K. M. Sheikh	Muhammad Hafizur Rahman

2. FEBRUARY 17, 1960—JUNE 8, 1962:

Lt. Gen. Azam Khan *	Habibur Rahman
Manzur Qadir	Zulfikar Ali Bhutto
Lt. Gen. W. A. Burki	Muhammad Hafizur Rahman *
Mohammad Ibrahim *	Akhter Husain *
Lt. Gen. K. M. Sheikh	Zakir Husain
Mohammad Shoaib	Abdul Qadir
Abul Kasem Khan	Mohammad Munir
F. M. Khan	

Note: * Completed assignment before June 8, 1962.

3. JUNE 8, 1962—JANUARY 2, 1965:

Mohammad Ali (Bogra) *	A. K. M. Fazlul Quadar Chowdhury *
Mohammad Munir *	Shaikh Khursheed Ahmad
Abdul Qadir *	Rana Abdul Hamid
Abdul Monem Khan *	Mohammad Shoaib
Habibulah Khan	A. T. M. Mustafa
Wahiduzzaman	Abdullah-al-Mahmood
Zulfikar Ali Bhutto	Abdul Waheed Khan
Abdus Sobur Khan	Al-Haj Abd-Allah Zaheer-ud-Din
	(Lal Mia)

Note: * Completed assignment before January 2, 1965.

4. January 2, 1965—August 31, 1966:

Zulfikar Ali Bhutto *   Kazi Anwarul Haque
Mohammad Shoaib *   A. H. M. Shams-ud-Doha
Khwaja Shahabuddin   Altaf Hussain
Ghulam Faruque   Ali Akbar Khan
Abdus Sobur Khan   N. M. Uquaili
S. M. Zafar   Sharifuddin Pirzada

Note: * Completed assignment before August 31, 1966.

5. August 31, 1966—March 25, 1969:

Ajmal Ali Chowdhury   S. M. Zafar
Ghulam Faruque †   Kazi Anwarul Haque
N. M. Uquaili   A. H. M. Shams-ud-Doha
Khwaja Shahabuddin   Altaf Hussain §
Sharifuddin Pirzada ‡   Ali Akbar Khan *
Abdus Sobur Khan   Nawabzada Abdul Ghaffar Khan
Vice Admiral A. R. Khan   of Hoti
                              Mian Arshad Husain

Note: * Completed assignment November 30, 1966. Portfolio transferred to Vice
Admiral A. R. Khan.
† Resigned 1967.   ‡ Resigned 1968.   § Resigned 1968.

In the fall of 1966 not a single member of Ayub Khan's first presidential cabinet remained. The last to leave were Zulfikar Ali Bhutto and Mohammad Shoaib. But they departed for entirely different reasons. Bhutto because he could no longer support Ayub's policies and Shoaib because he so closely identified with those same policies.[3] Bhutto represented the anti-United States faction in the President's cabinet whereas Shoaib was undeniably pro-West in his orientation. Pakistan's international posture affected Ayub's control and it was considered expedient to balance Bhutto's departure with that of the Finance Minister.

The Making of a Leader

Ayub never received high marks either as politician or statesman. There are even those who denigrate his military expertise. Looking back over the years, however, there is still much to be admired. Ayub was born on May 14, 1907, of Pathan parents with landed interests in Hazara in West Pakistan.[4] Educated in the Muslim University at Aligarh, he later joined the Royal Military College, Sandhurst, and was commissioned in 1928. He commanded an infantry battalion in World War II and opted for Pakistan when the British withdrew from South

Asia. While president of the Services Selection Board he was selected by Prime Minister Liaquat Ali Khan to represent Pakistan at the headquarters of the Punjab Boundary Force. Ayub Khan was a colonel on the day of Pakistan's independence. Later the Qaid-i-Azam, Mohammad Ali Jinnah, promoted him to brigadier. Posted in Waziristan on the North West Frontier, he was given responsibility for evacuating the troops from tribal territory; the withdrawal was a deliberate move aimed at securing the friendship of the warlike Pathans, who were also being wooed by the Afghans. After the successful handling of this operation he was promoted to major general and given his assignment in East Pakistan.

On January 7, 1948, he assumed his duties as General Officer Commanding in East Pakistan, replacing the ailing British GOC. East Pakistan was a depressing post in the years immediately following independence. The new GOC was compelled to operate with limited resources while the bulk of the Army was locked in a struggle with elements of the Indian Army in Kashmir. Ayub's task was to strengthen the defenses of the eastern province. Colonel Mohammed Ahmad insists that:

> He [Ayub] was the only Pakistani General who was virtually the Commander-in-Chief of an isolated province with all its problems and peculiarities.[5]

Major General Ayub Khan faced a multitude of critical problems in East Pakistan and his performance did not pass unnoticed; though junior to a number of other officers, Liaquat Ali Khan recommended to Governor General Khwaja Nazimuddin, Jinnah's successor, that Ayub Khan be given command of the Pakistani Army after the British General Sir Douglas D. Gracey retired. When the appointment was finally announced there was consternation in military ranks.[6] M. N. Bhatti recalls:

> The decision was a highly unexpected one. General Ayub was neither seniormost nor most distinct so far as his actual achievements were concerned.[7]

What Bhatti implies is that, unlike some of the more celebrated Pakistani generals, Ayub Khan did not participate in the Kashmir War of 1947–48. It is also interesting to note that Major General Ayub Khan was selected as the first Pakistani commander in chief on September 6, 1950, a time when the Pakistani and Indian Prime Ministers were hoping to reduce the tension existing between their two countries.

It is a known fact that Liaquat wanted peace with India and insisted his forces accept the U.N. cease-fire proposal for Kashmir.[8] It is also known that a number of high-ranking Pakistani military officers were conspiring against the Prime Minister and planned to resume the war in Kashmir. This would appear to be the principal reason for the selection of Ayub Khan. Serving in the remote province of East Pakistan he was insulated from the activities of his brother officers. Above all, a professional tradition was to be upheld and on becoming commander in chief Ayub was expected to support his political leaders. His Aligarh background was undoubtedly another important factor in his selection. The test of Ayub's loyalty was not long in coming. The dissatisfaction of the would-be conspirators apparently intensified with the appointment of Ayub Khan and six months after assuming his new responsibilities he was called upon to crush the military dissidents in the celebrated "Rawalpindi Conspiracy."

Although the Prime Minister reported that the attempt to overthrow the government was directed by forces under the control of international communism,[9] the Prime Minister's handling of the Kashmir problem was primary.[10]

General Ayub was first among those marked for elimination according to the President's biographer, Colonel Mohammed Ahmad, and he relates how the new commander in chief reported the news to his staff:

> Soon after the Commander-in-Chief's car arrived. There was absolute silence in the hall. General Ayub walked in with a very serious and sad look on his face. Like many others, I felt that the announcement was not going to be a happy one. I can still recall the first few sentences of General Ayub's announcement. He said, "Gentlemen, it is with a very sad heart that I have to inform you of a most unfortunate development." Then he paused and looked at the audience from one end to the other and continued, "The Government have conclusive evidence that there has been a conspiracy by some army officers for the overthrow of the Central Government and so they have arrested the C.G.S., and some other officers involved in this conspiracy."
>
> The entire audience gasped in shock, as the staggering announcement settled in their thoughts. After some more remarks about the conspiracy, General Ayub's face flushed with emotion and his choked voice and eyes full of tears gave vent to his pent-up feelings. He said, "Gentlemen, I hope you realize that Pakistan was created not for us, but for all our children and all the generations that will

follow. Had this conspiracy succeeded in its nefarious objectives, that would have resulted in the end of Pakistan." He then walked out of the conference room.[11]

Although the officers involved in the unsuccessful coup were first imprisoned (along with several civilians, among them the noted leftist journalist and poet, Faiz Ahmad Faiz) and dismissed from the service, they were eventually released to enter private life. Clearly, no one in high office wanted to publicize the facts behind the conspiracy and the affair was permitted to fade into the historical past. If Ayub Khan wished to make an example of the conspirators it is not on the record. As the officers were no longer in the Army, the matter was out of his jurisdiction, and he seemed to feel that a public trial would only result in the nation and Army becoming polarized.[12]

The Politics of Crisis

While playing a major role in rebuilding the Pakistan Army, Ayub also devoted considerable attention to the political system. The period 1951–58 was turbulent and on numerous occasions the Army was called upon to restore order. The riots and general lawlessness in East Pakistan in 1952, 1954, 1956, and 1958; the assassination of Liaquat Ali Khan in 1951; the Punjab disturbances of 1953; the persistent clashes with tribal and Afghan paramilitary forces on the North West Frontier; and the demonstrations in Karachi in 1953 and 1957 are cases in point. Ayub stood by as Khwaja Nazimuddin (who resigned the Governor General's office to become the Prime Minister after the death of Liaquat Ali Khan) was dismissed by Ghulam Mohammad. He acquiesced when, in October 1954, Ghulam Mohammad dissolved the Constituent Assembly. There can be no doubt that Ayub Khan supported these actions. Without the Army's support they would never have been successful.

The general was convinced that politicians were an irresponsible lot; with Qaid-i-Azam and Liaquat no longer present to restrain them, self-aggrandizement was their sole concern. This, he rationalized, was the major reason for disorder in the country. It also explained why the long-promised constitution was still in the talking stage many years after the grant of independence. Centrifugal forces were built into the Pakistani design. The country, split physically, was also culturally and economically disparate; poverty and illiteracy were widespread; and the general population was totally unfamiliar with the process of parliamentary government. Instead of laboring to correct these national problems the politicians exploited them for their private gain. This was Ayub's personal reading, as stated in his autobiography, but it helps to explain why he felt compelled to link forces with the bureaucrats and why he condescended to join the newly formed "Cabinet of Talents" as Defense Minister in 1954.

At that time Ayub Khan believed that the Army's primary role was to defend the country from would-be external enemies. And the general was convinced that the military building program he envisioned had only begun. Agreements had been entered into with the United States in 1953 and 1954, and soon Pakistan began receiving the sophisticated weapons it could not manufacture. But this preoccupation did not prevent him from analyzing the country's political activities and institutions. Ayub's political thinking in this early period will be found in a memorandum which he drafted before assuming the office of Defense Minister. The theme of the memorandum enunciated a position he would strive to give meaning to in the period to come. He wrote:

> The ultimate aim of Pakistan must be to become a sound, solid and cohesive nation to be able to play its destined role in world history. This can be achieved only if as a start a constitution is evolved that will suit the genius of the people and be based on the circumstances confronting them, so that they set on the path of unity, team work and creative progress.[13]

When the Second Constituent Assembly finally drafted and President Iskander Mirza declared the Constitution of the Islamic Republic of Pakistan in 1956, Ayub Khan had long since resigned his Defense Minister's post in order to devote his time exclusively to the expansion and modernization of the Army. But civil unrest did not cease with the coming into force of the Constitution. With the 1954 defeat of the Muslim League in East Pakistan and its rupture in West Pakistan, new political formations emerged. Coalition governments reflected the failure of any single party to develop a national following and, to compound the confusion, the political individualists who are so much a part of the Pakistani scene made a shambles of the political process.[14]

Political parties found it impossible to retain the loyalty of their members. Coalitions of parties were so tenuously organized that all efforts at holding them together also failed. Moreover, even with the added feature—the amalgamation of the provinces of West Pakistan into the One Unit of West Pakistan in 1955—the political life of the nation deteriorated rapidly. The cumulative impact threatened the nation's survival.[15]

The making and unmaking of governments both at the Center and in the provinces, the passionate exchanges of the advocates of joint electorate in East Pakistan as opposed to those championing the more traditional separate electorate in West Pakistan, or whether or not the One Unit should be dissolved and the old provinces of the Punjab, Sind, Baluchistan, and the North West Frontier reconstituted, all led to repeated breakdowns of law and order. With leftist movements on the upswing and separatist elements openly defying the government, with the Muslim League (under the leadership of the opportunist Abdul Qayyum Khan) plotting a renewal of the war in Kashmir, enough fuel existed to incinerate the fabric of Pakistani society.[16] But the match was never struck.

In the midst of mounting tension the Pakistan Army made its own plans. When Major General Umrao Khan's report reached General Ayub, describing events leading up to and highlighting the altercation in the East Pakistan Assembly which ultimately resulted in the death of the Deputy Speaker, those plans were activated.[17] It was President Iskander Mirza who informed the nation that the Constitution had been abrogated, the legislatures closed, the political parties abolished, and martial law imposed throughout the country; but it was not clear for almost three weeks who was really in charge. However, on October 27, 1958, all doubts were brushed aside. As General Ayub Khan became Pakistan's new President, Iskander Mirza was being rushed to Karachi Airport, placed on a plane destined for London, and told never to return to Pakistan. On November 13, 1969, he died in exile and was buried in alien soil in Teheran.

Mirza wanted to restore a semblance of the old order; he argued against introducing land reforms and was obviously frightened of Ayub Khan's power as Chief Martial Law Administrator.[18] After organizing a new cabinet and making Ayub his Prime Minister, he shifted control of the Army to Mohammad Musa. In this way Mirza hoped to slow the revolution while neutralizing his principal competitor. The Prime Minister's office was a hollow shell; its mystique had evaporated with the banishment of Nazimuddin as far back as 1953. Iskander Mirza knew this, and so did Ayub Khan. The President traditionally held greater power than the Prime Minister and Mirza's plan was to reduce Ayub's authority by appearing to promote him. General Musa was the key personality in this drama. When Mirza later ordered him to arrest Ayub the general balked, and reported the incident to his colleague. Ayub was furious. He ordered Generals Azam and Sheikh to confront Mirza with an ultimatum. Mirza was given the choice of leaving the country or going to prison, and within hours the erstwhile President was on his way into permanent exile. Later Ayub would write: "I was most unhappy making this decision. I was unhappy for him too. How unfortunate that he could not be loyal to anybody!" [19] On October 28, 1958, General Ayub Khan promulgated the Presidential Cabinet Order, leaving Mirza's cabinet intact but abolishing the office of Prime Minister. That office was now incorporated with the President's office, clearing the way for the switch to the presidental form of government.

THE MARTIAL LAW PERIOD

A new era has begun under General Ayub Khan and the Armed Forces have undertaken to root out the administrative malaise and the anti-social practices, to create a sense of confidence, security and stability and eventually to bring the country back to a state of normalcy. I hope and pray that God may give them wisdom and strength to achieve their objective.

With these words recorded by the *Morning News* of Karachi on October 29, 1958, Miss Fatima Jinnah, the sister of the Qaid-i-Azam, heralded the ouster of Iskander Mirza and "the completion" of the revolution. Little did she know that almost six years to the day later she would be standing as the candidate of the Combined Opposition Parties (COP) against the incumbency of President Ayub Khan.

One theme remains constant in what can now be called the Ayub Era. On October 8, 1958, acting in his capacity as Chief Martial Law Administrator, General Mohammad Ayub Khan declared: "Our ultimate aim is to restore democracy but of the type that people can understand and work." [20] Ayub was fully aware that the intelligentsia equated "democracy" with parliamentary systems, and the fear now persisted that the abandonment of parliamentary government would mean the end of self-government as well. Ayub, however, harbored fears of his own. Convinced that parliamentary government in Pakistan's sociocultural milieu was synonymous with political instability, he steadfastly refused to consider its reinstatement. Hence holding his critics at bay absorbed much of his energy. The election campaign which culminated in his reelection on January 2, 1965, did not reconcile critics of the presidential system. Although the personalities of the President and Miss Fatima

Jinnah dominated the proceedings, the principal issue was the virtue of the parliamentary as against the presidential form of government and vice versa. The official spokesman for the President, Z. A. Suleri, juxtaposed the two systems in these terms:

> If the one-party system with all its undemocratic hazards is not to be adopted, then the presidential system alone holds the field. For, while it does not bind the people hand and foot to highly organised, political parties and they can enjoy their freedom from party loyalty and duty, they are nonetheless given the chance to exercise their franchise and elect the government of their liking . . . the presidential system lends itself to the mobilisation of unorganised votes to serve a supreme national purpose, namely, to produce a government for a fixed period. . . . And this is the job which the parliamentary system failed to do in Pakistan; it excited and involved the elect and the few at the top whose permutations and combinations never gave this country a government which could attend to the basic needs of national uplift and development.
>
> Now Miss Jinnah is not challenging President Ayub in merely personal terms; she is equally questioning the validity of the presidential system and wants it to be substituted by the old parliamentary system . . . the people cannot vote for anarchy; they will prefer the presidential system which bestowed stability and made for phenomenal progress in every field of national activity.[21]

There was little discussion of these contentious issues in the months and years immediately following the revolution, however. Martial law remained in force until June 8, 1962. For almost forty-four months the voices of dissent, so commonplace heretofore, were muted. President Ayub issued one regulation after another prescribing severe punishment for antisocial activities which included such malfeasances as smuggling, hoarding, black-marketeering, and abduction of women and children. Bank balances of the abolished political parties were frozen. Some of the more intemperate politicians like Khan Abdul Ghaffar Khan, leader of the frontier Red Shirts, G. M. Syed, a Sindhi leader, and Maulana Bhashani of East Pakistan—all members of the National Awami Party —were detained.[22] Anticorruption councils were set up to hear charges brought against members of the civil service; and a Land Reforms Commission was organized in West Pakistan, supposedly to break the hold of the landed gentry. A high-powered Rehabilitation Committee organized under the chairmanship of Lieutenant General Mohammad Azam Khan tackled the long-festering refugee problem, and 40,000 new quarters were constructed in and around Karachi in a six-month period. The new town was called Korangi and several hundred thousand people, who had lived for a decade in wretched, squalid conditions, suddenly had a new environment in which to raise their families. The human objection to being uprooted caused people grown accustomed to living in the Karachi "shanty towns" to refuse to leave, however, and they had to be forcibly evicted. They complained that the new housing development was far from the city and that transportation was faulty or too expensive.

Although martial law remained in force, it is interesting to note that the troops were soon relieved of their civil duties and ordered back to their barracks on November 10, 1958. The bureaucracy, the "steel frame" of British administration, continued as one of the two pillars of government throughout this period. However, in the months leading up to the revolution it, too, had become associated with the political malaise and rampant corruption. In an effort to cleanse the administration, Ayub Khan appointed a Screening Committee to investigate the integrity and efficiency of thousands of officers in all the services. Under Martial Law Regulation No. 61 and the Public Conduct (Scrutiny) Ordinance of 1959 the government expanded the examination to include judicial and civil officers. On March 10, 1959, the President promulgated an order under which government servants found guilty of corruption, misconduct, subversive activities, and inexcusable inefficiency could be suspended, compulsorily retired, reduced in rank, or dismissed from service. The Special Police Establishment reported against 997 officials, including 250 gazetted officers. Similar operations were carried out in the provinces. As a direct result of these efforts 526 officers were either compelled to retire or removed from service. Eighty-four officers of the All-Pakistan and Class I Service of the Central Government and 106 gazetted officers of the East Pakistan Government were included in these statistics. Other officials were treated less drastically. Some were reduced in rank, had their increments curtailed, or received other forms of punishment.[23]

The impact on the bureaucracy of the investigations caused considerable demoralization, however, and although the public found it salutary the authorities soon had second thoughts. It would not be an exaggeration to say that the administrators were becoming panicky. It was generally held that some officers had been unjustifiably accused and sentenced while others more guilty had escaped the security net. Administration, therefore, began to suffer under the strain and it was soon obvious that the pressure would have to be reduced. To this day critics of Ayub Khan's martial law government cite the fact that just when corrective measures began achieving results the call went out to slow the investigations. A high-ranking police official who was in the thick of these operations notes: "Martial law was more reformative than punitive. The result was that people began to think that the Law was even more lenient than the ordinary civil law . . . the main weakness of the regime was its leniency." [24]

Despite initial fears it soon became apparent that the martial law regime of Ayub Khan was not set on "revolutionizing" the country. There is much validity in the remark that it was lenient, but it cannot be said that it was weak. If it was found necessary to halt the wholesale investigation of the services it was simply because the "steel frame" was displaying signs of fatigue. Torn between continuing the public spectacle and restoring the equilibrium of the services, the government adopted the latter course. Nevertheless, the regime did not turn its back on corruption. A senior Enquiry Officer with a sizable staff was appointed to scrutinize the activities of officers suspected of malpractices in the Central Government. Cases of corruption normally were turned over to the appropriate head of the department concerned. The individual department then recommended the type of punishment to be given the offender.

It is true that this procedure affected only a few officers, and the feeling persists that responsible departmental officers were either too protective of their own personnel or indifferent to the recommendations of the investigating agencies. In the provinces, the anticorruption agencies, councils, and committees had more direct control over miscreants and lists of officials charged with malpractices were published regularly. But corruption continued nonetheless. The fact that there was no "all-out" drive on administrative corruption cannot be labeled a weakness of the regime, however. Although in desperate need of reform, the bureaucratic system had to be kept intact at least until such time as other sectors of society changed. This seemed to be the more immediate dilemma; without the active cooperation of the "steel frame" the hoped-for transformation would be less likely.[25] This knowledge also helps to explain why the Pay and Services Commission, which was established in 1959 and submitted its report in 1962, failed to have its recommendations publicized, let alone implemented.[26] Hence it is necessary to observe those areas where the martial law regime tried to act more resolutely.

ORDER AND REFORM

General Ayub Khan set up the Law Reforms Commission on November 23, 1958. On December 12th he announced the appointment of a Commission on National Education. By January 20, 1959, the final report of the Land Reforms Commission was in his hands and six days later another body was established to implement its recommendations. On March 25, 1959, the Public Offices (Disqualification) Order (PODO) was promulgated, which prescribed disqualification from becoming a member of an elective body for up to 15 years if the accused went before a tribunal and was found guilty of corruption. In August the Elective Bodies (Disqualification) Order (EBDO) was introduced, providing certain former political leaders with the option of being tried for "misconduct" or disqualifying themselves from engaging in political activity.[27] Acording to Sher Hasan Khan, the Special Police Establishment undertook investigations of thirty-eight cases under EBDO and seventeen persons were convicted and debarred from politics.[28] The great majority, however, accepted the option to disqualify themselves and withdrew from public life. On March 5, 1960, EBDO was amended so as to include all persons who had retired, resigned, or been dismissed from government service.[29]

After checkmating the politicians the President moved to reduce what was left of the opposition. The Progressive Papers, Limited, of Lahore, owned by Mian Iftikharuddin, another NAP leader, were seized by the government. The English daily, *The Pakistan Times,* and two Urdu newspapers, *Imroze* and *Lail-o-Nahar* were either to be liquidated or brought under new management with strong government controls.[30] On April 26, 1960, the Press and Publications Ordinance was issued. It was aimed at amending and consolidating the press laws which emerged in the first hours after the revolution. The Ordinance extended to the whole of Pakistan and specified under what conditions a newspaper could be commandeered by the authorities. One of the salient clauses specified

> [Anything which might] tend directly or indirectly to bring into hatred or contempt the Government established by law in Pakistan or the administration of justice in Pakistan or any class or section of the citizens of Pakistan or to excite disaffection towards the said Government . . .[31]

Other newspapers, such as the prominent English dailies *Dawn* of Karachi, *Morning News* of Karachi and Dacca, and *The Observer* of

Dacca, were allowed to remain under original management. The same was generally true of some vernacular papers in both wings of the country. All of these journals more or less adhered to the dictates of the martial law regime and refrained from making critical judgments on government policies.

On May 1, 1959, President Ayub announced the most important experiment of his administration. After meeting with the governors of East and West Pakistan and members of his cabinet, he revealed that a decision had been taken to go ahead with a scheme to be known thereafter as Basic Democracies. The principal reasons given for the introduction of the new program were the need to accelerate rural development, improve social welfare facilities, and to create a new politically conscious class of leaders with administrative skills capable of mobilizing the rural population. While the urban population was included in the Basic Democracies scheme it was obvious that the union committees in the cities would be given considerably less attention. On the first anniversary of the revolution, October 27, 1959, the President promulgated the Basic Democracies Order providing for the establishment of a five-tiered structure at the base of which were to be union councils in the rural areas and union committees in the cities. This structure was reduced to four tiers with the opening of the new provincial legislatures in 1962, but with the establishment of the wards below the union council in 1965–66 it can be said that the system again had five tiers. These primary bodies were to be directly elected on the basis of universal adult franchise with one councillor or Basic Democrat representing from 800 to 1,500 persons. In all there would be 80,000 Basic Democrats (later increased to 120,000), half representing constituencies in East Pakistan and half representing those of West Pakistan.

In addition to these Basic Democrats the government nominated an additional number, not to exceed one-third of the elected members, who would be voting members of the councils/committees. All the four tiers above the union, although including representatives from among the elected, were under the direct control of the bureaucracy, however. Basic Democracies was just what the name implied. It was a device employed by government to educate the inarticulate rural and urban masses. For example, even though martial law was still in force, views expressed in meetings of the different councils in the Basic Democracies system were immune from legal proceedings. Step by tedious step the President envisaged a system capable of transforming the sociopsychological character of the people as well as laying the foundation for local self-government. Given a reasonable amount of success, he opined,

Basic Democracies could become more democratic and less basic. However, this would take time. The immediate problem seemed to require some form of tutelary system.

Political socialization, a favorable popular response to symbols and values in the existing political system, could be achieved only after the nation had been mobilized to participate in the process of national reconstruction. It is important to note that one method for the attainment of this goal was lost with the abolition of the political parties. Another was rejected by disassociating the professional and urban elites from the experiment. The mechanism chosen was that of political bureaucratization. Before the people's elected representatives could become real exponents of the popular will they had to learn the meaning of civic responsibility. Thus the Basic Democrats would be "taught" to understand what it meant to have a stake in the preservation of the state; how to recognize their responsibility in maintaining law and order; and, above all, how to distinguish between fear and pride in upholding the political system.[32]

Basic Democracies were originally conceived as devoid of political party activity. When Ayub Khan publicized his dissatisfaction with politicians generally and the former political system in particular, it was obvious that only a new political order would satisfy him. While firm in the conviction that this new order must include the historically inattentive rural population, he was also aware of their susceptibility to the charm and promises of the political elite. When Ayub stated that a governmental system had to be devised which was "suited to the genius" of the Pakistani people,[33] he pondered how this could be accomplished free from the intrigues of professional politicians. Hence the decision was taken to bypass the politically conscious intelligentsia and to put full faith in the bureaucracy.

In the President's eyes, the people required guidance not so much in the politics of give and take but more in the realm of constructive community development. The bureaucrats not only possessed the necessary skills but seemed more apt to unify the population for the specific goals of rural uplift. Divisive or not, politics is not something that can be wished away, however, and the East Pakistanis were especially suspicious of the new system. Their more vocal elements insisted it was nothing more than the old union and district board structure in disguise; that it was a clandestine and unsophisticated technique employed to ensure the dominance of the military-bureaucratic elite and to keep the eastern province in a condition of servitude. It was repeated over and again that the administration, like the Army, was in the control of West Pakistanis.

Hence the restrictions imposed on the politicians to all intents and purpose eliminated the eastern province's "real" representatives and placed the region once more under a form of colonial occupation.

SEARCH FOR LEGITIMACY

Ayub took a serious view of opposition to his Basic Democracies system, but it was not his intention to ram it down the throats of his countrymen. Accepting the proposition that people naturally resist innovation, but convinced that the system must be tried, he set out on a nationwide speaking tour. A special train called the *Pak Jamhuriat* became the vehicle for spreading the news about Basic Democracies throughout the country. On December 14, 1959, the President boarded the train at Karachi and was to spend seven days on what was advertised as a "meet-the-people tour" of West Pakistan. On January 22, 1960, he repeated the performance in East Pakistan. Between these two tours the President accepted the advice of his cabinet that he legitimate his authority by seeking a vote of confidence from the people. The President then promulgated an order empowering the Election Commission to arrange for the election of the 80,000 Basic Democrats. The object was not only to get the experiment started but to have the popularly elected representatives express their faith, or lack of it, in the President. According to S. A. Saeed, it was Manzur Qadir who insisted on the need for a vote of confidence.

> Manzoor Qadir advised Ayub that he was popular with the masses, let him show it to the world that he is not there atop the state of Pakistan, not because of any ruthlessness, but because the people worship him as a Hindu worships his god. But how was the proof to come of his popularity? Qadir suggested him the way—asked him to take a leaf from de Gaulle's life and seek a vote.[34]

Saeed's book is enough to embarrass the most self-centered leader, but a careful scrutiny of the record offers convincing proof that there is truth in his comments despite the obvious emotional exaggerations. The President may not have enjoyed the popularity the author attributes to him, but there is little reason to doubt that Ayub acted on Manzur Qadir's advice. The election of the Basic Democrats began on December 26, 1959. Official figures indicate that less than three-quarters of the eligible population voted in West Pakistan. The percentage casting ballots in East Pakistan was closer to 50 percent. Some observers would conclude that this demonstrated the unpopularity of the new system.[35] Nevertheless, the 80,000 elected representatives assumed their new responsibilities in February 1960, and on the fourth of that month the Election Commission summoned them to register by secret ballot whether or not they had confidence in President Mohammad Ayub Khan.

On February 14th the Basic Democrats expressed themselves overwhelmingly in favor of the President; the official tabulation indicated that 95.6 percent of those casting ballots had confidence in Ayub's leadership. The very next day Ayub addressed the nation and, after acknowledging his gratitude, announced that a commission would be appointed to help frame a new constitution for the nation. On February 17th the capstone was added to the new political edifice. Ayub Khan officially took the oath making him the first elected President of Pakistan.

Cynics decried the swearing-in ceremony as a farce and sham which would only make Pakistan a laughingstock. They argued that the result was inconclusive; that the Basic Democrats owed their existence to the President and could not be expected to commit political suicide by casting a vote against him. But except for these verbal comments (uttered discreetly), and the basic apathy of the urban intelligentsia, there was no opposition. After the oath-taking ritual the President identified his eleven-member Constitution Commission headed by Chief Justice Mohammad Shahabuddin. One week later the new capital to be built on the Potwar Plateau outside Rawalpindi was given the official name of Islamabad. By this date there could be no doubt either of Ayub Khan's intentions or the direction in which he had chosen to lead the nation.

On April 11, 1960, President Ayub enlisted the support of two trusted friends and confidants. They were men known for their strong character and sense of responsibility. In West Pakistan, in April 1960, Governor Akhter Husain relinquished his office to Malik Amir Mohammad Khan. Akhter Husain, a dedicated, honest, and efficient civil servant had chaired the Land Reforms Commission and also served as Election Commissioner. He was later to serve as Minister of Information and Broadcasting and, finally, as Minister of Education before stepping down because of age and failing health.

The new Governor was a hunting partner and neighbor of the President. A pious individual, the Amir was also a symbol of traditional Muslim life. Often referred to as the Khan of Kalabagh, he was one of Pakistan's wealthiest landowners, who heretofore had avoided the center of the political stage. Malik Amir Mohammad Khan had been a member of the National Assembly and West Pakistan Interim Legislature. Before 1958 he declined a portfolio in the Central Cabinet as well as a provincial governorship. After the revolution he was appointed chairman of the Pakistan Industrial Development Corporation and held the rank of minister. Given Ayub's determination to push his reforms, he clearly needed someone who represented the dominant interests in West Pakistan's rural areas.

The land reforms in West Pakistan did not eliminate the influence of the zamindars, although it reduced the importance of some. Landlords were permitted to retain up to 1,000 acres of rain-fed land and 500 acres of irrigated land.[36] Khalid bin Sayeed suggests that the minimum figures for landholdings were not lower because the regime did not want to antagonize the middle-sized landlords, who were mainly Army officers. Concessions were also permitted whereby gifts of land could be made to heirs and orchards retained. The land reforms, therefore, did not break the hold of the landlords except in the case of jagirdaris ("feūdal" landholdings) which were completely eliminated. Martial Law Regulation 64—fixing a 36,000 produce-unit ceiling on landholdings—was left for the new Governor to implement, and it is important to note that the Amir surrendered 22,000 acres of his own land to the Land Commission.[37] On the one side, the new Governor was in a position to influence the landlord class and through them, the peasant masses; on the other, his somewhat apolitical background, traditional biases, and strict methods were exactly what the President desired in order to maintain political stability in a time of anticipated change. Malik Amir Mohammad Khan had a reputation for being a hard taskmaster, however, and during his term as Governor was labeled, *sotto voce,* a ruthless tyrant.

Ayub's other appointment was Lieutenant General Azam Khan, who was appointed Governor of East Pakistan. Governor Zakir Husain (no relation to Akhter Husain) had been appointed at the time of the revolution and was a despised and hated official. A former police officer, he never succeeded in winning the confidence of the Bengalis and his unpopularity undermined all attempts at building the President's prestige in the province. Azam Khan had done a remarkable job as Minister of Rehabilitation and earned the reputation of being a difficult but forthright public official. He never allowed his concern for development and social reform to obscure the need for law and order, however. While the resettlement of the Karachi refugees was still fresh in the minds of his countrymen they could not forget that it was Major General Azam Khan who was charged with quelling the Punjab disturbances of 1953.

At the time of the declaration of martial law, Lieutenant General
Azam Khan was given responsibility for the whole of West Pakistan
with the exception of Karachi. Thus, President Ayub had installed in
each wing of the country trusted strongmen who stood a reasonable
chance of furthering his reforms. In time, however, both men would
earn his displeasure and would be forced to relinquish authority. Azam,
because he became too popular with the East Pakistanis and hence
rivaled Ayub's leadership; and Kalabagh, essentially because after six
years his strong-arm tactics evoked bitterness and more and more proved
a liabilty for the regime. Although there were few to mourn the passing
of Malik Amir Mohammad Khan, Azam Khan still claims many ad-
mirers. But while Azam campaigned strenuously for Miss Fatima
Jinnah and the COP coalition in the 1964–65 election, and thus
remained very much anti-Ayub, he played no role in forcing him from
office.

By 1961 the world knew that Ayub Khan was not a passing shadow.
While he strengthened his hold on the nation, political stability permitted
a relaxation in the field of economic restraints. Private enterprise was
encouraged and the Second Five Year Plan, after a hesitant beginning,
began making advances. The annual report of the State Bank of Pakistan
announced record production and investment levels for 1960–61. And
on October 14, 1961, Pakistan and the United States signed a $621
million agricultural commodities agreement which was to finance the
Rural Works Program and further bolster the experiment in Basic
Democracies.

In an effort to improve Pakistan's image abroad, the President undertook a number of international tours, first to the Middle East and then to
Japan and Southeast Asia. In February 1961, Queen Elizabeth and the
Duke of Edinburgh arrived in Pakistan for a sixteen-day visit. In that
same month Pakistan signed an agreement with the Soviet Union en-
abling the latter to prospect for oil in both wings of the country. Three
days later President Ayub affirmed Pakistan's right to settle its border
problems with Communist China. In the following month President Ayub
attended the Commonwealth Conference in London and accepted President John F. Kennedy's invitation to visit the United States later that
year. Vice President Lyndon B. Johnson visited Pakistan on May 20,
1961. There were indications in these activities that Pakistan was modifying foreign policies that had remained more or less on dead center
from 1953 to 1960. Although the country was heavily dependent on
Western—and especially American economic and military assistance,
Pakistan's peculiar geographic position and continuing criticism of

CENTO and SEATO military commitments caused the President to reappraise Pakistan's international posture. Talk circulated about the need to develop a more rational and independent foreign policy, and Ayub could not afford to ignore its impact on his domestic policies or personal position.

India was less of a problem than Afghanistan in 1961. Although there were several minor altercations, and India's plans to construct the Farakka Barrage in West Bengal threatened to ruin the Ganges-Kobadak irrigation project in East Pakistan, President Ayub and Prime Minister Nehru took the opportunity to discuss their outstanding differences at the Commonwealth meeting in London. But Afghanistan presented a more immediate threat. Always coveting the North West Frontier region with its hardy Pathan population, the Afghans massed troops on the Pakistan border, forcing the authorities to close it. On Afghan initiative, diplomatic relations were broken on September 6, 1961.[38] Landlocked Afghanistan, dependent on the port of Karachi and the West Pakistan land route that leads through the Khyber for its commerce, thus was forced to seek an alternative outlet through the Soviet Union.

When hostilities erupted the Pakistani Army proved more than a match for the Afghan forces, but this only tended to aggravate Pakistan's relations with the United States. American congressmen were disturbed over the knowledge that Pakistan had employed U.S. arms in crushing the Afghan maneuver, arms which they had hoped would only be used in response to Communist aggression. When the Pakistanis were informed of this American reaction they stated that the country was entitled to defend and preserve its territorial integrity with whatever weapons it could muster. The reason for the congressional outburst was that certain American officials and journalists reported that Afghanistan was being driven into the Soviet camp by the Pakistani action. Although the United States Defense and State Departments were somewhat familiar with the Pakhtunistan issue (the claim of Afghan irredenta on the North West Frontier), and hence sympathized with the Pakistanis, those condemning them did not or could not grasp its significance.

With relations strained over this and other issues, such as the oil-prospecting agreement with the U.S.S.R. and the overture to settle boundary differences with Communist China, President Ayub's November trip to Washington was moved up to July. In Washington, President Ayub addressed the United States Congress, and *The New York Times* on July 31, 1961, recorded these words: "If there is trouble, there is no other country in Asia where you will be able to even put your foot in. The only people who will stand by you are the people of Pakistan."

Pakistan was at that time one of the West's strongest bastions in Asia. By population count it was the United States' biggest ally. It was, after all, the most "allied" ally in Asia, being associated with the United States in four separate mutual security agreements. General Ayub was the architect of all these arrangements, and it is fair to state that he had ample reason to feel let down. But still not to the degree that he would in another seventeen months when American arms shipments to India increased; or again in September 1965, faced with an Indian attack on his most sensitive frontier; or finally, in April 1967 when the United States announced it would refrain from supplying military equipment and that its military advisory groups would be withdrawn from Pakistan altogether. (The United States Government decided to resume selling arms to Pakistan on October 10, 1970.)

Chapter 2

Political Renaissance: Old Issues, New Dimensions

AFTER the Constitution Commission submitted its report it remained for the President and his advisers to survey its recommendations and decide how the new constitution would be drafted.[1] On October 26, 1961, the eve of the third anniversary of the revolution, President Ayub informed the nation that a document would be produced guaranteeing a strong, stable government. Before the month was out a two-man committee, of which Manzur Qadir was the dominant member, was appointed. Manzur Qadir had chaired one of the two presidential committees which were charged with systematically analyzing the Constitution Commission's recommendations. His predilections, therefore, were well known. Not only was he close to the President's thinking on the substance of a new constitution, he was also recognized as one of the few people whose advice the President respected. This also explains why Ayub bypassed his Law Minister and preferred that his Minister of External Affairs prepare the new constitution. Reference has already been made to S. A. Saeed's embellished prose, but it is still revealing to note what he says about the relationship of the President and Manzur Qadir. It should be emphasized that this comment was published almost a year before the Foreign Minister received responsibility for drafting the new constitution. Saeed writes:

> The understanding between the two is both deep and mysterious. If Ayub claims "a faculty of judging human beings," Qadir has no less. Both understand the people of Pakistan so well that before the people would act or open their lips they can read what they intend, and deeper than that is the way Qadir understands Ayub. And this is the secret of their power.[2]

It is an established fact that Manzur Qadir, like the President, could not reconcile himself to some of the fundamental features of the Constitution Commission's report.[3] Furthermore, the Commission's recommendations were purely advisory and hence not binding. The President

23

and his martial law government at no time indicated that in establishing the Commission they relinquished the prerogative to disagree with its recommendations. This could be interpreted as an apologia for the President and what was to follow, but it is not meant to be one. Ayub Khan took great pains to explain his philosophy of government. From the inception of martial law he was heard to exclaim that the conditions necessary for the establishment of a sophisticated democratic system were absent in Pakistan. Overwhelming illiteracy, widespread poverty, and an almost universal lack of national political consciousness dictated another course from the one seemingly determined by the British legacy. Ayub was convinced that there should be democracy but, in order for it to be truly effective, it had to be built from the ground up.[4] The President never questioned the integrity of the members of the Commission and he held its chairman, Chief Justice Shahabuddin, in high respect. All the same, the Commission's recommendations were noticeably short of the President's initial objectives, far from his public statements, and completely in conflict with his own thinking. The single most important institution which the President sought to nourish, the only one which he felt could reach down and touch the largest portion of Pakistani society, was in his judgment irreverently treated. In arguing against writing the Basic Democracies scheme into the constitution the Commission declared:

> We would have included it in the constitution under the heading "local government," had it not been for the fact that, even for minor changes, which may become necessary as experience of the working of the scheme is gained, amendment of the constitution would be required. We would, therefore, regard it only as an existing law.[5]

Karl Von Vorys points out the "glaring" influence of the "modernized segment of the society on the Commission." [6] The Basic Democracies system, conceived by President Ayub Khan with assistance from Manzur Qadir, had been and now was the prime target of articulate urban interests. Having been disenfranchised by the proclamation of martial law, the Constitution Commission appeared to afford the intelligentsia their last opportunity to alter the Basic Democracies system before it became enshrined in a constitutional document. Thus, despite the President's insistence on sustaining and invigorating the Basic Democracies, it was with considerable distress that Ayub witnessed its virtual repudiation by the Commission. It was the electoral college of Basic Democrats which had elected President Ayub Khan, thereby theoretically, if not *de jure,* legitimating his rule. Now the Constitution

Commission Report chose to reject this electoral college in favor of direct suffrage "restricted" to literates and property owners.[7] If he had accepted the Constitution Commission Report Ayub would have been compelled to all but discard the Basic Democracies and accept limitations on his authority.

A member of the intelligentsia, the former Prime Minister Choudhri Mohammad Ali, was only one of the 6,269 respondents to the questionaire circulated by the Commission, but his reply was the most significant and received the greatest publicity. Appearing in *The Pakistan Times* of Lahore on June 13, 1960, it stressed the importance of reviving the parliamentary system. The presidential system, he cautioned, will lead to a "personal dictatorship." Later Ayub would write of Choudhri Mohammad Ali as one of his "bitterest" critics, and that as "author of the 1956 Constitution: he felt robbed of immortality." [8]

While the Constitution Commission went along with the idea of a presidential system, the legislative institution again would be dominant. The Commission was absolutely opposed to the banning of political parties and the continuance of martial law.[9] To the President and Manzur Qadir such recommendations implied the loss of the revolution and a reversion to the older pattern of government with all its latent conflicts. It was in this light that the Commission Report was eventually rejected. The President has been criticized for reneging on his original promise to give the people what they wanted in the way of a constitution; instead, it was said he placed himself in a position where only he knew what was best for the people. The passage of events may now show that the President was wrong by insisting on a drastic modification of the Commission's recommendations, but he was at that time convinced that the future of the nation rested on mobilizing the rural people and the Basic Democracies scheme was the only device ready at hand. At the same time, it would be wrong to conclude that Ayub was oblivious to the reactions of the sophisticated urban elite and its following. In his Constitution Speech on March 1, 1962, he said:

> I am conscious of the fact that some sections of [the] intelligentsia and those with vested interests may have cause to complain. I do not see any reason why a suitable formula cannot be evolved *later which will give them a feeling of full participation.*[10] (Italics added.)

The President could not have been more explicit. *The intelligentsia would be asked and made to mark time while the government went about the business of inducting the rural population into a "new" political process.* Those members of the intelligentsia who wished to contribute their time and energy in this activity would be welcome. However, so long as the masses remained politically immature, dissent and opposition to government policies would be constrained. The President could not be dissuaded from the view that the country required political stability and continuity of leadership before anything else. While respecting the parliamentary system, he could not bring himself to believe that Pakistan could afford another go at it; that is, without what he considered to be the preconditions for the constructive employment of a parliamentary system—representative institutions at all levels of society, trade unions and cooperatives on a country-wide basis, and other institutions which would give Pakistanis training in the fundamentals of give and take. In their absence, the parliamentary system meant a return to older conflicts and hence the eventual subversion of the nation.[11]

Controversies, Ayub was to acknowledge, were acceptable, but what he feared was interminable bickering and bitterness. If the country was to survive, let alone prosper, a system had to be developed which would allow for maximum social mobilization. Ayub acknowledged that the political dialogue had to be extended, recruitment into the political process had to be broadened—but not at the expense of material progress. The President emphasized that this was his constitution and that it was based on his own philosophy of government. Ayub concluded by noting his experience and long association with the most senior members of the administration. He prided himself on knowing his countrymen. His grasp of national priorities developed from "wide study, deep and prolonged thought and a burning desire to help the people in building the country into a sound, vigorous, progressive and powerful State." [12] He argued that his constitution be given a chance.

SELLING THE 1962 CONSTITUTION

Advance copies of the Ayub Constitution had been circulated to members of the press, who prepared questions on those features which needed elaboration. His response to these queries came a day before his broadcast to the nation and the actual signing of the document. Before proceeding with his Gaullist version of a press conference, Ayub emphasized that his martial law powers would terminate the moment he affixed his signature to the new constitution. "As soon as I sign it, it becomes law and it can only be altered in accordance with the manner

that any other law can be altered. Of course," he added, "this Constitutional law has a special way of alteration." [13] The President did his
utmost to convince the journalists that he would be accountable to the
people; but he also let it be known that the chief executive must be
insulated from irresponsible and "illegitimate" harassment. Moreover,
it was crystal clear that he would not tolerate the undermining of those
institutions upon which the stability of his system rested.

Ayub cited the principal objections to the constitution such as the
presidential system, the indirect franchise, and the non-justiciability of
fundamental rights. He also acknowledged that his chief opposition might
well be found in the attitude of the press. The press would be permitted to express its views, but, he cautioned, "if the object is to pres-
surize me, then you are not going to succeed. . . . I cannot retrace my
steps. I suggest that you ask people, as I am asking you, to give this
[constitution] a trial." [14] He then gave his word that the constitution
could be amended by the National Assembly without unreasonable in-
terference by the executive:

> I would go even further and say that our Constitution, and, for
> that matter, any constitution of a country which has to go or is
> going through a transitory evolutionary period, should be looked
> into carefully every 15 or 20 years. When the conditions of the
> society change, the Constitution must also reflect these changes.
> This is the only way you can prevent revolutions.[15]

The President was obviously trying to avoid an ideological commitment. His actions were conditioned by pragmatism. Change would be
the result of trial and error and proven need. But he also clung to extremely strong convictions from which he could not deviate. For example, he was fully aware of the East Pakistani preference for a parliamentary and not a presidential system. But he feared the consequences
flowing from Bengali entreaties. Urged by his interrogators to say what
was on his mind, the President explained that the removal of "any vital
element from this constitution" would cause the whole edifice to collapse. "If East Pakistan wants to have a Parliamentary form of Government and here [in West Pakistan] somebody else wants to have something else, really you have got to have two countries then!" [16] The
President insisted that only an enemy would want to see the separation
of East and West Pakistan. Thus he felt reinforced in his view that only
a presidential form of government could insure Pakistan's unity and
hence there could be no tampering with this feature of the constitution.
On the other hand, suggestions for change within the framework of the

constitution would receive a proper hearing and neither he nor his administration would prevent constructive criticism.

NEW SYSTEM, OLD DILEMMAS

After the promulgation of the Constitution the country awaited the election of the members of the national and provincial legislatures. As the 1960 "vote of confidence" in the President was determined to have retroactive effect, and as the President was granted a five-year term under the Constitution, Ayub Khan would not stand for election again until 1965. This first series of indirect elections under the new Constitution would be conducted solely for the legislatures and without political parties. The electorate, as in the case of the earlier presidential election, would be the 80,000 Basic Democrats and although Ayub addressed the nation shortly before the election his remarks were really intended for them.

The speech was labeled by the President as "My Manifesto," and it took the form of a statement of guidelines to be followed in electing suitable people to the parliamentary posts. He listed four objectives of national policy. First, Pakistan was an ideological state founded and nourished on Islamic tenets but not unmindful of its obligation to the country's minorities. Second, the security, stability, and unity of Pakistan must be protected at all costs. Again he reiterated his belief that "East Pakistan and West Pakistan can remain free and sovereign only if they remain together. Separated, it may be a matter of a few years, if not a few months, before they disappear, disintegrate, or are destroyed." [17] Third, the government's resources would be harnessed in an effort to improve the material existence of the Pakistani people. The President emphasized that this was not only needed for progress at home but for prestige abroad. "A weak nation, like a weak man, may invoke pity but gains no respect." [18] (Later actions were to show that the President was almost as keenly interested in improving Pakistan's international position as he was in modernizing the domestic condition.) And finally, democracy was declared to be the cornerstone of Pakistan's political system. Democracy was identified as a fundamental principle of Islam and Muslims were enjoined to follow its precepts. With this in mind, the foundations for democratic development were already laid "in the shape of the Basic Democracies." Ayub explained:

> Participation of the people in a sensible, understandable and workable fashion has been introduced at all levels of government. As the national character solidifies, I have no doubt that the roots

of these institutions will *Insha-Allah,* become deeper and firmer. The new Constitution—a pragmatic rather than a dogmatic scheme —is designed to fulfill this objective of inducing a sane and balanced political life in the country.[19]

The President then identified the means for the fulfillment of these objectives. He cited support of the Constitution and the awakening of the masses through Basic Democracies [20] as well as changes in the socio-economic life of the nation, responsible leadership both at the public and private level, strong and stable government with efficient administration, justice and equity for all, and multidimensional programs for development. Above all, he declared, there must be "a relentless passion for work, ceaseless work, and nothing but work." [21]

The polling for the members of the National Assembly were held on April 28th. This was followed on May 6th with the elections to the provincial assemblies. While 96.6 percent of the electors cast their ballots in the former election, 97.8 percent voted in the latter. It is important to note, however, that only a minority of those elected to the various legislatures received a majority of the votes cast. This was because of the number of candidates competing for each seat. On the other hand, a considerable number won their seats unopposed.[22] The elections were conducted without fanfare or demonstrations, and the absence of political party affiliations was deemed to be the reason for the tranquility. It need not be emphasized that martial law was still in force, which also helped to dampen the ardor of the more politically minded.

Despite the prevailing quiet, the government felt obliged to issue the Political Organisations (Prohibition of Unregulated Activity) Ordinance on May 9th. This new ordinance was mainly directed against the possibility of political turbulence in East Pakistan. Lieutenant General Azam Khan had been abruptly and unceremoniously removed from his governor's post in East Pakistan and replaced by Ghulam Faruque. Already unhappy with the elections, this act added to the displeasure of the inhabitants of the eastern province. The arbitrary and coercive aspects of the Ayub regime were too visible, and few could detect any significant differences between the new system and the martial law which had preceded it.

POLITICAL REALIGNMENT

On June 8, 1962, the National Assembly met in its first session. The place was Ayub Hall at Rawalpindi. President Mohammad Ayub Khan addressed the legislators and announced that martial law had been

terminated. After almost forty-four months of quasi-military rule the
civilian leaders supposedly were back in authority. The new Constitution
also came into effect on this date. In his speech the President repeated
he would support all efforts aimed at ensuring the stability and development of the nation but that he would deal harshly with those who sought
to disrupt the country by undermining the people's confidence in their
government. On this matter there would be no room for compromise.
In order to facilitate the operation of the National Assembly, seventeen
parliamentary secretaries (drawn from the membership) and one Chief
Parliamentary Secretary and Chief Whip were appointed. They were
to maintain close liaison between all Members of the National Assembly
(MNAs), the Ministers-in-Charge of Divisions and their administrative
secretaries; essentially they were to assist the ministers in their parliamentary activities. The parliamentary secretaries were also entrusted
with public relations duties for their respective divisions. Thus, like
the Basic Democracies which were linked to and dominated by the
bureaucracy, the legislators were brought under administrative influence.
This arrangement also insured needed expertise as well as coordination
in the governmental process, especially where developmental activities
were concerned.[23]

It is important to note that the central and provincial government
secretariats were reorganized in this same period. In addition, many of
the heretofore centrally directed activities were provincialized. The railways, the Water and Power Development Authority, and the Industrial
Development Corporation were bifurcated, and Agricultural Development Corporations were established in each province. Each provincial
government was given its own Planning and Development and Basic
Democracies departments while the Central Government promised funds
for numerous new projects. The Second Five Year Plan initiated in 1960
was suddenly everyone's responsibility. With the President acting as
chairman of the Central Planning Commission and the National Economic Council it was apparent that a concerted effort would be made
at energizing the development program and accelerating economic progress. The Central Planning Board set up in 1953, which was responsible
for drafting Pakistan's First Five Year Plan (1955–60), was converted
into the Planning Commission and Development Boards in the provinces.
By 1961 the President assumed the chairmanship of the Planning Commission and the Deputy Chairman, a high-ranking CSP officer, was
given the status of a Central Minister. At the same time, the Commission
was given the status of a Division in the President's Secretariat, and the
scope of its functions and powers was enhanced by the inclusion of

responsibility for implementation and review as well as formulation of national plans. The delegation of planning authority to the provinces followed after the promulgation of the Constitution. Similarly, the Rural Works Program, which was launched in East Pakistan as a pilot project in 1961, became a country-wide operation by 1963.

The President's cabinet underwent some sweeping changes in this same period. The new advisory group reflected the political climate which suddenly enveloped the country. Manzur Qadir retired from public life and resumed his legal practice in Lahore. Some believe he was simply exhausted and had requested the President to relieve him. Others thought his role as chief draftsman of the Constitution made it necessary for him to step down. Rumors also circulated that he disagreed with the President's intention to politicize the administration and possibly yield to pressure and reinstate the political parties. The new cabinet indeed included a number of politician-types. A former Prime Minister, Mohammad Ali (Bogra), succeeded Manzur Qadir as Foreign Minister.[24] Similarly, Abdul Monem Khan (soon to replace Ghulam Faruque as Governor of East Pakistan), Wahiduzzaman, Abdus Sobur Khan, A. K. M. Fazlul Quader Chowdhury, Shaikh Khursheed Ahmad, Abdullah-al-Mahmood, Abdul Waheed Khan, and Al Haj Abd-Allah Zaheer-ud-Din (Lal Mia) were selected from among the victorious members of the National Assembly to fill the ministerial positions.

The President's tactics were obvious, but also unconstitutional. Article 104 of the new Constitution specifically prevented a minister from serving in the National Assembly. The President ignored this section of the Constitution, however, and proceeded to issue Order 37 which allowed the ministers to keep their legislative positions. When the President's action was challenged in the High Court of East Pakistan it was ruled unconstitutional and later sustained by the Supreme Court. Although the ministers were thus declared to be ineligible for their legislative posts, their appearance in the Assembly as members of the government was judged permissible. Sitting in the front Treasury benches they were in a position to answer questions, rebut the opposition, or speak in support of the President's legislative program.[25]

The inability of the President to modify the Constitution in this instance can be contrasted with the success of his growing political opposition. Article 173 virtually banned the existence of political parties, and the issuance of the Prohibition of Unregulated Activity Ordinance prior to the convening of the National Assembly left no doubt as to the government's original intentions. In this, the role of Manzur Qadir cannot be minimized. As already noted, the national and provincial legislators were elected on the basis of individual performance and/or personality.

The absence of political parties meant there could be no platforms and no responsible organizational programs that the electors might consider; but it also meant the legislators would have great difficulty in organizing their affairs once the assemblies convened. This latter dilemma was especially evident when the speakers and deputy speakers had to be elected from among the members of the legislatures. The initial impulse, therefore, was to organize along provincial lines, and the members from East and West Pakistan huddled in separate caucuses to work out their respective strategies. This was certainly not what the President desired, and the fear that a continuation of the ban on political parties would only lead to deepening cleavages and more intense conflict between the East and West Pakistani contingents compelled him to reconsider his position. Hence, when the President indicated a slackening in his hostility to the political parties, some organized but mostly *ad hoc* activity followed.

THE OPPOSITION REACTS

The political discussion that followed centered on the Constitution; those opposing it condemned it on its face as being autocratic and undemocratic. The banning of the political parties, the continuation of the restrictions on the EBDO'ed politicians (those convicted under the Security of Pakistan Act), the forced detention of other political figures, the indirect process of elections, and the non-justiciability of fundamental rights were offered as justification of this judgment. The silence of the President on these expressions of political disfavor encouraged some of the more vocal members to seek legislation in the Assembly for the legalization of the political parties. In point of fact, the National Awami Party (NAP), Muslim League, Jamaat-i-Islami, Awami League, and Krishak Sramik Party were already operating with impunity outside the legislatures. On July 4, 1962, a bill providing for the formation and regulation of political parties was drafted by the government and referred to a select committee of the Assembly.

The select committee was composed of persons representing different shades of opinion, and three days after becoming seized of the draft they returned it to the floor of the Assembly citing their inability to agree on a *modus operandi*. Nevertheless, on July 14th the draft bill, virtually unmodified, was put up to a vote and passed. On the next day the National Assembly passed another bill liberalizing the Preventive

Detention Laws. The President gave his assent on July 16th and the Political Parties Bill became law. Despite many controversial features making it difficult for the opposition in the National Assembly to associate itself with the new law (i.e., the law prevented persons imprisoned for three months or more under the Security of Pakistan Act from participating in political activities, and it gave the government authority to declare other persons ineligible should they engage in activities considered detrimental to the health and security of the nation), the political parties were quick to legitimate their operations after its enactment.

Within a few days the Jamaat-i-Islami announced that it was back in business. In August the Nizam-i-Islam revealed its intention to engage in political activity. Although President Ayub acknowledged he was a prisoner of events and hence forced to accept the return of the political parties, he was still convinced that the country would be better off without them. Nonetheless, on July 20th, accepting the *fait accompli,* he made a fervent plea for a broad-based nationalist political party which could unify the nation and direct its energies toward constructive endeavors. At the time it did not seem that he would consider joining any political party. In an article in *Dawn* on July 31, 1962, the President emphasized his concern that a party organized and led by himself would receive the opprobrium of the people in that it would be considered a "King's Party." However, Ayub urged his followers to get on with the job of building a party that would represent the government in the assemblies, and it was known that he urged government party leaders to take the name of the defunct Muslim League. The President was criticized for using the name of the Muslim League, but no one disputed the fact that it was important as a political symbol to the party in power which still sought to legitimate its activity.

Thus all the resources of the government were placed at the disposal of pro-government politicians in the legislatures. In effect, a political party was being formed in reverse order. On September 4, 1962, the Muslim League (Conventionists) became the official government party. The Conventionists comprised the ministers, a majority of members of the Assembly, and other followers of the government. Almost all were relatively new to politics and had not held posts in the pre-1958 Muslim League. Of the older, more seasoned Muslim Leaguers, those who were allowed to participate in politics formed their own Muslim League Party, which was distinguished by the term "Councillors." The Councillors derived their name from the Muslim League Council, which refused to accept the Conventionists as genuine Muslim Leaguers.

Abdul Qayyum Khan, the last president of the Muslim League before the imposition of martial law, was imprisoned by the authorities a few days after the passage of the Political Parties Bill. He did not rejoin the Council Muslim League until February 1967 when his EBDO term expired. Therefore, the Muslim League Councillors selected former Prime Minister Khwaja Nazimuddin to lead them. When he died in 1964, Nurul Amin took control of the party. Nurul Amin was also made leader of the National Democratic Front after the death of H. S. Suhrawardy in 1963. He was leader of the opposition in the National Assembly, helped form the Pakistan Democratic Movement, and led the Democratic Action Committee, coalition of eight opposition parties which sought to displace Ayub Khan.

AYUB'S RESPONSE

The Conventionists had as their chief organizer Chaudhri Khaliquzzaman, president of the Muslim League after the death of Mohammad Ali Jinnah; but he was too old and too weak a figure to lead the party. On December 15, 1962, the only obvious choice for a leader was identified, and President Ayub Khan was requested to assume the post. In being asked to take the assignment he was reminded that not only Jinnah but Liaquat Ali Khan, the first Prime Minister, had held the presidency of the party while simultaneously administering the affairs of state. The President agreed to consider the proposal but first stressed the need for the party to restructure itself; to lay down the guidelines that it intended to follow. On May 23, 1963, *Dawn* of Karachi printed an article by the President stating that he had joined the Conventionists "as a two-anna member from both East and West Pakistan."

In the same article the President made it clear that he would be more than just a symbolic leader, however. He proceeded to list the party's objectives. They were:

1. Take such steps in religious, educational, social, economic and other fields as would bring about unity of thought and action amongst people. Make them take pride in their homeland and its achievements and bring self-respect, self-reliance and a sense of responsibility and discipline.

2. Build a society with spiritual, moral and civic sense capable of moving with the modern age.

3. Encourage such activities as will enable us to enter the age of science and technology within the shortest possible time.

4. Encourage industrialisation to the maximum extent possible and modernize agriculture so as to get the maximum benefit from our lands and remove economic disparities wherever possible.

5. Take such measures as will enable the benefits of development to be shared by as many people as possible.

6. To do that, take steps to see that while private enterprise is encouraged, undue accumulation of wealth is not allowed in a few hands.

7. Establish Islamic political ideology, social justice and economic order and move in the direction of a welfare state in accordance with the resources of the country.

8. Meanwhile, encourage people to regulate charities on a local, collective and national basis so as to take care of the needy and deserving.

9. Stand by our solemn promise to assist the people of Jammu and Kashmir to attain their freedom.

10. Conduct foreign relations in a manner that will gain us friends and ensure the maximum security and development of the country.

Seven months later in Dacca on December 24, 1963, President Mohammad Ayub Khan accepted the unanimous vote of the Pakistan Muslim League and became its president. Despite his aversion to politics, Ayub Khan hoped to prove that through organizational politics he could rule a divided society without excessive coercion and without violence.[26]

THE POLITICS OF CONTROL

Having given in to the demand to reinstate political parties the President let it be believed he would yield on other major issues as well. In his question and answer meeting with the press on March 1, 1962, President Ayub disclosed that he would appoint a Franchise Commission to investigate all sides of the issue surrounding direct or indirect elections. (A Franchise Commission had also been recommended by the Constitution Committee.) Taking cognizance of the opposition to the Basic Democracies electoral college with its power to elect the President and the members of the national and provincial legislatures, Ayub intimated that he would welcome a better system than the one he had designed—but he was assuredly skeptical. Commenting at the time he said:

They can produce two more qualifications and say that anyone who is educated beyond a certain level, or anyone who owns property beyond a certain level or pays taxes beyond a certain level, might be given the right to vote. What else can they say? Very well, as soon as you do that, you are going to create a tremendous imbalance between your city population and your rural population. You are going to disenfranchise 80 per cent of your people. You are going to set them at a disadvantage straight-away. One may well say that this is not an insurmountable problem because if a constituency has 500 voters, shall we say, by a certain criteria to elect one man and another constituency has 5,000 or 50,000 voters on the same criteria, it does not make all that difference. But then how are you going to select your President on that basis? Can you make certain that the number of voters in East and West Pakistan would be equal? Can you say that East and West Pakistan are going to be at par with each other in so far as the numerical strength of votes is concerned, and if they are not thus at par, then can you say that 100 East Pakistanis will count as 80 West Pakistanis? The position would obviously be absurd. But I am going to set up a Commission and I will be interested to see what they bring up *but I beg of you please to get it into your head that direct universal franchise in Pakistan, other than on the basis of which I am suggesting, is not a practical proposition for the present at least.*[27] (Italics added.)

In spite of his firm conviction that the process of indirect elections was the only one presently suited to Pakistani society, Ayub gave in to the pressure of the intelligentsia. On July 30, 1962, he appointed a five-member Franchise Commission to investigate alternative propositions.

Akhter Husain, the chairman of the Commission, and his associates were requested to address themselves to two principal questions:

1. Whether the system of election of the President and Members of the Assemblies through Basic Democracies was [an] efficacious and appropriate instrument for a realistic representation of the people; and

2. If the Commission recommended universal suffrage, whether any qualifications of the electors should be imposed?

The Commission submitted its report on February 12, 1963, with two members, including the chairman, dissenting. It was an embarrassing moment for Ayub Khan. The majority report, like the Constitution

Commission before it, ruled against indirect elections and insisted that only universal adult franchise should be the basis of election for the President and members of the assemblies. The minority report was in keeping with the President's ideas, however. With opinions of the members of the Commission divided (3–2), the Law Ministry was ordered by the President to appoint a Special Committee to examine all recommendations dispassionately and "keeping in view the socio-economic and administrative requirements of the country." [28] Later, when the Special Committee submitted its report, no one was surprised to find it in favor of the minority view that the indirect election should remain. "Until such time as a majority of the people become literate, any election based on direct voting would be an unreliable index of responsible public opinion and will provide an opportunity to unpatriotic and hostile elements to create confusion and arrest the progress of the country." [29]

To this, five opposition members on the Special Committee courageously contributed a note of dissent which read in part: "We are finally of the opinion that the present system is a denial of the rights of the people and that it would only perpetuate a thinly veiled dictatorship in the country." [30] Not everyone would go so far as to use the language that Maulvi Farid Ahmad employed in his personal note of dissent, but it illustrated the disillusionment and frustration of the opposition in this fretful exercise: "It is, perhaps, unique and unheard of in the annals of running the government and the appointment of Commissions that a Commission, the child of its own creation, has been neglected and consigned ingloriously to the gutters. This is a matter which the country should not fail to notice except with the gravest concern." [31]

It is open to question whether the President was wise in appointing the Franchise Commission. On the one side, he wished to show his proper intentions (the same was true when he appointed the Constitution Commission) but on the other, he was unprepared from the outset to listen to and accept recommendations running counter to his own judgments. Also, with the Constitution already in force and with Basic Democracies being given increasing consideration, it was already too late to consider a new approach—that is, unless a drastic revision of the new political structure was contemplated. A somewhat independent but apologetic analysis of the Ayub Constitution concluded that:

> While the present constitution has rightly taken steps against the political and economic instability as experienced in Pakistan in the past, it may be necessary in the course of the working of the constitution, to provide some additional safeguards against the

danger of arbitrary government. With a sincere and well meaning President such as the present President of Pakistan there may not be any such risk.[32]

In the end, however, Ayub only added fuel to the fire set by his detractors, who now felt all the more justified in accusing him of dictatorial acts. If anything was gained from the episode it was that the President, for the time being at least, would insist and would be successful in having things done his way; but opposition to his ideas and policies was clearly on the upswing.

From the moment the political parties were permitted to operate President Ayub was on the defensive. Overtures went out to both Khwaja Nazimuddin and H. S. Suhrawardy to cease their criticism and join with the Conventionist Muslim League in the forging of a strong national party. Both men chose to rebuff the invitations, however. Suhrawardy had been arrested on January 30, 1962, under the Security of Pakistan Act, and his imprisonment without trial disturbed his followers as well as the volatile student community. Demonstrations erupted in and around Dacca and some of the other municipalities of East Pakistan in defiance of martial law which resulted in the jailing of a number of political leaders. When he was finally released from prison on August 19, 1962, Suhrawardy not only refused to accept Chaudhri Khaliquzzaman's invitation to join the Conventionists (an interesting invitation in view of Suhrawardy's EBDO status) but was intent on organizing the entire opposition against Ayub Khan. In order to do this he severed his ties with the Awami League and formed the National Democratic Front (NDF). The NDF, according to Suhrawardy, was not a political party and therefore permitted him to skirt the disqualification order. He was to toil in its behalf until illness forced him to seek medical attention in Beirut, where he died on December 5, 1963. At the news of Suhrawardy's death there was wide and persistent speculation in Pakistan that the President had him poisoned so he could no longer threaten his authority. In point of fact, Suhrawardy had been ailing for many years and his multifarious activities, both political and social, simply took their final toll. But there was no convincing those who both loved the former Prime Minister and despised the President.

Nazimuddin refused to join with the Conventionists for virtually the same reasons as Suhrawardy. Despite having been decorated by the President in the year following the revolution, Nazimuddin grew disenchanted with Ayub's handling of the affairs of state. He was especially critical of the new Constitution and the presidential form of government, which he felt gave far too much power to the executive. And as for the Conventionists, he could not accept them as fellow Muslim Leaguers. Instead, he agreed to accept the leadership of the Council Muslim League. Nazimuddin joined both Suhrawardy's NDF and, at the outset of the electoral campaign in 1964, the Combined Opposition Parties (COP). In October 1964, when he was being considered as the possible COP candidate for the presidency, death overtook him.

It is one of the ironies of Pakistan's history that just when the political opposition returned to the main stage and a decisive election was in the offing they should be shorn of their national leaders. The only other personality who might have tested the President's power was Tamizuddin Khan, Speaker in the National Assembly; but his sudden death in 1963 also removed his name from contention. It was no wonder, then, that the COP in looking for someone to stand against the President was compelled to request the assistance of Miss Fatima Jinnah.

There was simply no one else the numerous opposition parties could trust and rally around. But it was also a dismal commentary on the political shape of things in the opposition camp. In the two and a half years which extended from the promulgation of the new Constitution to the second election of the Basic Democracies in the autumn of 1964 and the election of the President on January 2, 1965, popular dissatisfaction would be obvious. However, mobilization of this discontent beyond the confines of the major cities was never significant. The opposition would offer the view that they had little chance of winning in the rural areas because of the strength of the rural power structure and the bureaucracy which favored the government. Although this is in part correct, it is also true that the opposition displayed very little ingenuity in wooing the rural Basic Democrats. Another argument offered by the opposition is worthy of further study. The Basic Democrats, they insist, were elected for the most part on independent platforms in 1964. It was only after the election that the government "enticed" them into joining the Muslim League Conventionists.

THE POLITICS OF REGIONALISM

The unsettled situation in East Pakistan was particularly distressing to the President. His regime gave more attention to the provincial disparity issue than had any previous government, and the 1962 Constitution devoted a passage to this dilemma. It declared that all efforts would be made to satisfy the economic demands of the people of the

East wing. But even with increased investment of government money, the granting of greater provincial autonomy in virtually all the developmental and public utility spheres, and the determination to "Bengalize" the administration, there was no quelling the anti-government disturbances. Governor Ghulam Faruque was unable to fill the shoes of Lieutenant General Azam Khan and powerless to control the demands of the politicians, students, and laboring elements. He resigned in frustration hardly six months after assuming his office.

The new Governor was a Bengali, Abdul Monem Khan, and it was hoped he could calm the passions of his provincial countrymen. Abdul Monem Khan, a lawyer from the district of Mymensingh, had only membership on a school board to show for his experience in public life before the onset of Basic Democracies. The Basic Democrats elected him to a seat in the National Assembly, and from there President Ayub took him into his cabinet as Minister for Health. It was from this position that he was called to assume the office of Governor of East Pakistan. His appointment came as a shock to members of the East Pakistani intelligentsia who suspected Monem Khan of dishonest practices. Given this record and his loyalty to the President, he could not be expected to earn the respect of the East Pakistanis. Needless to add, he was also incapable of coping with the province's economic and social problems.

With its limited resource base East Pakistan will have difficulty in equalling West Pakistan's development, no matter how much preference is given to the former. West Pakistan's greater potential is obvious and investments already made will inevitably draw more in their wake. Hence the gap must widen, and as West Pakistan improves its standard of living repercussions are bound to be felt in East Pakistan. Thus the disparity problem will remain to plague any government despite all efforts and sincere intentions to correct the imbalance.

Disparity, whether it be considered a slogan or an unfortunate circumstance, will remain a grievance of significant political proportions. "We have been turned into a colony" is a familiar East Pakistani claim when a discussion of the Central Government is raised. The thrust of the East Pakistani argument is simple: East Pakistan's jute is the nation's chief earner of foreign exchange. Nonetheless, profits from the sale of the commodity are being spent to develop West Pakistan. In one sense the argument is valid; but the larger problems which cannot be answered are linked to East Pakistan's absorptive capacity, its limited resources, and the overwhelming population pressure.

Even Pakistan's faulty statistics cannot hide the fact that West Pakistan is six times again the size of East Pakistan, that the natural endowments of West Pakistan although not extraordinary are more impressive than those of East Pakistan, and finally, that the density of population in West Pakistan is under 200 persons per square mile whereas in East Pakistan it is now well over 1,000. Supposing the province were permitted to retain all the profits earned from its jute crop, the income received would still be insufficient to raise the standard of living of the average peasant; clearly, money is not the only factor—even if in Pakistan it is scarce in the extreme. It is cruel realism which dictates how a country allocates its priorities and scarce treasure. Only a firm hand and compassionate attitude can deal with the nightmare of underdevelopment and its inevitable consequences.

Ruling out the possibility of a clash which would terminate in the establishment of a separate sovereign entity in East Pakistan, an anonymous observer from Great Britain wrote in 1963:

> The future of an independent East Pakistan is not clearly visualized, but one thing is clear—there is no thought at all to any closer connexion with West Bengal; indeed fear of economic domination by the Hindu [and Indian] part of Bengal is one factor that will go to induce wariness when the pros and cons of separation are weighed.

> What can be done to reinforce the unity of the country? Economically, not much; disparity has already gone too far to be removed and it will be immensely difficult even to prevent the gap widening further. One hope expressed in Dacca by those who are dismayed by the present trend is the emergence of a new and ideological party with mass support in both wings and a programme of radical social and economic reform. For the moment there is no sign of such an alignment. The Government might be tempted to lean upon Islam as the strongest unifying force, but already in Dacca even those who are anxious to preserve unity dismiss religion as an effective binding agent. Perhaps the best that can be hoped for is that Pakistan will move towards a looser association between the two wings, with a high degree of political and economic autonomy for each, and that in such a relationship the East Pakistanis would find new reasons for maintaining the nation as one.[33]

In the early Spring of 1969 it appeared that the latter course was finally being pursued.

In a relatively unknown document prepared by five members of the Finance Commission in 1963 the disparity enigma was dissected. They found that it would take twenty-five years for the provinces to be brought abreast of one another economically; and that this target could only be achieved if development in the West wing was drastically curtailed. The intimation was that deceleration would have to be almost total.[34] Obviously this was an impossible proposal.

The momentum of development in West Pakistan could not be slowed without calamitous consequences. Nor would the government encourage such a suggestion. But reports like this made urgent a more equitable distribution of development benefits. This meant the building of two new capital cities instead of just the one originally planned at Islamabad. East Pakistan was declared by the new Constitution to be the legislative capital and work was started on building a "second capital" outside the immediate limits of metropolitan Dacca. Similarly, if a fertilizer factory, steel mill, or sugar refinery was to be built in West Pakistan, East Pakistan had to be given one too. The furor over the building of nuclear power plants is another case in point. But no matter how much pressure the East Pakistanis place on their government, one fact remains self-evident. East Pakistan cannot yet compete with its sister province in the development race, and it will take decades before advances in West Pakistan materially improve the economic picture in East Pakistan.

Pessimistic though it be, the inevitable conclusion is that East Pakistan's demands cannot presently be met no matter how much effort the Pakistan government gives to the dilemma, no matter how sincere its intentions.[35] Thus more political turbulence can be expected and more restraints will undoubtedly be imposed.

As recently as the winter of 1966, demands could be heard reverberating throughout Pakistan for an arrangement which would give the East Pakistanis greater control over their destiny. In the forefront of this movement was Sheikh Mujibur Rahman, the leader of the East Pakistan Awami League. His Six Point Program, which he presented to the Subjects Committee of the Conference of Opposition Parties in Lahore and which appeared in a letter to *The Pakistan Times* published on February 13, 1966, specified those areas which would free the East Pakistanis from the grip of the Central Government and hence from the dominance of the West Pakistanis. It argued in favor of still another constitution, not the restitution of the one promulgated in 1956. A new edifice would be constructed along confederal lines. The Central Government would be supreme in only two areas—defense and foreign affairs. And in the former category each province, now labeled states, would be free to raise and maintain paramilitary and territorial forces.

The Central Government would give up its power to tax and the two states would have their own currencies which would be freely convertible. The Central Government would receive its working revenues from the states in the amount that the states deemed necessary. Each state would control its own foreign trade, and the exchange earned from this trade would be left at the disposal of the state earning it.

Mujibur's Six Point Program frightened his associates in the West Pakistani opposition. Most of them feared the proposal contained the seeds of national disintegration and rejected it on that count alone. Others, perhaps more sympathetic, found it unacceptable on grounds that it would invite government reprisals against the political parties, and forty-four months of martial law had proved to be a sobering experience. No one in West Pakistan wanted a repetition of the 1958–62 period. And although they were prepared to risk arrest in order to publicize their demands, they were not interested in supporting a policy which, as Ayub suggested, might lead to "civil war" in the country.[36]

In December 1966, and in the early months of 1967, the United States was accused of plotting to establish a "United States of Bengal." The United States categorically denied any such clandestine action and it appears, given the prevalence of anti-Americanism, that this was one more attempt at discrediting a segment of the opposition. But a more bizarre charge was to be made in January 1968, when Mujibur Rahman and some thirty-four other Bengalis were implicated in what has come to be known as the Agartala Conspiracy. Charged with working with Indian agents, they were rumored to be planning the assassination of Ayub as a prelude to declaring East Pakistan an independent state. Arraigned before a public tribunal in mid-1968, their trial only highlighted the degeneration of the judicial, administrative, and political systems.[37]

Chapter 3

International Events: The Domestic Impact

IN THE AUTUMN of 1962 India and China engaged in a border clash which reverberated round the world. The Indians were no match for the Chinese armies which swarmed through and over the Himalayas and quickly put the hapless defenders to flight. As Chinese successes mounted, the Western powers, but especially the United States and Great Britain, were drawn into the picture. India's poor showing was attributed to an outmoded defense posture which relied too heavily on diplomatic niceties and very little on military muscle.[1] When the Chinese unilaterally withdrew their forces, a dazed Indian Government began to review the shambles of its foreign policy. At the same time it opened its doors wide to receive military hardware which the United States soon made available.

In Pakistan, this gesture of American goodwill toward India was interpreted as ill will directed at a loyal and steadfast ally. India was Pakistan's unreconciled enemy, and the arms shipments were described as a threat to Pakistan's security. It has already been noted that President Ayub was endeavoring to weather the political storms which he himself had created by allowing the "free" play of political party activity. This new situation, far beyond his power to control, provided still another opportunity for his opponents to undermine his authority.

Given the President's adherence to the military pacts and his unconcealed friendship with the Western powers, especially his reliance on the United States, he was exposed to criticism from those who had long argued against sustaining these tight relationships and dependencies. Now the criticism grew louder and it obviously had considerable popular backing. The President was in a poor position from which to defend himself. His foreign policy had already undergone several reappraisals and, as noted, windows had been opened to the Communist world more than a year before. But now even more drastic changes were required.

On November 21, 1962, the President convened an emergency session of the National Assembly to consider the situation arising out of the

Sino-Indian conflict and the arms that the latter country was receiving from the United States. It was Ayub's considered opinion that the large-scale supply of weapons to India disturbed the balance of military power in South Asia and posed a direct threat to Pakistan's security. Although in 1959 President Ayub offered India a plan for the joint defense of the subcontinent, which even then appeared threatened by China, now he claimed that the "threat" was merely a ploy used by the Indians to acquire large quantities of free arms from the United States. Ayub could not forget that Prime Minister Nehru rejected his 1959 joint-defense offer out of hand; nor could he dismiss from his mind the feeling that Nehru had provoked China into the 1962 border conflict by calling upon his troops to clear the Chinese from lands they had occupied earlier in Ladakh and the North East Frontier Agency.

When the Chinese voluntarily withdrew their forces to the original line of control, Ayub was even more convinced that the Chinese were less interested in invading India than in teaching the Indians a lesson.[2] Thus Ayub insisted that India was using "the Chinese bogey" to improve its war-making capabilities. The President concluded that India would never fight China as an ally of the United States and that China would never launch an isolated full-scale attack on India. Hence the weapons which India received from the United States would only be used against those countries from which India had least to fear. And as Pakistan and India each considered the other its primary enemy, the expanding of the Indian Armed Forces would embolden the Indians to possible adventures. Moreover, it would make it impossible for Pakistan to resolve the Kashmir dispute.

The intertwining of international and domestic politics is neither unique nor a consequence of modernity. All governments throughout history have been prisoners at one time or other of international events. Pakistan is no exception. Every alert person in Pakistan knew Ayub Khan's role in allying the country with the West—even if some could not understand his reasons. Many articulate individuals, especially those who were displeased with the manner in which Ayub came to power, concluded long ago that the President conspired with the United States in overthrowing the parliamentary government of Feroz Khan Noon.

They believed that the imposition of martial law was merely a shield behind which the whole edifice of Pakistan's Government could be dismantled, that the destruction of the political party system was necessary because Washington had decided the leftists in the National Awami Party, the Ganatantri Dal, the Awami League, and the Youth League— as well as Bhashani's Krishak Samiti—were growing too powerful.

Whether or not Ayub admitted the accuracy of this judgment was un-important because he was compelled to follow the dictates of "his mas-ters." But, insist his antagonists, he also had little to lose and much to gain. Ayub Khan is pictured as having fancied himself a great leader and the rightful heir to Jinnah's mantle. That he found the Americans useful explains their happy if limited alliance.

Ayub's policies identifying Pakistan with the West were never so pro-nounced as in May 1960 when the famous U–2 incident took place. The flight over the Soviet Union was reported to have originated from Pesha-war, and when the Russian Premier announced that a "red ring" had been drawn around the frontier city most Pakistanis were understandably alarmed. What price must Pakistan pay for its alliances with the West? This was a question that was debated in the bazaars, universities, indus-tries, and wherever the more "sophisticated" masses congregated. It was fortunate for the President that the incident occurred in a period of martial law when an absolute ban on political parties obtained. Had it been mid- or late 1962, the U–2 incident might well have led to serious demonstrations. As it was, people murmured their dissatisfaction with the country's foreign policy but there was no overt reaction.

THE OPPOSITION AND FOREIGN POLICY

Muslim pride was another reason for the discontent. Pakistan's heavy dependence on the West in the economic sphere as well as the military, and the resulting impact on the political system and social life, riled the sensitive, concerned elements in the population. It was their argument that this dependence prevented Pakistan from molding a society true to Islamic traditions. Maulana Maudoodi was only one of their spokesmen. Whereas Maudoodi emphasized religious aspects, intellectuals like Faiz Ahmad Faiz developed the same theme but his more secular propensities urged him to declare that broader aspects of Islamic and Oriental "cul-ture" were also in danger.

At the Seventh Anniversary celebrations of the Pakistan Writers Guild, Faiz Ahmad Faiz, holder of the Soviet Union's Lenin Peace Prize, struck this chord again. In a paper entitled "Some Cultural Problems of Afro-Asian Countries," published in *The Pakistan Times Sunday Supple-ment* on February 20, 1966, he made the following points:

> The qualitative political change from colonialism to independence must be followed by a similar qualitative change in the social struc-

ture left behind by colonialism. . . . Imperialist domination tried to weaken and destroy whatever was good progressive and forward-looking . . . it tried to sustain and perpetuate whatever was bad, reactionary and backward-looking, ignorance, superstition, servility and class exploitation. What was handed back to the newly liberated countries, therefore, was not the social structure which it took over but the perverted and emasculated remnants of cheap, spurious, second-hand imitations of its own capitalist cultural patterns by way of language, custom, manners, art forms and ideological values . . . these problems can be effectively solved only when the political revolution of national liberation is followed by a social revolution to complete national independence.

To men like Faiz and Maudoodi the Christian West was a corrupting element, and they cautioned their followers that only with the banishment of Ayub Khan could "the decay and degeneration" of Pakistan's Muslim society be arrested. Despite all these attacks on his authority, direct and indirect, Ayub stubbornly adhered to friendship with the West, however.

Relations with Pakistan's allies were strained earlier, as was noted in the bitter exchange between Pakistan and Afghanistan in 1961; nevertheless, the denouement did not come until the extensive shipment of arms to India by the United States in 1962. Ayub could no longer avoid the issue of his Western entanglements. What he said about India and China he believed up to the day he left office: the years spent in building the Pakistani Army were not wasted; Pakistan's enemy was no illusion. Ayub looked upon India as a threat to Pakistan's integrity, and he was deeply worried about the growing disparity in military capability. Ayub also had to take cognizance of the existence of the political parties, most of whom persistently clamored for a withdrawal from the military alliances and a wider association with the Muslim countries (notably in the Arab world), and Communist or Socialist states.

ZULFIKAR ALI BHUTTO: POLITICIAN WITH A DIFFERENCE

The sudden death of Mohammad Ali (Bogra), Pakistan's Foreign Minister, on January 23, 1963, elevated Zulfikar Ali Bhutto to one of the three highest offices in the President's cabinet. His appointment could not have come at a more auspicious moment. Bhutto held a variety of portfolios in Ayub's government after the declaration of martial law. From October 10, 1958, to his appointment as head of the Ministry of External Affairs on January 24, 1963, he occupied the top posts in the

Commerce, Industries, Information and Broadcasting, Kashmir Affairs, Natural Resources and Rehabilitation, and Works ministries. Born in 1928, he was just under thirty when he assumed his first cabinet position, and was the most youthful, energetic, and ambitious of the President's confidants.

Bhutto was a bright, intelligent, and sensitive individual and the President treated him like a family member. And Bhutto returned this affection, practically worshipping Ayub. In a way, Ayub was betrayed by Bhutto's youth. The President valued his presence in the cabinet because he worked arduously at his assigned tasks, but Ayub could not anticipate that Bhutto, in Pakistan's age-graded society, would contest the dictates of his superior. Nor could he foresee how the personality of the young minister would mature in the hard realities of international and domestic politics; how his emotionally charged but articulate speeches would affect the Pakistanis who listened to or read them; or how one day he would disagree with the wisdom of his President's decision and be forced into the vortex of a national controversy.

Born in Larkana District in Sind, the son of Sir Shah Nawaz Khan Bhutto, an influential landlord and former minister in the Bombay Government before Independence, he was the scion of an aristocratic family whose importance was recognized in Sind, Baluchistan, the Punjab, and Rajputana in India. Z. A. Bhutto graduated from the University of California with honors in political science in 1950 and received an M.A. in jurisprudence from Oxford in 1952. In that same year he obtained his Barrister-at-Law certification from Lincoln's Inn.

After completing his education Bhutto was appointed lecturer in international law in the University of Southampton in England. He returned to Pakistan in 1953, and after a brief stint as a teacher took up legal practice in Sind. In 1957 he was made a member of the Pakistani Delegation to the United Nations General Assembly and in 1958, just before the October revolution, led Pakistan's delegation to the United Nations Conference on the "Law of the Sea." Bhutto's training and interests were in the field of international affairs, and it can be speculated that the President was grooming him for a post in the Foreign Ministry from the moment he selected him for his cabinet. The young man learned much in his more than four years as a cabinet official, and although the President might have preferred greater maturity before moving him into the Ministry of External Affairs, destiny ruled otherwise.

Mohammad Ali's death left Ayub in a difficult situation. The government had assumed a posture which, while critical of the United

States, enabled Pakistan to remain in the alliances. The President understood the implications of this policy and trusted no one but himself to sustain it. Mohammad Ali was an ideal choice in that he acted like a transmission belt. Twice Ambassador to the United States, congenial and accustomed to carrying out orders, he had implemented the President's policies to the letter.[3] But it was not easy to find a successor. In selecting Bhutto, Ayub obviously believed he had an obedient subordinate. Although inexperienced, he seemed to be what the times required.

United States arms shipments to India intensified anti-American feeling in Pakistan and the President wanted someone with rapport among the students and urban intelligentsia. And Zulfikar Ali Bhutto's performance up through Ayub's reelection in January 1965 leaves no doubt that he served a very useful purpose. Bhutto, unlike the President but undoubtedly with his consent, publicly castigated the United States. He also openly supported a number of new organizations such as the Pakistan Afro-Asian Society whose Anti-Americanism became its *raison d'être*. While the President had no intention of duplicating his style, all this was considered good domestic politics. Nevertheless, a new problem had arisen. Bhutto accumulated a following of his own.

The new Foreign Minister was a true representative of the educated and determined younger generation. He was one of them, spoke their language, knew their thoughts, and shared their aspirations. It would not be in error to suggest that he, like so many young intellectuals, found socialist policies appealing—and this reinforced his prejudices against things Western.[4] Bhutto was often carried away by his own rhetoric, and his emotionally charged speeches were often more than Ayub had bargained for.

But even then the Foreign Minister was an asset. Through him the Ayub regime acquired a degree of creditability it could ill afford to discount. Bhutto played his role so well that some observers believed the President would eventually name him his heir apparent. Hasan Askari analyzes the leadership dilemma in Pakistan and concludes with the view that the Ayub regime "did succeed in giving us new ideas, new priorities and new men. The reason behind the EBDOing of the leading lights in the Opposition was to neutralize them for a certain number of years and in that period to groom up a new set of young leaders." Although holding the opinion that the regime failed in this endeavor, Askari comments that there are one or two new luminaries. "The most probable heir for the mantle of Savior is Mr. Zulfikar Ali Bhutto. Mr. Bhutto seems to be idolised by practically everyone."[5]

THE KASHMIR DILEMMA

The Kashmir dispute remains the key to India-Pakistan relations. It caused the two countries to clash at the very moment of independence in 1947 and it has been responsible for the subsequent tense situation, the intermittent conflict, and the brief Indo-Pakistani War of September 1965. It is also interesting to note how the Kashmir dilemma weaves itself into the fabric of Pakistan's domestic life. Ayub Khan emerged as commander-in-chief of the Army in 1950 in part because the government of Liaquat Ali Khan could not trust the "older" officers who insisted on renewing the war in Kashmir. It was left to Ayub to neutralize the conspiracy that these generals were hatching.

In like fashion, Kashmir played a prominent role in Ayub's decision to oust the parliamentary government and abrogate the 1956 Constitution. Under the leadership of Abdul Qayyum Khan, the Muslim League in 1958 tried to make a comeback at a time of widespread political instability. Essentially, the party sought to rally the public behind its banners by declaring that the Muslim League would actively support the Kashmiris in their liberation movement. As commander in chief it fell to Ayub to order the Army to intercept and disarm paramilitary Muslim League forces. Under Army pressures, the government later agreed to force the Muslim League to disband its private force. It was the Kashmir dispute which again perplexed the government in the early sixties, but with the emergence of Zulfikar Ali Bhutto as Foreign Minister restraint did not seem to be a valuable tactic.

Ayub Khan's popularity sank to a new low at the start of 1963. Popular sentiment in Pakistan ran against the President when he failed to take advantage of the Sino-Indian border war and march his armies into Kashmir. Ayub was perceived as following the dictates of his United States advisers—a prisoner in his own country. It was the Foreign Minister's task to ease Ayub over this hurdle. Bhutto counseled resoluteness and advised the President to take a hard line on Kashmir, not only because a Muslim population was being denied the right of self-determination, but because it would immeasurably improve the President's image at home. And lest it be lost from view, the President's primary objective lay in the establishment of institutions capable of putting the country on the road to eventual modernization. This elusive objective could only be attained if Ayub was supported and received the cooperation of the articulate reference groups.

As a military figure Ayub could never acquire popularity with the intelligentsia through political means. Nor would economic progress bring in its wake a satisfied and dedicated following. Only a military success could earn him this reward; and the battleground for such a test was readily available in Kashmir. Thus Bhutto could say:

> I remember that when the struggle for the achievement of Pakistan was being waged, it was said that it should be a now or never struggle. The problem of Kashmir has now become so urgent, so critical in its consequences, that it should be thought of in the same way. Kashmir must be liberated if Pakistan is to have its full meaning.[6]

It is not intended to compare the "patriotism" of Ayub with that of his Foreign Minister. Both men were dedicated to the proposition that the Kashmiris must be given the opportunity to determine their own destiny. The major distinction to be drawn here is that Ayub Khan, as a practitioner of military science, knew the hard realities of national capabilities and modern warfare. Emotional responses may momentarily intoxicate but they also blur issues. Ayub, by temperament, pondered the consequences of his pronouncements. But Ayub learned this the hard way. Bhutto, on the other hand, was less apt to practice caution or self-restraint. Bhutto wrote of Nehru that "he [Nehru] sprang out of that greatest of all contradictions called India and that is why Nehru was India." [7] The man who spoke of Nehru in these terms must have given some consideration to his own leader. To Bhutto, Pakistan is not a contradiction, and if he observed closely he must have realized that neither was Ayub Khan.

Ayub was without mystique or popularity, possibly because he addressed himself to specific issues, practiced rationalism, and refused to be carried away by sentiment. It is not that he was so out of touch with his people; simply put, his pragmatism was too stark, perhaps too calculated for Pakistanis to appreciate. All the same, it is obvious that Ayub Khan personified Pakistan for a decade.[8]

FOREIGN ENTANGLEMENTS

The new Foreign Minister soon realized he had taken on a terrible responsibility. Talks with India were underway, and he was called upon to take up where his predecessor left off. He played host to the Eleventh Session of the Central Treaty Organization's Economic Committee and welcomed the United States Assistant Secretary of State, who was in

Pakistan to reassure President Ayub that American arms going to India would never be used against Pakistan. But what was undoubtedly his most celebrated activity was the journey to Communist China and the signing of the border agreement between the two countries on March 2, 1963.

Bhutto was neither responsible for the settlement nor the drafting of the document. The initial work and, by and large, the most difficult phase of the negotiations were carried through under Manzur Qadir. Mohammad Ali (Bogra) completed the arrangements. It was Bhutto's task to represent Pakistan at the ceremony honoring the accord. Again, this is not to suggest that the Foreign Minister was a rubber stamp to the proceedings. As a long-time member of the President's cabinet his advice had often been requested. On other occasions he was impetuous enough to present his views, requested or not. And although Manzur Qadir may not have always appreciated the advice of Z. A. Bhutto, the fact that the President listened was significant.

Bhutto encountered less resistance from Mohammad Ali, who was unimpressed with Qadir. (On one occasion Mohammad Ali publicly called Qadir a "Rasputin.") Nonetheless, the fact remains that it was during Manzur Qadir's tenure as Foreign Minister that the first real change in Pakistan's foreign policy came about. It is interesting to note, however, that it was Bhutto who received credit for Pakistan's *more* independent foreign policy.

In one way or another foreign affairs dominates the Pakistani scene, and its impact on the political system cannot be minimized. On April 7, 1963, President Ayub explained the policy that his Foreign Minister would later develop. The President was doubtful, despite the assurance of numerous United States emissaries (W. W. Rostow visited with Ayub on April 5th), that American shipments of military hardware to India would not be employed against Pakistan. The President noted that this was an improper reading of Indian intentions and betrayed American ignorance of the Indo-Pakistani conflict. On the following day Pakistan presented its case to a meeting of the SEATO powers and the Foreign Minister emphasized that the balance of power in South Asia must be maintained if peace was to be preserved.

On his return to Pakistan Bhutto addressed the National Assembly and informed his countrymen that the government would not bow to India's might, nor would Pakistan accept any solution for Kashmir which was not both honorable and just. By no means would the Pakistanis desert the Kashmiris in their struggle for self-determination. The Foreign Minister followed up this speech with a declaration on April 17th that Pakistan might have to consider taking a "fundamental decision": specifically, to withdraw from the Western military alliances if long-term military aid to India was not coupled with a settlement of the Kashmir dispute.

Pakistan had not taken advantage of India while that country was struggling with the Chinese in the Himalayas, and the Pakistan Government had a right to believe this act of forbearance would not be overlooked once the hostilities were at an end. In fact, the Pakistani authorities thought this was the most opportune moment for the Western allies to put pressure on India for a Kashmir settlement. Even after the Chinese withdrew and the United States military supplies began arriving in India it was thought the United States would insist on some reciprocal action. At the very least, India would be expected to reduce the tension existing between itself and Pakistan. But this did not happen and the Pakistanis were sadly disillusioned. Pakistan's leaders therefore drew the conclusion that if a settlement was possible in Kashmir it would come only through Pakistan's own initiative.

Initial efforts, therefore, were directed at negotiations. In addition to the six rounds of ministerial talks which finally terminated without agreement on May 16, 1963, Pakistan presented its case to the CENTO Ministerial Council which met in Karachi that year. The American Secretary of State and the British Foreign Secretary were both present, and they learned from President Ayub that no Pakistani government could consider abandoning the Kashmiris. He also emphasized that increasing domestic pressures were causing the government to assume risks it had long sought to avoid. Picking up on this theme, Z. A. Bhutto told newsmen in Dacca on May 9, 1963, that Pakistan was firmly opposed to the partition of the Kashmir Valley or its joint control by India and Pakistan. In other words, the only way to solve the dispute was to agree to the plebiscite which the United Nations had recommended many years before. Pakistan's stand vis-à-vis Kashmir had not really changed, but with the Foreign Ministry under the direction of Bhutto the impression grew that its line had hardened considerably.

THE POLITICS OF THE KASHMIR DISPUTE

The Kashmir dispute was a constant source of irritation and posed some perplexing questions for the Ayub Government. It was by far the most popular issue in West Pakistan. No government could afford to ignore this fact. At the same time solutions were virtually impossible to come by. Pakistan had tested many approaches in the years following independence.[9] First, it sought to gain the territory in a covert and and later open struggle; second, it accepted the good offices of the United Nations; third, it allied itself with the Western powers and hoped alliance commitments would pressure India into a compromise solution; fourth, it went to war with India in September 1965; and finally, it now has associations with Communist China and seeks the support of the Soviet Union.[10] Despite all these efforts, the situation which prevailed shortly after partition remains to haunt the Pakistan Government. And as the Kashmir problem continues to defy solution the temper and frustration of the Pakistanis is magnified.

In the absence of an outlet for their pent-up energies, Pakistani displeasure is usually directed at the government. In meeting periodic outbursts the authorities have been firm, but they cannot indefinitely promise that which to date has proven unattainable. It is time to ask whether Pakistan can really achieve its much publicized goal of freeing Kashmir from Indian control. Similarly, is the pursuance of such a liberation policy in Pakistan's interest? What consequences might flow from the continued pursuit of this policy? What would happen if it were discontinued? How does the continued pursuit of such a policy affect Pakistan's relations with the great powers? What does this portend for its relations with the United States? If it should decide to chance a rupture in its relations with the United States, how might this influence Pakistan's political and economic development? These questions can only be raised here, but perhaps some of the answers may be seen in the events of the period 1963–69.

On December 14, 1963, Pakistan lodged a strong protest with India against the move to formally integrate Kashmir into the Indian Union. Ever since 1957 India had planned on giving Kashmir the same status as its other states, but internal opposition and Pakistan's reaction always prevented the completion of this program. Now the Indian Government intended to go ahead with its original arrangements. However, on December 27th a sacred relic, a hair of the Prophet, was reported stolen from the Hazratbal Shrine in Srinagar. In Kashmir, news of the theft resulted in severe disorders, and rioting soon spread to India and Pakistan. In the midst of mounting unrest the Jammu and Kashmir Liberation League Executive called an emergency meeting in Azad Kashmir (the western area under Pakistan's control) to consider the situation and its impact on Muslims all over the subcontinent.

Meetings were held in Pakistan to condemn the disappearance of the sacred relic and rumors circulated that right-wing Hindu organizations were behind the theft. Reports spread throughout Pakistan that Jan Sanghis and members of the Hindu Mahasaba had begun a reign of terror in Kashmir and some of India's northern states, and were set on destroying Muslim life and property. At the same time riots broke out in East Pakistan, where a large Hindu minority resides. On January 2, 1964, the West Pakistan Assembly unanimously adopted a resolution expressing a deep sense of anger and sorrow at the theft of the holy relic and the attacks perpetrated on defenseless Muslims. Similar protests emanated from the Indian legislatures, where concern was voiced for the Hindus in East Pakistan.

On January 3rd Pakistan brought its case before the U.N. Security Council and cautioned against the consequences of the plan to merge Kashmir with the Indian union. Pakistan's Chief Delegate Chaudhri Muhammad Zafrullah Khan insisted in a letter to the Council that Prime Minister Nehru was seeking to consolidate India's hold over the disputed territory in defiance of U.N. resolutions which repeatedly called for a plebiscite. On the same day that he was restating his country's case before the United Nations, Pakistan held a "Protest Day" as an expression of its resentment. When the exchange in the U.N. began to peter out, Foreign Minister Bhutto intervened personally, but to no avail.

As in numerous meetings of this kind in the past, the Council listened attentively, deliberated, but was unable to convince the disputants that a compromise formula was in their mutual interest. On February 17th a frustrated Zulfikar Ali Bhutto requested an adjournment of the Security Council on the grounds that he had to consult his government. Chinese Communist Prime Minister Chou-en-Lai was scheduled to arrive in Pakistan, and it can be speculated that the Foreign Minister felt his cause would be better served in Karachi than in New York City. It should be mentioned that, ever since the Chinese attack on India, visits by Chinese leaders to Pakistan have been interpreted by the Indian Government as part of the general Pakistani strategy to intimidate or pressure them into arriving at a settlement of their outstanding differences. On February 23rd, after lengthy talks with President Ayub and Zulfikar Ali Bhutto, Chou-en-Lai publicly declared his country's support for the Muslim Liberation Front in Kashmir.

With international pressure increasing for some interim, if not permanent solution for Kashmir, Prime Minister Nehru ordered the release of Sheikh Mohammad Abdullah, the "Lion of Kashmir," after almost eleven years of continuous imprisonment. The freeing of the

Kashmiri leader on April 8, 1964, sparked optimism in international circles that a solution for the long, bitter dispute would at last be found. Nehru's action was interpreted as a first giant step in the direction of securing a satisfactory solution. Zulfikar Ali Bhutto's verbal invitation to Sheikh Abdullah to visit Pakistan, although disconcerting to conservative Indian opinion, was greeted with enthusiasm in other quarters. On receiving President Ayub's formal invitation Sheikh Abdullah requested authority to leave the country. Permission was granted quickly, and on May 24th Sheikh Abdullah arrived in Rawalpindi where he was given a tumultuous welcome.

The Foreign Minister, who was again in New York City, hurried home in time to receive him. Pakistan and India never appeared so close to a *via media* on Kashmir as when Sheikh Abdullah announced in Rawalpindi on May 26th that Prime Minister Nehru and President Ayub would meet in June in an effort to reach a satisfactory solution. But it is another irony of history that the destiny of nations often rests on the most fragile circumstances. Prime Minister Nehru had suffered a stroke earlier in the year and although advised to relinquish his responsibilities and take an extended rest decided against leaving his post. Having reconsidered India's foreign policy position in light of the country's increasing domestic and international problems (and possibly feeling that he did not have long to live) the Prime Minister, it can be surmised, concluded that a settlement with Pakistan over Kashmir was now absolutely essential. It could be suggested that Nehru had deceived himself as to Chinese intentions. Perhaps he realized that India could not continue to ignore the claims of both China and Pakistan. At least one of these neighbors might be friendly to India. At this late stage he appears to have selected Pakistan.

The release of Sheikh Abdullah and his freedom to visit Pakistan is a case in point. Abdullah, although not strictly speaking an emissary of the Prime Minister, was nonetheless convinced that a settlement had to be arrived at which took into account opposing views and allowed for a meaningful and honorable compromise. It appears that President Ayub and Prime Minister Nehru held the identical opinion, that both were prepared to back away from their original positions. But the June meeting would never be held. On the day following Abdullah's announcement, Prime Minister Nehru suffered another stroke and died almost immediately. Although Sheikh Abdullah returned to India to attend the funeral, followed later by Zulfikar Ali Bhutto, this event represented a watershed in India-Pakistan relations.

HOSTILITIES RENEWED

The new government of Lal Bahadur Shastri permitted Sheikh Abdullah to leave India again in order to visit the holy city of Mecca, but it was not expected that the Kashmiri leader would exploit his new freedom so as to embarrass the Shastri government. Abdullah must have known that the new government could not relent on Kashmir without causing its own downfall, and he discarded the diplomatic niceties for a blistering attack on the administration. When he was pictured with Chinese leaders, India's more vocal elements no longer pretended tolerance. Prime Minister Shastri was imposed upon to order Abdullah to return and answer for his crimes. At this point Sheikh Abdullah had the option of going to Pakistan or returning to India. Curiously, he chose to return to India. On his return to New Delhi in May 1965 he and his closest advisers were arrested and incarcerated. Abdullah would not be freed again until December 8, 1967. Nehru's death created a leadership vacuum in India and the Shastri government was far too weak to deal with the Kashmir dilemma. What perhaps saved it from collapse was the Indo-Pakistani War of 1965.

Pakistan's reaction was not unexpected. Violent outbursts and condemnation of the Indian Government, which was accused of going back on its promises, once again reverberated through the country. It is also important to point out that the arrest and imprisonment of Sheikh Abdullah and the rekindling of the Kashmir dispute coincided with Pakistan's elections for the second generation of Basic Democrats, followed by the campaigns for the presidency and the legislatures. It was inevitable, therefore, that the Kashmir dispute should fit prominently in the electioneering. It was also impossible to keep the role of the United States out of the debate that ensued.

Anti-Americanism reached a new peak of intensity in late 1964 and the burden of criticism focused on U.S. military assistance to India. On the one side, the Pakistani opposition parties organized under the COP and, with Miss Fatima Jinnah as their agreed candidate standing against President Ayub, exploited this anti-Americanism. On the other, the government did virtually nothing to abate it and in fact took a relatively similar position. The government claimed the COP was being sponsored by the United States through the CIA. It was the government's argument, as expounded by Bhutto and other ministers in the central and provincial governments, that Pakistan's new independent foreign policy disturbed the Americans; that they had actually engineered a plan to unseat President Ayub and thereby reverse this policy.

Bhutto and his confreres made mention of the air agreement between China and Pakistan as well as the boundary settlement.[11] They also cited the air pact with the Soviet Union, the barter agreement with Poland, and the trade agreements with Albania, Czechoslovakia, and Hungary as having distressed the United States Government.[12] Almost on the eve of the election for President, Ghulam Nabi Memon, West Pakistan Minister for Law, Information and Parliamentary Affairs, accused the United States of financing the election campaign of Miss Fatima Jinnah and her COP cohort. The Minister declared in a public address that the United States "was meeting the expenditure in West Pakistan" whereas "the Indian Government was footing the bills in East Pakistan." *Dawn* of Karachi on December 30, 1964, insisted that the Americans were providing funds for the opposition campaign in East Pakistan as well. "The latest disclosures have made many Pakistanis ask whether Pakistan has now become the latest playground of America's 'Invisible Government'—the CIA." A few weeks earlier Miss Jinnah had been condemned for suggesting that Pakistan, because of its government's new foreign policy, had lost its "only friend," the United States. It may be interesting to point out that the U.S. was also accused of supporting opposition candidates in the Indian general elections in February 1967. The CIA was again the prime target, and American denials registered no effect whatsoever. Irrespective of the outcome, the United States was caught in the middle of a tenacious political contest in which it had to suffer for the ills and weaknesses on both sides. Moreover, official U.S. denials of the allegations usually fell on deaf ears.[13]

At about the same time, Foreign Minister Zulfikar Ali Bhutto made a solemn promise to the Pakistani nation. Pakistan would continue its independent foreign policy and would renew its efforts to gain the freedom of the Kashmiri people. He publicly declared—as reported in the *Morning News* (Karachi) on December 28, 1964, six days before the presidential election—that after the polling on January 2nd the Pakistan Government would "take retaliatory steps to counter the Indian attempt to merge the occupied parts of Kashmir with India. And you will see better results in the very short future." There is still no way of knowing if this was more than campaign oratory. Still, it proved to be a prophetic statement. It is also difficult to learn if the President sanctioned all the speeches made by his ministers. What is certainly obvious, however, is that he could not be expected to know what each and every one of his supporters would say in the course of the campaign. Nevertheless, the fact that Bhutto's Kashmir statement was inflated into banner headlines emphasizes its importance.

In political campaigns much is said in the heat of battle and promises are clearly made to be broken. Nonetheless, politicians are on surer ground when they keep their pronouncements ambiguous. Certainly, this provides them with more flexibility and it leaves a way out from otherwise hard commitments. For the professional politician it is almost a rule of thumb to deliberately leave "solutions" for pressing and difficult issues fuzzy and inchoate. But the Pakistani Foreign Minister, like other politicians before him, chose to violate this political dictum and the President, whether he realized it or not, was committed to a policy which soon became irrevocable.

It is virtually impossible to gauge the level of importance of foreign issues in the presidential campaign which culminated in the reelection of President Ayub on January 2, 1965. Many observers seem to agree that the most vital issue before the Pakistanis, whether they voted or not, was the presidential versus the parliamentary system of government. Nonetheless, there is little question that the political ideologues in the NAP and the Jamaat-i-Islami considered foreign policy a key feature of the campaign.[14] Representing extremist components within the COP, they did not take seriously the government protestations condemning the United States. In their view these were smokescreen tactics, employed to delude the people. The government, they argued, was more than ever allied with the West.

The opposition continued to point to the government's policy which kept the country tied, no matter how loosely, to Western alliances. Bhutto worked arduously to correct this impression, and publicly declared the pacts served to aid Pakistan in a number of ways not originally envisioned when they were first entered into. Membership in the pacts did not mean Pakistan identified itself with the West's anti-Communist activities. But, in all candor, Bhutto was embarrassed by Pakistan's remaining a party to the Alliances. Moreover, early in 1964 he began to pressure President Ayub to reconsider Pakistan's commitments.

THE DETERMINANTS OF FOREIGN POLICY

While remaining in the Western alliances, Pakistan was compelled to cultivate "friends" in all parts of the world. In this regard, President Ayub emulated de Gaulle's performance.[15] Thus non-participation in military exercises would be one way of minimizing alliance entanglements. Another would be delimitations on the use of Pakistani territory by alliance members. Still another would be the organizing of new groupings, free from Western controls or influence. Despite many provocations, Ayub did not subscribe to the undermining of the alliances. He knew full well, however, the need to develop new arrangements which might better guarantee Pakistan's security. Here the parallel with de Gaulle's method is striking.

Regional organizations insuring the friendly relations of Pakistan's neighbors always held a prominent place in Ayub's thinking. From the outset of his rule he sought to settle differences with India, e.g., the 1959 suggestion for joint defense of the subcontinent. Despite many differences with Afghanistan he tried to develop amicable relations. His decision to legalize Pakistan's borders with China, Burma, and Iran were aimed solely at removing possible sources of conflict. The same can be said for his attempt to develop satisfactory arrangements with the Soviet Union. As Ayub was quick to point out, Pakistan's foreign policy must reflect global changes and should be determined by geography, not ideology.

Pakistan is on reasonably good terms with China and since September 1965 has been the recipient of limited Chinese military supplies.[16] Its relations with Afghanistan have also improved. Through the good offices of the Shah of Iran, diplomatic relations were re-established between Pakistan and Afghanistan on May 29, 1963. Although Afghanistan still covets Pakhtunistan its demands have been somewhat muted. Iran and Turkey joined with Pakistan in the establishment of the Regional Cooperation for Development (RCD) [17] in July 1964, and the arrangement has drawn the three countries into intimate contact. At the same time Pakistan remains in CENTO and SEATO, as does Turkey in CENTO and NATO despite that country's growing disillusionment with the U.S. Similarly, Iran remains in CENTO. All three RCD countries have sought to change their policies vis-à-vis the Soviet Union. Not only Pakistan but Iran and Turkey have "rationalized" their foreign policies and, in addition to exchanging visits at the highest level, are trading with and receiving assistance from the Soviet Union.

No wonder the then Secretary General of CENTO, Dr. Ali Abbas Khalatbary (himself an Iranian), was reported in *The New York Times* of February 19, 1967, as declaring that CENTO appears to have outlived its purpose. "It [CENTO] is like insuring your house against fire; the policy does not cover damages by earthquake or theft."

U.S.–PAKISTAN RELATIONS AND THE INDO-PAKISTANI WAR OF 1965

The Pakistanis believe their cause in Kashmir is just. Kashmir is disputed territory and has been so recognized by the international community. Thus they distinguish between their support for the Kashmiri Liberation Front and an overt attack upon what they perceive as India proper. Most Pakistanis freely admit and indeed publicize their support for the Kashmiri Muslims. Although the Pakistan Government hedges on whether or not it is responsible for arming and training forces for conflict in Kashmir, the activities of the Pakistan Army in the summer and fall of 1965, as in 1948, are known and substantiated. But it is hardly likely that Pakistan ever seriously contemplated launching a full-scale war against her South Asian neighbor.

That India did not hesitate to strike directly at Pakistan in 1965 indicates that she had other plans, however. Some would argue that this was a correct military response under the circumstances. It forced the Pakistanis to defend an area much larger than their forces were equipped to handle; more important, it prevented the Pakistan Army from continuing its offensive in Kashmir since the troops involved in that campaign of necessity had to be diverted to the Lahore and Sialkot fronts. India thus retained control of Kashmir. Although both sides paid a heavy cost in lives, the Pakistanis were more seriously affected. Pakistan's heavy military hardware and weapons systems, with the exception of its aging aircraft, were largely consumed in the war. Although some vehicles, tanks, and heavy arms could be salvaged, none of these vital items could be replaced locally. Only small-arms ammunition could be provided, and Pakistan could not supply the large-caliber shells needed for its fieldpieces. Pakistan's dependence on external means of supply were underlined by President Ayub's appeal to President Lyndon Johnson. (One of President Ayub's last calls to President Johnson came in April 1967 after the American decision not to resume arms shipments to Pakistan.) Ayub noted again that India is in a more advantageous position and the suspension of American military assistance to that country was not nearly as serious as the cut-off of shipments to Pakistan.

The United States refused to be committed to a conflict which it felt should have been avoided, however. Nor did the United States Government want to choose between two countries with which it had no outstanding quarrels. Pakistan, of course, did not hold the same view.

It was an ally of the United States in a number of military arrangements and, although the alliances had always been interpreted as defense mechanisms against international communism, Pakistan had been invaded and the country anticipated that its partners would take some action in its behalf. But the United States and most other alliance members were determined to play an absolutely neutral role. In point of fact, the United States insisted that all alliance members should abstain from the conflict. Hence even Iran and Turkey, which pledged material assistance to Pakistan, were more or less pressured into accepting the American policy.

SEATO announced in the first days of the war that the Indo-Pakistani hostilities were outside its jurisdiction. CENTO refrained from making a similar statement, and Turkey and Iran did manage to send some small arms despite American displeasure. These latter shipments had little bearing on the outcome of the conflict, however, and Pakistan faced the harsh and frustrating reality of watching its military stores diminish rapidly. The refusal or inability of Pakistan's allies to shape the course of events in the subcontinent provided the Communist world with an opportunity to fill a vacuum. The Chinese ultimatum calling upon India to vacate a number of border posts in the Himalayas brought joy to every Pakistani heart. Indonesia, still under Sukarno's leadership, offered help in the form of limited arms shipments and sent a contingent of doctors and nurses. The Arab world sent words of encouragement. (It is significant that the Pakistan Government returned this support with its own verbal offering when the Arabs confronted the Israelis in May 1967. The reported presence of Pakistani troops in Jordan in 1970 is clearly something which Ayub Khan would not have sanctioned.) The Soviet Union, while continuing to send weapons to India, offered its good offices and urged the belligerents to settle their differences amicably.

The intervention of the leading Communist powers had an immediate impact on Pakistan's domestic life. Although President Ayub at first rejected the Soviet offer to mediate the dispute, he welcomed the Communist Chinese pressure on India because it forced India to do what Pakistan itself had done when the Indians struck at West Pakistan; that is, to divert its forces. While all assistance was gratefully received, Ayub worried about the future.

Without trying to ascertain whether or not the Chinese were bluffing, it seems fair to state that Ayub did not want them to enter the subcontinent. Neither the physical presence nor the ideological influence of the Chinese was desirable or in the long-term interest of Pakistan. At the same time, Pakistan could not continue the war at the level of intensity at which it was being fought. But the population of West Pakistan, especially in those areas where the major battles were occuring, did not hold the same view. Nor did many in the ranks of the Armed Forces, but for different reasons. Few knew what was happening on the front lines. Only the highest ranking military leaders and civil servants knew how rapidly Army and Air Force stores were being consumed. Hence lower grade officers were eager to protract the hostilities, and the urban population was convinced Pakistan could win Kashmir. While the population of East Pakistan was less optimistic, West Pakistani sentiment exhorted the government to continue the struggle. "Now that the showdown has come let us see it through to a conclusion," was the prevailing opinion. The more excitable elements went so far as to demand that everything be placed on the line. No risk was too great, no cost too high. "Even if Pakistan loses, India will not win." Nothing else was of comparable importance. India had to be destroyed even if it meant Pakistan must be brought to ruin with it.

The military officers who differed with Ayub were not different from military officers in other parts of the world in similar situations. Although the battles were devastating to the forces under their command, no decisive struggle had been fought. It was also their view that Indian will would weaken in a protracted conflict and give Pakistan an opportunity to press home its demands. The feeling prevailed that something tangible had to be achieved given the large cost in men and materiel; and that this could only be done by continuing the fight with whatever was available. It was apparent that Pathan tribesmen were fighting on the Lahore front one week after the outbreak of hostilities. It can also be added that many officers were less wary of Chinese Communist intentions than Ayub Khan.

Most military leaders are rarely credited with political acumen, nor can they be blamed for not acquiring it. A sizable contingent in the officer corps welcomed Chinese intervention for they believed it would help balance the forces facing Pakistan. They were less concerned with the political implications of a new Sino-Indian clash. President Ayub, however, did not seek a military victory. His objective was a political settlement. He wanted the Kashmiris to have the opportunity to organize their own society but also wished to see India remain intact. An India in chaos could not leave Pakistan unaffected.

Ayub's vision of a free, independent, and sovereign Pakistan left no place for Communist organization or ideology. Although disillusioned with the West, he argued against intimacies with communism. Islam would be as much in danger from communism as it was from extreme Hindu nationalism. Hence Ayub refused to entertain the thought of an alliance with the Chinese. Hasan Askari, no ally of Ayub, put the problem this way:

> Just what are China's real intentions towards Pakistan? So far, they have been understandably on good behaviour. But for how long? The Chinese make no secret of their global intentions. . . . How long will it be before they begin to take a more than academic interest in our domestic politics? The Appeal of their particular brand of politics is undoubted. The Communists . . . are (especially in East Pakistan) Peking-oriented . . . any alternatives to the present mad rush into China's arms would be an improvement. Right now we are allowing ourselves to be hustled into a position from which any future disengagement will be painful and embarrassing.[18]

Ayub's decision was discussed with opposition political leaders as well as his supporters in advance of the official pronouncement accepting the terms of the U.N. resolution calling for a cease-fire. Most accepted his position calmly despite their displeasure. Others, however, were unconvinced, and the processions which were organized in Karachi and Lahore in the closing hours of the war were obviously politically inspired. In Karachi, where controls on public activity are traditionally more difficult to enforce, the demonstrations were transformed into rampaging, hysterical mobs composed mainly of youths. Carrying placards and shouting slogans against the acceptance of the anticipated cease-fire arrangement, human torrents swept through Karachi's principal thoroughfares. On arriving at the United States Information Service Library, they proceeded to smash the windows before setting the building ablaze.

Not yet satisfied the crowd moved down Victoria Road and assembled in front of the United States Embassy, which unlike the library was cordoned by police, and all efforts to storm the Embassy were thwarted. After bricks smashed the glass doors of the building and broke several windows, the demonstrators were beaten off by a fierce attack by police armed with lathis. Frustrated, the demonstrators moved back up the street and on passing the Metropole Hotel, which houses the Pan American Airways office, paused to vent what was left of their unexpended fury. Neither this outburst of popular disfavor nor the lesser ones in Lahore and Rawalpindi caused the President to reconsider his decision, however. On September 24, 1965, he called upon his troops to halt their operations and ordered the Governors of West and East

Pakistan to impose a curfew on the population. Although clashes between Indian and Pakistani forces continued intermittently into December the war was officially over.

AFTERMATH OF WAR

Zulfikar Ali Bhutto was dispatched to New York City with orders to insist that the United Nations Security Council honor its pledge and bring about an equitable settlement of the Kashmir dispute. The Foreign Minister emotionally announced that Pakistan was ready to withdraw from the United Nations if the organization reneged on its promise; no time limit was specified, however. In Pakistan the people were urged to resume daily routines disrupted by the war. The bureaucracy heeded the wishes of the President though many officers were visibly disturbed. Others, it should be noted, were obviously relieved. The commercial and entrepreneurial elements were also glad that the hostilities had been terminated. But these were a very small, though important minority. The West Pakistan intelligentsia, the student community, the lower middle-class urbanites, were noticeably unreconciled.

Popular sentiment in the municipalities ran decidedly against the President. Adding to Ayub's dilemmas was the knowledge that the two armies still faced one another and the cease-fire was tenuous at best. Domestically, the President had to contend with intemperate opinion and internationally, with the small United Nations Observer Force which desired a general withdrawal of the opposing armies. Moreover, he had to console his unreconciled countrymen and explain that he was not "selling out" the Kashmiris. No one in the West, and least of all the United States, could assist Ayub in dealing with these problems. With all other opportunities foreclosed the one remaining option was the offer of the Soviet Prime Minister for a meeting to be convened in Tashkent in which he and Prime Minister Lal Bahadur Shastri would attempt to restore the *status quo ante*.

Acceptance of the United Nations resolution *in toto* would have been interpreted in Pakistan as bowing to Western influence; and with anti-American passions at a peak of intensity this was politically dangerous. But Soviet offers of mediation put matters in a different light. By agreeing to meet in Tashkent, Pakistan's leftist opposition groups could be adequately neutralized. The remaining opposition, never a serious threat to the government, might then be isolated and controlled within the normal operations of the President's emergency powers.

Therefore Ayub and Zulfikar Ali Bhutto traveled to Tashkent on January 4, 1966.

In Tashkent, Ayub struggled to find a suitable formula for accepting the remaining clauses of the U.N. Resolution, particularly that which called upon the two armies to withdraw from their forward positions. As the days passed the Pakistani press and radio reported one story; the two leaders could find no common ground for agreement. Even an agreed agenda, it was said, could not be arrived at. All indications pointed to a breakdown in the negotiations and a possible resumption of the hostilities. Although arms shipments to Pakistan and India had been curtailed by the United States, it was known that India was still receiving substantial quanities from the Soviet Union. Pakistan had begun receiving some military hardware from China and Iran; it also opened a campaign to recruit and train an infantry force far in excess of the numbers considered necessary before the September war. It appears now that Foreign Minister Bhutto counseled the President against accepting anything less than an agreement for the holding of a plebiscite in Kashmir.

In Bhutto's opinion Pakistan could no longer rely on the United States or the Western nations. The American decision to force a postponement of the Aid-to-Pakistan Consortium in July 1965 was still another reason for the irritation. The events of the preceding months were proof-positive that India's interests would never be sacrificed for those of Pakistan. Hence Chinese support should be exploited in order to gain some leverage with the Soviet Union. If this were done carefully the Soviet Union might conceivably curtail its arms shipments to India and in turn make Pakistan a recipient of its largess. Bhutto was adamant: Pakistan must seek Chinese assistance! Ayub gave considerable thought to Bhutto's appraisal of the contingencies and his recommendations but at the last minute decided to disregard his advice. When the President revealed he would sign the Tashkent Declaration drafted by the Soviet Union, Bhutto asked that he be permitted to publicly disassociate himself from it. He also insisted on resigning from the cabinet. The President, however, refused to accept his resignation and ordered him to remain at his post. Depressed and powerless, Bhutto offered no resistance. When the President put his signature to the Tashkent Declaration the Foreign Minister is reported to have looked on dejectedly.

Chapter 4

Post-Tashkent Politics

ALMOST two months after the termination of the Indo-Pakistani War and some weeks before President Ayub met with his Indian counterpart in Tashkent the mood of Pakistani society seemed poised for a resumption of hostilities. At no other time since the independence of the nation had there been so clear a display of unity. The following statement summed up the feelings of a wide segment of the public:

> No Government in Pakistan ever had such a healthy climate and opportunity to mould the Pakistani people into a nation of which not only posterity will feel proud, but which would command the respect and admiration of the world at large. Such moments and opportunities in the lives of nations are rarely witnessed. It is a moment whose significance should be fully realised. It is a moment which should not be allowed to go unheeded. It is a moment of destiny for Pakistan.[1]

News of the agreement in Tashkent shocked the Pakistanis, who had expected something quite different. Virtually everyone believed the talks would fail, and preparations were underway to welcome Ayub back to Pakistan as a hero of the people. But when the news was relayed in the evening over Radio Pakistan there was only surprise and dismay. The following morning, when it was learned the Indian Prime Minister had suffered a heart attack and died shortly after the signing ceremony, the public's attention was still riveted on the agreement. How were the Pakistanis to mourn the passing of the Indian Prime Minister? Shastri was the villain of the piece and memories of the last few months could not be expected to fade. Had Pakistan made so great a sacrifice only to accept the restoration of the *status quo ante?* When the President finally returned to Rawalpindi there were no celebrations, no press conferences, and no high-level meetings. Ayub did not even seem inclined to explain why he chose to sign the agreement and went into immediate seclusion. The reasons for the President's silence are not known, but it can be

67

conjectured that he was deeply affected by the sudden passing of Lal Bahadur Shastri. Undoubtedly he also wondered how the Prime Minister's death would affect the agreement he had just signed. Zulfikar Ali Bhutto likewise refused to comment, and went directly to his ancestral home in Sind.

THE STUDENTS

On January 13, 1966, *The Pakistan Times* of Lahore printed an article which stated: "The breakthrough, kept secret until the last moment, came as one of diplomacy's big surprises." Moreover, Ayub's reluctance to explain his reasons for accepting the Tashkent Declaration was more than the aroused Pakistanis could tolerate. Hence, after an impatient pause of almost forty-eight hours demonstrations erupted in several areas of West Pakistan. Not unexpectedly, the student community stood in the forefront of this activity and the public peace was shattered.

The most serious disorder occurred in Lahore, the most celebrated city in the seventeen-day war. Section 144 of the Code of Criminal Procedure was in force in Lahore as in other parts of West Pakistan, making it a violation to take out processions or hold public meetings of more than five people. Nevertheless, defying the order, students from Panjab University and other local colleges moved out of their school compounds and proceeded to march on the downtown area. Earlier a band of students, dressed in black and bearing banners calling upon the government to reconsider the position taken at Tashkent, camped outside the main gate leading to the Governor's residence. Efforts to persuade the students to leave proved futile and police reinforcements arrived to bolster the detachment already on the scene.

Rioting began some time after noon. The police ordered a halt to the marchers converging on the city, many of whom were joined by veiled women who carried children said to be the dependents of men killed in the war. Shouts of "Give us back our husbands, fathers, and brothers" pierced the air and the crowds became more difficult to manage. From Regal Chowk and Charing Cross the students marched toward Government House several hundred yards down the Mall Road where they sought to petition the Governor. It was at this juncture that the police asserted themselves.

All attempts to stop the students were answered with increased resistance and rowdiness. Soon the brick-throwing began and the police were ordered to counterattack by using their tear gas cannisters. The battle raged for several hours but damage to public utilities was not extensive, though a double-decked omnibus of the West Pakistan Road Transport Corporation was attacked, its windows smashed, and an attempt made to set it afire. The fluorescent tubes lighting the downtown area and the traffic lights were also easy targets. The disorder spread around the areas surrounding the city colleges where the police, on the defensive, resorted to shooting. An official government announcement stated that the first victim was a policeman and that the struggle grew as a result.

The rioting in Lahore continued into the night and when it was finally brought under control four persons were dead, many injured, and several hundred in jail. Panjab University, local colleges, and schools were ordered closed for an indefinite period; parts of the city were littered with debris and hastily scrawled obscenities were to be seen in a number of localities. One theme explained everything. The President, according to the demonstrators, had "sold Kashmir" to the Hindu "babus" and "warlords." Many people were outraged, more were quietly bitter, but hardly a person could be found who was not prepared to voice his displeasure with the unexpected turn of events in Tashkent. In this instance, sympathy was with the students—they reflected the feelings of West Pakistan's urban population.

Concerned with the violent reaction to the Tashkent Declaration and urged by his advisers to lay the matter before the people, President Ayub broke his self-imposed silence with a mid-day radio address to the nation on January 14th. Speaking in Urdu he explained that the Tashkent Declaration had in no way detracted from or damaged the country's position on Kashmir. "The Kashmiris' right to choose their future remained inviolable," he reiterated. (All the President's speeches were now delivered in Urdu. On the day the Indians attacked West Pakistan the President spoke to the nation in English, but a few days later the government decided that all future addresses would be in Urdu. It is also noteworthy that English-language news reports were eliminated from television programming and a few weeks later Radio Pakistan announced that English news programs would be reduced to two each day. By contrast, at the beginning of the hostilities there were English news programs almost every two hours.) The President declared that once the withdrawal of the armed forces had taken place, Pakistan would be in a position to request the Security Council to mediate the dispute. This was in keeping wtih the resolution of September 20, 1965, he explained. But no matter what happens in the future, he continued, Pakistan would never abandon the Kashmiris and the country would never enter a "No-War Pact" with India "unless the Jammu and Kashmir dispute was settled honourably and equitably."

Taking note of the sentiment aroused against his policies, the President remarked: "There may be some amongst us who will take advantage of your feelings and will try to mislead you. They are not more patriotic perhaps than you or me. The ordeal is not yet over." Clearly, the President held to the view that the demonstrations were the work of his political antagonists. It was the judgment of most impartial observers, however, that he had failed to gauge the temper of the population; that, in fact, the violent reaction was a predictable response and was absolutely spontaneous. The politicians had reacted much more slowly to Tashkent and, though they had not created the disturbances, sought to reap some advantages from them.

After the President's broadcast *The Pakistan Times* of Lahore ran a headline declaring: "All Misgivings Dispelled"; and followed with the comment that the "people left their radio sets with a sense of relief, satisfied when they heard their President declare that the Declaration had in no way harmed our view-point on the Jammu and Kashmir issue." Despite these pronouncements by the government press it was obvious that everyone was not "relieved" and that popular misgivings were the rule rather than the exception.

Before the President's radio address, no government official made any effort to calm the students or the population at large. But now, with renewed confidence, they agreed to face their constituents and discuss the issues. On January 22 West Pakistan Minister of Education Malik Khuda Bakhsh Bucha gave an audience to a deputation of students and informed them that their demands would be given sympathetic consideration by the government. The deputation of the Qaumi-Jamiat-Tulaba-e-Pakistan (National Assembly of Pakistani Students), led by its convenor Irshad Ali Khan, exchanged views freely with the Minister who advised them to seek their objectives without putting the national interest in jeopardy. He further noted that all the government asked of the students was that they should conscientiously and diligently pursue their studies. In return, the government would safeguard their interests. He added that a judicial inquiry into the firing by police would be held under a High Court judge and that the government would be lenient in its attitude toward those students whose passions caused them to break the law.

Already efforts were underway to redress student grievances. "Kindness is needed not persecution," wrote Mohammad Idrees in his weekly student column in *The Pakistan Times* (January 19, 1966), and the government was quick to heed his words. By January 22nd virtually all of the approximately 200 students arrested in the rioting were released on bail and the government announced it was contemplating reopening the educational institutions. By the end of January the institutions in Peshawar and Rawalpindi resumed normal activity. Those in Lahore followed in late February. In Karachi they remained closed for a longer period. In East Pakistan, which was virtually unaffected by the student disturbances in the West wing, the educational institutions remained open until a disturbance caused by student dissatisfaction with educational policies in Dacca University, unconnected with the government's foreign policy, brought about its closing for an indefinite period.

It should be mentioned that schools throughout Pakistan had been more or less closed since the fall of 1964. The election campaign had absorbed the attention of the students and they occupied themselves in making life miserable for the authorities.[2] The 1965 war followed on the heels of the summer vacation; the emergency caused a suspension in educational operations, to say nothing of the paralysis that gripped society generally. When the schools finally reopened in November of 1965, the adverse reaction to the Tashkent Declaration once more forced their closing. The fact that the government considered it possible to open the schools at the end of January 1966 reflects its "success" in weathering a severe political storm.

Malik Khuda Bakhsh Bucha used the occasion to issue an official handout commenting on the situation which stated: "The character of the student is built either in his home atmosphere or in the educational institution where the students spend most of their time. Therefore the parents and teachers should provide the required conditions for the development of the personality of the students on proper lines."[3] Chaudhri Muhammad Zafrullah Khan, Pakistan's celebrated member of the Court of International Justice and one of the nation's leading personalities, varied this theme. Speaking in defense of the Tashkent Declaration, he chided the opposition politicians who were condemning it and added: "Politicians should think twice before inciting students and the people to lead processions against the Tashkent Declaration. Their angle of vision should be constructive and in the interest of peace."

Douglas Ashford has analyzed the linkages between education and politics and uses the phrase "politically over-developed youth"[4] to describe student involvement in politics in the developing countries. "Political over-development" is a complex concept, but there is no mistaking the pivotal role played by the student generation in this century—and South Asia is no exception. Examples are numerous, but one of the earliest successful and most sustained performances was in reaction to the British policy to partition Bengal in 1905. Students sometimes seem able to do what politicians cannot, and it is often assumed that they are being used or exploited. But students are also eager to do battle. This was especially true in the struggle to free the subcontinent from British rule; and it is true today. The young, enthusiastic, often idealistic students take pride in their capacity to obstruct government —not simply because they have an immature distaste for authority or need an outlet for their energies, but because they feel a certain responsibility to the society of which they are a part:

> Even those who are very apprehensive of the fact that a greater involvement in politics will lead to neglect of studies and possibly to indiscipline as well, will agree that at this moment when there is so much apathy among the masses, the students are the only segment relatively alert to the country's social problems. By denying them the freedom of expression we'll only be strengthening the hands of those who want to remove the last traces of freedom of expression in our country.[5]

This fact has never been clearly discerned by any of Pakistan's governments, past or present, and the tendency has been to use the same old arguments and techniques in quelling student disorder. But there is a ray of light even at this late hour. The *Report of the Commission on Student Problems and Welfare* recognizes that in developing countries the students form a sizable section of the intelligentsia

> . . . and feels by reason of its education that it has the right to take a leading part in the building up of the political consciousness of the illiterate and uneducated masses.
>
> After the demagogues and politicians proper, they form a very influential political element, whose support is sought for by almost all politicians, whether in power or out of power. Leaders of the opposition and Ministers alike woo students and seek to be popular amongst them, for in political campaigns they are found to be useful and loyal workers.[6]

But the Commission also demonstrates misunderstanding. They prescribe a remedy that would prevent the students from engaging in their "national pastime." Little consideration is given to guiding them into constructive channels where they can actually make a positive contribution in raising the "political consciousness" of an inert population. Instead, the Commission earnestly believes that if "legitimate" student grievances are given attention—i.e., improved teaching, better living conditions, carefully regulated tuition, and limitations on police behavior—they will quietly retire from the "political wars." With the cooperation of the parents, guidance counselors, and the press, the students, the report leads one to believe, can be transformed into model citizens. This is obviously wishful thinking. Student involvement in politics is too deeply rooted in the traditions of the subcontinent to be eliminated in this fashion. It also explains why the report was greeted with such contempt.

Granted, there are also traditions which seek to remove the students from politics and these too are deeply rooted. It has been pointed out that: "The moral and political traditions of our society have always given it to the elders—in age or power—to dictate to young people, and in cases of disobedience to use the rod." [7] One of these traditions eventually will yield to the other; and it would seem that the latter, despite its stubborn resistance, will be the inevitable loser. Youth is in widespread rebellion against the values and practices of its elders. "In a society where understanding is termed weakness, and tolerance is regarded as capitulation, it is natural that false notions of prestige should stand in the way of any settlement." [8] All the same, youth can be expected to persist in its demands.

In Pakistan, the students seek the restructuring of society in order to improve opportunities for a more productive existence. They also seek to assure their individual satisfaction. Irrespective of their education and with few exceptions, the majority of these young people are unable to find work commensurate with their attainments. In most instances these youthful members of society feel they are treated like second-class citizens.

> . . . there are some fortunate people for whom the government have opened special institutions with the express purpose of "producing future leaders of the country." [This was the British educational policy and the system evolved by the British is virtually intact today.] There go the sons and daughters of the rich and the privileged. After finishing their studies, replete with our idea of an English accent, these favourites will be sent abroad through government scholarships, through connections of their parents. On return they will be fixed up in jobs which their elders have already prepared for them. The openings in industry and trade will be filled by the proprietors, or the sons of senior civil and military officials. By accident of birth they move into positions of privilege

without ability or effort, and without having any sympathy and feeling for the country which will now be called upon to bear the expenses of their lavish living.[9]

This indictment is subjective and somewhat exagerated but it cannot be brushed aside. The statement contains well known truisms, even if it is only partially valid. The large majority of the student community has been alienated by authority—it always has been. However, the negative attitude displayed by government must give way to a new appraisal of student demands. Students will have to be treated with tact if something constructive is ever to emerge. Force has never succeeded, and will not succeed now or in the future. Using students to betray other students is also a futile policy. Silencing students is impossible short of absolute terrorism and repression. "The Government of Pakistan has not yet reconciled to the idea that the students, like other humans, have their problems and like other citizens have a right to talk about these problems" [10]

President Ayub hoped to establish workable institutions that Pakistanis could also revere. He wanted to weld Pakistan into a strong and integrated nation. But he and his government, like those before him, overlooked the obvious. Institutions require time to achieve legitimacy and can only prosper if the people for whom they are meant take pride in operating them. It is the young enlightened generation that must be wooed, for it is they who ultimately determine the success or failure of officialdom's design. It is this group that must be won over, who must see in their government's program the prospects of a better future—for themselves and their society. It was the Ayub government's inability to develop a flexible response to student demands that resulted in the disorders leading to the President's resignation and the reimposition of martial law.

The students had no confidence in the Ayub regime, and all government acts were interpreted as tactics aimed at neutralizing student activism. Conflict, not cooperation, became the norm. The Commission on Student Problems proposed reordering student government along the lines of Basic Democracies, but the students feared this recommendation would place their unions under the control of the government bureaucracy.

> The student government based on the Basic Democracies system was tried in Karachi and it failed miserably as it should have. Now by proposing it again the Commission is not only suggesting a denial of democratic process, but it is hurling insults at the

intelligentsia as the very inventors of the B.D. system had made clear that their system was meant to "suit the genius" of the "illiterate masses." [11]

Students in Pakistan, as in other developing countries, are destined to play ever more significant roles in the process of change. The Pakistani student is resolute and defiant, and future governments will have to devote more thought to accepting student involvement in politics. As the students themselves have announced, whether their "role is going to be in conformity with the wishes of the Government or in antagonism to it, depends largely upon the Government's attitudes." [12]

THE POLITICIANS

Reaction of the political opposition to the Tashkent Declaration is edifying. On the one hand, there were those like Choudhri Mohammad Ali (Nizam-i-Islam) and Shaukat Hyat Khan (Council Muslim League) who condemned every feature of the agreement; on the other, there were personalities like Sheikh Mujibur Rahman (East Pakistan Awami League) and Maulana Abdul Hamid Khan Bhashani (National Awami Party) who refrained from criticism. Bhashani's NAP seldom argued the cause of Kashmir, and consistent with its previous stand, avoided taking sides in this clash. Maulana Maudoodi's Jamaat-i-Islami also vehemently criticized the Tashkent Agreement. Although his party was extremely well organized it neither captured the popular imagination nor harnessed the sentiments of important and articulate interest groups. Explanations for these differences are not difficult to come by. Whereas the more conservative West Pakistani opposition emphasized the limited objective of removing the Ayub Khan regime it remained divided on questions of organization and program. The forces led by Bhashani, like those which rally round Mujibur Rahman in East Pakistan, by contrast represent radical interests with rather explicit platforms. For them, President Ayub was only a preliminary target.

Both the NAP and EPAL seek comprehensive changes in the nation's political system. Their goals are to revolutionize society's lifestyle, particularly its socioeconomic structure. Theirs has been a positive program which seeks over-all social reform, and it is little wonder that they refused to be associated with the anti-Tashkent agitation.

Bhashani became a leading spokesman of Socialist-Communist causes from the moment he quit the Muslim League in the months following independence in 1947. He broke from the Awami League to form the

NAP in 1957 when the late H. S. Suhrawardy, then Prime Minister and a co-founder with Bhashani of the former party, refused to heed his advice and take Pakistan out of the Western military pacts. Suhrawardy further infuriated Bhashani by keeping the Communist countries at a comfortable distance.

It is significant that Suhrawardy visited Communist China and entertained Chou-en-Lai in Pakistan during his tenure as Prime Minister. Like Ayub Khan, Suhrawardy did not find his relations with the West incompatible with those of the Communist countries. Despite Pakistan's apparently one-sided relationship with the West, the historic record reveals that succeeding governments have followed a curiously middle-of-the-road policy in foreign affairs. By Western standards, Pakistani leaders have also maintained a calm, statesmanlike demeanor in times of highly emotional international crisis such as the 1956 Suez War and conflict between Israel and the Arab countries in June 1967. In the 1957 clash Sheikh Mujibur Rahman sided with Suhrawardy, and the split between Mujib and Bhashani has been sustained to the present period. While Sheikh Mujibur Rahman is often critical of the West, his detractors frequently accuse him of being in the pay of the United States. But both the EPAL and NAP represent leftist interests. Hence it is important to distinguish between them.

The East Pakistan Awami League is only loosely tied to its West Pakistan affiliate and stressed the replacement of Ayub's presidential government with the pre-1958 parliamentary system. Principal emphasis has always been on greater regional autonomy for East Pakistan. In this respect, Sheikh Mujibur Rahman is the most outspoken proponent of provincialism. The NAP, however, embraces all of Pakistan. While insisting on severing all ties with the western countries, it desires more intimate relations with socialist countries. Its domestic program, unlike that of the Awami League, flows from this reorientation in foreign policy. Parochialism, as distinguished from "provincialism" mentioned above—the break-up of the single province of West Pakistan into its pre-1955 constituent parts of the Punjab, Sind, Baluchistan, and the North West Frontier Province—is a prime feature. Divide and rule is a game that is still played in the subcontinent, and parochialism is provincialism carried to an extreme. President Yahya Khan's decision to accept NAP demands to destroy the One Unit and return West Pakistan to its pre-1955 status is ominous when seen in this context.

The NAP program not only feeds local passions but bears a striking resemblance to the policies of the Indian Communist Party prior to 1947. At that time the CPI insisted that the only "real solution to the present communal differences lies in the creation of a Socialist Republic of free States and a Central Union of them all." [13] The NAP, like the other Pakistani opposition parties, seeks a return to the parliamentary system, at least for the time being. Prominent in their program is the call to nationalize industries and socialize the economy. As industry expands in Pakistan, the constantly increasing disparity in wealth is a made-to-order target for their political barbs, and it is no secret that a score of families dominate Pakistan's industrial complex.

The NAP leaders could not overlook the fact that the Tashkent Declaration was drafted and signed in the Soviet Union; or for that matter that it had been countersigned by the Soviet Prime Minister. For Bhashani and his associates, Soviet assistance in helping reduce tension between India and Pakistan was the first step on the road to the re-creation of Pakistani society. M. H. Usmani, general secretary of the NAP, praised the Soviet Union and voiced the opinion that the Tashkent Declaration would prove to be a turning point. Stressing the party's program, Usmani remarked that the war between India and Pakistan had brought the common man into the national picture as never before.

It also showed that the "imperialist" countries were not friends of Pakistan and the arms race was suicidal to developing countries. "An independent economy was imperative to defend national sovereignty without having to depend on unreliable alliances," he concluded.[14] Echoing him, Bhashani declared that the Tashkent Declaration had "slackened the hold of the imperialists" on Pakistan and brought about a closer relationship with the socialist countries. Bhashani offered the view that "imperialism" was the cause of all the sufferings of the people of Asia, Africa, and Latin America. Citing the United States as the greatest threat to world peace, he has repeatedly called for a united effort to defeat it. The NAP has gone on record (*The Pakistan Times,* February 12, 1967) with the statement that it would go to the assistance of Communist China if it were attacked by the United States.

Undaunted by the dissension in their ranks, the more rightist political parties refused to alter their course, however. Tashkent seemed to be an issue worth exploiting and they diligently set about their task. Their tactics were simple and conventional. In spite of government directives imposing Section 144 in all the major urban centers of West Pakistan, the politicians held their public meetings and offered themselves for arrest when the police appeared. The feeling persisted that a politician could not earn his credentials until he proved his contempt for authority and served a period in jail. It is doubtful that this tactic had more than symbolic or sentimental importace, however. All the same, members of the Council Muslim League, Nizam-i-Islam, Jamaat-i-Islami, and West Pakistan Awami League pursued their original plans. Having violated Section 144, they went one by one to prison.

In Dacca, Nurul Amin—a moderate, former Chief Minister of East Pakistan, convenor of the National Democratic Front (NDF), and leader of the opposition in the National Assembly—called upon the authorities to end the state of emergency proclaimed during the war under which the politicians in West Pakistan were being arrested. While seeking the release of all political prisoners and the rescinding of Section 144 he avoided condoning the anti-Tashkent agitation, however. Nurul Amin intimated that the Tashkent Declaration was in the best interest of the country but he deplored the government's action denying the right of dissent to those who opposed it. Still another opposition leader who sympathized with the dissenters while supporting the agreement was Z. H. Lari, president of the Karachi Zonal Council Muslim League. Though acknowledging that some features of the arrangement were disappointing, he believed the government required time to work out the difficulties implicit in the dispute. Like Nurul Amin he condemned the government for preventing public expression on a vital issue. Nevertheless, he felt it was a question of war and peace and that it would be best to avoid taking a partisan stand. Apparently Lari was not speaking for the membership, however, and he was soon expelled from his party. Miss Fatima Jinnah was silent on Tashkent. Farid Ahmad, general secretary of the Nizam-i-Islam, came out in favor of the agreement. But both agreed with Nurul Amin and Lari that the government should avoid using repressive tactics.

The government at first treated the opposition leniently. Important West Pakistani leaders like Sardar Shaukat Hyat Khan, Inayatullah, and Sardar Zafrullah Khan of the CML and Hamid Sarfraz of the Awami League (West Pakistan) were arrested by the police after violating the law; instead of being jailed they were driven out into the rural region and deposited in a distant location far from Lahore. This ignominious treatment exemplified the contempt in which they were held. It also suggested that the government had little to fear from these estranged politicians.

The remarkable stability of the administration in this period is reflected in the government's insistence on holding the long-postponed elections for the chairmen of the Basic Democracies Union Councils in West Pakistan. Rumors circulated that the Basic Democrats had lost all interest in the system and would refuse to hold the election, but the polling was conducted without a hitch. Another illustration of the government's strength was the signing of an agreement by Lieutenant General Bakhtiar Rana, one of the celebrated heroes of the Indo-Pakistani War, calling for the official withdrawal of Pakistani forces from those areas occupied during the hostilities. It is interesting to note that General Rana was Martial Law Administrator for West Pakistan during most of the forty-four months after Ayub's take-over in October 1958.

Frustrated by the government and their own inability to agree on important issues, the West Pakistani leaders announced that a National Conference would be held in Lahore on February 5–6, 1966, to thrash out differences. But even before the conference convened it was announced that the central issue would be the Tashkent Declaration. On learning this the East Pakistanis, with the exception of a small contingent led by Mujibur Rahman, declined the invitation. The NAP insisted they were never invited, but the West Pakistani president of the Awami League (who went to East Pakistan in an effort to gather support for the meeting) said they had flatly refused to join. In fact, the Working Committee of the NAP in the Punjab and Bahawalpur passed a resolution condemning the Lahore meeting, noting that not only would it disrupt the solidarity of the country but would also "further the sinister interests of the imperialists." The clash between the right-wing and left-wing parties was clearly defined.[15] The moderate East Pakistani opposition may have declined the invitation because the Kashmir issue was too remote. At any rate, they believed issues with much higher priorities needed tackling. They did not want to risk going to prison for a cause they could not fully support.

The Jamaat-i-Islami, Nizam-i-Islam, Council Muslim League of West Pakistan, and Awami League of West Pakistan sponsored the meeting, maintaining their individual identities throughout the proceedings. As anticipated, Nurul Amin's NDF and the NAP boycotted the conference. Even Choudhri Mohammad Ali's request that they send observers went unheeded. With the absence of these "antagonists" it might have been expected that the convention could agree on a common program but this was not the case. The only East Pakistanis to turn up in Lahore were those led by Mujibur Rahman, and their demands were enough to fracture what little unity the conference could muster.[16]

When the meeting was finally called to order more than 700 delegates were present but only 21 represented East Pakistan. It was something less than an auspicious beginning for what had been billed as a "unity conference," and prospects were dim that a single national party could emerge from the deliberations. None of the delegates indicated a desire to risk sacrificing their extant organizations, no matter how feeble, for another of vague and nebulous proportions. The fear persisted that a new coalition party would be short-lived, thus making restoration of even the present political base questionable. Some delegates therefore suggested objectives falling short of actual unification. A joint command was mooted for coordinating political activities but agreement proved impossible. The compromisers recommended something more "realistic" like a broad understanding on means to a common goal, but even this very limited objective was rejected.

Hence from the outset there was bickering and indecision. Each delegation's leader harangued the government and condemned it for resorting to "undemocratic practices"; all the arguments had been heard before, however, and their impact was negligible. Also, publication of the speeches was banned by the government and thus they were to have little effect on the population at large.

The National Conference ended in two days. From most standpoints it failed to attain any of the objectives for which it had been organized. A proposal for launching a civil disobedience movement aimed at gaining the revocation of the Tashkent Declaration was presented by some members of the West Pakistan Council Muslim League and West Pakistani Awami League, but it was not taken up for want of a consensus. Some young firebrands held the view that the matter should be pressed with deliberate force anyway, but the more senior politicians were unimpressed and indicated a desire to pursue their objectives through constitutional means. Later, however, the conference passed resolutions condemning the Tashkent Agreement and urged the government to abrogate it. Mujibur Rahman, having met with stiff opposition on his own proposals centered on giving more autonomy to East Pakistan, not only rejected these resolutions but marched his small delegation out of the conference and returned to his native province. To all intents and purposes the meeting was a dismal failure.

With the conference over and the opposition hopelessly divided, the government moved to silence some of the West Pakistani dissidents. On February 17 the government arrested three West Pakistan Awami League and two West Pakistan Council Muslim League leaders in Lahore. The politicians were taken in custody under Rule 32 of the Defense of Pakistan Rules (1965) for what was called "persistently indulging in activities which were highly prejudicial to the maintenance of public order." The leaders were: Nawabzada Nasrullah Khan, president of the All-Pakistan Awami League; Sardar Shaukat Hyat Khan, general secretary of the Council Muslim League; Malik Ghulam Jilani, a former member of the National Assembly, and Khwaja Mohammad Rafiq—both members of the Central Working Committee of the Awami League; and Sardar Mohammad Zafrullah, president of the Lahore branch of the Council Muslim League. They were seized in the early hours of the morning under an order issued by the District Magistrate. A press note in *The Pakistan Times* (February 18, 1966) issued following their arrests read as follows:

> Reports of prejudicial activities of these five persons, both individually and cojointly, were being received for some time past. In particular evidence is available to show that they had been persistently indulging in activities which were highly prejudicial to the maintenance of public order and peaceful conditions in the city of Lahore in particular and the Province in general. They had been advocating the use of force and violent methods, including the use of firearms. They had also started a regular campaign of creating discontentment and hatred among the public.
>
> In order to prevent them from pursuing their unlawful activities, it has been found necessary to order their immediate detention.

On hearing of the arrests, virtually all the opposition parties issued severe condemnations of the government. In such matters there was no disunity. Tufail Mohammad, president of the National Conference's convening committee challenged the government to substantiate the bona fides of its actions in a court of law. He described the arrests as a "misuse of the powers assumed in the name of the defence of the sacred soil of Pakistan." [17] Mian Arif Iftikhar, MNA and NAP leader, condemned the arrests on behalf of his party. If the government had evidence let it proceed through proper judicial channels. He added: "The citizens of Pakistan would be right in supposing that after the great sacrifices made and the great trial undergone during the Indian aggression against Pakistan, they are at least entitled to discuss and debate and think about the war and its consequences for their country." In his opinion, free discussion was essential to arrive at a rational appreciation of different views. [18]

But even this event did not bring the opposition an inch closer to coalescing. On the same day that the leaders were apprehended, Khwaja Mohammad Safdar, leader of the opposition in the West Pakistan Assembly, ruled out the possibility of a merger of all the opposition parties. The Council Muslim League leader insisted the amalgamation of the opposition parties would only mean the addition of one more party to the existing number. A complete merger was neither possible nor advisable; most people were decidedly against abandoning their traditional organizations because they served local interests. The alternative he suggested was a unified command of all the opposition parties which would be solely directed at achieving "national" objectives. He held the opinion that all the leaders could agree to such an arrangement, and went on to note that in their meeting at Lahore it was all but agreed that a fifty-man national council should be set up to be selected from each of the five major parties.

Safdar admitted, however, that because of the special conditions laid down by Mujibur Rahman the establishment of such a unified command would have to wait until other leaders in East Pakistan were consulted. Khwaja Safdar complained bitterly about the "atmosphere of political suffocation prevailing in the country." He cautioned that this hampered the growth of political activity. The Council Muslim League leader who was touring various districts of the West Pakistan province in an effort to reorganize his party on a more popular basis agreed with a questioner that no political party, including his own, had roots among the masses. Lack of political unity and the absence of popular support neutralized the effectiveness of the parties and must have been very reassuring to the President.

Despite the entreaties of various groups and personalities, the administration methodically imprisoned many of those West Pakistani politicians who insisted on keeping the Tashkent issue alive. And once in jail they remained there irrespective of the legal exertions in their behalf. In fact, they were neither released nor put on trial. As is customary with political prisoners they were simply detained, thus frustrating their rank and file. And as the months passed, enthusiasm waned and the Tashkent Declaration ceased to be a real political issue. Shaukat Hyat Khan, Nawabzada Nasrullah Khan, and Malik Ghulam Jilani gained their release only when the government felt they no longer represented a threat to the public peace. In mid-December, almost a year after their imprisonment, they were set free.

In the meantime, the administration was not idle. After first hesitating to deal forcibly with Mujibur Rahman, it soon became evident that his persistent efforts were beginning to gain adherents. In a sudden display of official determination Mujib was ordered arrested along with many of his followers. All were detained under the same Defense of Pakistan Rules. Among those imprisoned with the Awami Leaguers was Tafazzal Hussain, the editor of *Ittefaq,* a leading Bengali newspaper, which was also seized by the government. Two additional political leaders from East Pakistan, Mushtaq Ahmad and Zahur Ahmed Chowdhury, were likewise incarcerated. These two were later reported to be seriously ill (as were their counterparts Shaukat Hyat Khan and Malik Jilani in West Pakistan), but they remained in detention.

It is important to note that the government refrained from attacking the NAP, although that party virtually adopted Mujib's Six Point Program for greater East Pakistani provincial autonomy and added six points of its own. The Twelve Point Charter of Demands prepared by the NAP was laid before the National Assembly on December 9, 1966. It not only demanded autonomy for East Pakistan but again called for the dissolution of the One Unit in West Pakistan. Furthermore, it urged the release of all political prisoners, the introduction of rationing throughout East Pakistan, restoration of the parliamentary system, introduction of direct elections on the basis of universal adult franchise, "full support to the heroic people of Viet Nam in their struggle for National Liberation," withdrawal from the military pacts, and restoration of civil liberties and freedom of the press.[19]

Ayub Khan's Dilemma

It might be asked why Ayub could not successfully move against all the opposition leaders, such as those representing the NAP. The following explanation could be offered. Only the NAP had a program that excited the disenchanted intelligentsia. It was the only party with the potential for receiving foreign assistance. Thus it was both politically dangerous and too "popular" to crush. (Popularity refers to the NAP program, not its personalities, however.) Although Ayub now hesitated to act against the NAP this was not the case when he took power in 1958. The NAP was one of the first organizations to feel his authority and its leaders were easily sidelined. Nonetheless, since 1962 leftist parties had become respectable and the NAP derived increasing benefits. The Communist Party, which was banned in 1955, has never been reinstated, however, and in many respects the NAP could be considered its proxy.

The furor the United States raised by supplying arms to India was accelerated to a frenetic pitch in September 1965. Both Communist China's support of Pakistan and American neutrality reinforced the power and hence the threat of the NAP. Similarly, the "good offices" provided by the Soviet Union made Pakistani society even more conscious of its immediate Communist neighbors. President Ayub was compelled to walk a domestic tightrope and this involved accepting the criticism of the NAP.

Rumors were rampant after Tashkent. One that was on the lips of most urbanites concerned the President's cabinet. Speaking at a gathering of intellectuals at Ayub Hall in Rawalpindi on January 29, 1966, the President ridiculed all those who predicted that trouble would develop in his administration. Digressing from his speech, he pointed to the rumor citing differences between himself and Foreign Minister Zulfikar Ali Bhutto. The President acknowledged that it had been circulated by a number of newspapers in the country and he caustically remarked "how fertile some brains are." His critics interpreted a recent visit to the Governor's home at Kalabagh as a maneuver to oust the Foreign Minister. "All these rumors are absolutely untrue. This, however, shows that we are very good at manufacturing and I do hope that when manufacturing in general expands in our country we will be equally good at that." President Ayub then commented that "such false stories did no good to the country."

Shortly thereafter the Foreign Minister appeared to confirm the President's comment. Speaking from Larkana, Bhutto did not mention his differences with Ayub or his intention to leave the government; instead he chose to restate the government's policy on Kashmir. It was reported in *The Pakistan Times* (February 10, 1966) that "a just and honourable settlement of the Jammu and Kashmir issue remained the only path towards the goal of a lasting peace and a relationship of true cordiality between India and Pakistan." Bhutto was officially interpreted as answering the opposition attacks on the administration when he declared: "It is inconceivable for anyone to think that we can go back on our solemn pledge to assist them [the people of Kashmir] in their liberation." Unofficially, his remarks were viewed as subtle criticism of the President's policies, however.

It was obvious to the public that a permanent split was only a question of time; and these views were justified a few months later when, in the summer of 1966, Zulfikar Ali Bhutto presented and Ayub Khan accepted his resignation from the cabinet. In his place the President put a virtual unknown, Syed Sharifuddin Pirzada, who was before his appointment Attorney General for Pakistan. Pirzada would in turn be succeeded in May 1968 by Mian Arshad Husain, Pakistan's High Commissioner to India. In September another former stalwart, Malik Amir Mohammad Khan—while apparently on a routine visit to the President's House at Rawalpindi—suddenly "resigned" and General Muhammad Musa, whose bags were already packed for the journey to Iran where he was to become Pakistan's new Ambassador, was named to succeed him. It is said the Governor put his support behind rival candidates in some

Karachi bye-elections and thus had angered Ayub. Malik Amir Mohammad Khan retired in seclusion at Kalabagh where, on November 26,
1967, he was shot and killed by his son because of a personal quarrel.

Musa's advancement to Governor of West Pakistan undoubtedly
satisfied the Army; similarly, when Ayub relinquished his control over
the Defense portfolio and named Vice Admiral A. R. Khan Minister for
Defense and Home Affairs he pleased another branch of the Armed
Forces. Nevertheless, the military, irritated over the Tashkent Declaration, was beginning to show more than simple concern with the President's inability to acquire more and newer weapons systems.

Chapter 5

Riots, Repression, and Retreat

DESPITE the trappings of civil government Ayub Khan's authority rested on the loyalty and solidarity of the Armed Forces. He seized power with their assistance and successfully perpetuated his rule with their complicity. Had they remained neutral after July 1962 it is highly doubtful that Ayub would have been returned to office in January 1965. It is not surprising, therefore, that the President's fortunes should wane with the growing estrangement of the military. Ayub had to ward off threats posed by his erstwhile Foreign Minister and sundry leaders of the political opposition, but his primary challenge came from a bitter urban middle class which could only be held in check by a determined military establishment.

THE DEVELOPMENT DECADE

Ayub Khan's creative emphasis lay in economic development. Agriculture, along with industry and commerce, made significant strides during his tenure. A traditional subsistence agrarian economy was restructured during the Second Five Year Plan (1960–65). The 3.4 percent annual growth rate for agriculture over the plan period compared favorably with the annual rate of 1.3 percent in the earlier period following independence. Food-grain output increased 27 percent and per capita income was up 14 percent. The Third Five Year Plan (1965–70) sought to sustain this momentum and aimed at a 5 percent growth rate. Although the Indo-Pakistani War and major droughts in 1965 and 1966 threatened agricultural objectives, the introduction of new wheat and rice varieties brought crop yields almost in line with projected goals. Statistically, the country was making progress, and the administration was hardly modest about its handiwork.[1]

The Fourth Five Year Plan (1970–75) was publicized by a demonstrably confident government which now talked of self-sustained growth.

In addition to achieving self-sufficiency in food production, schemes were prepared to encourage more diversified farming, higher rural incomes, and a sharp reduction in unemployment and underemployment. Pakistan possessed little additional land which could be brought under cultivation by the impoverished peasants, but government assistance in irrigation, transportation, procurement and production of fertilizer, improved seeds, and agricultural extension encouraged new endeavor. Generous price policies were no less important, however.

Private initiative was stimulated and positive payoffs created incentives for further investment. The most surprising result in the early 1960's was the proliferation of private tube-wells throughout West Pakistan.[2] Thus with government providing for major infrastructure, credit, subsidies, price stabilization, and demonstration and extension services, agricultural development was said to be entering a revolutionary phase. The Commission on International Development listed these striking statistics: [3]

RATES OF GROWTH IN AGRICULTURE

	1949–50/1959–60	1959–60/1967–68
West Pakistan		
Wheat	1.1	4.0
All major crops	2.3	5.0
East Pakistan		
Rice	0.3	2.4
All major crops	0.5	2.6

While listing accomplishments and identifying agricultural breakthroughs, shortcomings cannot go unnoticed. Though agriculture accounts for 48.2 percent of the GNP (1964–65) and carries the burden of the nation's foreign exchange earnings, yields remain among the lowest in the world. The average farm holding is a mere 6.8 acres which fact, coupled with the rapid increase in population (approximately 3 percent per annum), makes it difficult to be sanguine. Even with food production presently exceeding the population increase, prospects are not propitious. Furthermore, only a very small portion of Pakistan's population has genuinely prospered.

Gustav Papanek's reference to the "average" consumer whose lot was improved in the 1960's is instructive. The "average" consumer represents a minute fraction of the people. Groups that did well are identified as civil servants, businessmen, landlords, and some peasants engaged in industrial occupations. *Agricultural workers are not in-*

cluded. "Losers included the bulk of the population—families dependent on agriculture and particularly landless workers. They paid higher prices for manufactures, while agricultural prices remained relatively low." [4]

The agricultural story compares with and is related to advances in industrial development. Manufacturing accelerated during the Ayub decade. The way was eased for private investment. Liberal tax concessions were granted, and credit facilities were expanded through the establishment of the Industrial Development Bank and the Pakistan Industrial Credit and Investment Corporation (PICIC). In general, the government permitted greater freedom of action by shifting from direct to indirect controls. As a consequence of the stress on industrialization and the apparent ease with which profits could be made, landlords, professionals, traders, civil servants, and retired military officers "increasingly clamored for permits that would let them in on an obviously good thing." [5] Thus, as Papanek relates, the growing ranks of prestigious private industrial entrepreneurs was exceptionally rapid and, most important, the result of deliberate government policy during the Ayub era. [6]

The new industrialists included among their numbers members of Ayub's immediate family. The President insisted there was nothing wrong in this but his critics could not be expected to remain silent. Resentment increased during the 1965 war with India when Ayub's sons remained at their business posts while older retired officers were called up. Moreover, the relationship between government and business had altered drastically. "Businessmen and especially industrialists had become wealthier, more powerful and more sophisticated. Now that they owned newspapers and financed political groups, their support was increasingly valuable in political life." [7] Intermarriages between leading industrial families and civil-service families become commonplace. Hence along wth sizable increases in industrial capacity (an 8.6 percent rise in 1966–67) came a not unexpected reaction. The government-industrial relationship was a ready target for underpaid labor, the students, political dissidents, and lower middle-class income groups.

Pakistan was making significant gains in all economic sectors, but precious little advantage was filtering down to poor urban and rural people. Concentration of capital was justified on the grounds that profits were being plowed back into the economy,[8] but only twenty-four economic units controlled almost half of all private industrial assets. In addition, the resources, experience, and contacts of the leading private families made them strong contenders for ownership when semi-governmental corporations put their plants on the open market. It is estimated that over two-thirds of the assets thus sold have been bought by the leading families.[9] This accumulation of wealth and power was naturally viewed with rising indignation.

Amid the squalor and wretched poverty of the Pakistani masses a new elite now flaunted its prowess and privilege. Judged to be in violation of Islamic principle, it was also politically unconscionable. Those who possessed wealth were perceived as having gotten it illegally. And Ayub Khan not only bore chief responsibility but was accused of filling his personal coffers. In contrast with the situation of the privileged few, the knowledge that industrial wages were stationary or declining, per capita income among the lowest in the world, food prices skyrocketing, and little being done to provide adequate urban housing, health, or welfare services exacerbated the situation.

Given the unchanging misery of the multitude of poor peasants, the decade of development begins to look like something less than a statistical success. When Speaker of the National Assembly Jabbar Khan suggested that Ayub be given a life-presidency so that economic development might continue uninterrupted, more grist was provided for the mills of the discontented. It is not surprising to note, therefore, that the disturbances which eventually forced Ayub from office were precipitated by the government's elaborate festivities saluting ten years of economic progress.

It did not require a savant to recognize that the country was in deep trouble. Government propaganda could hardly be expected to placate those who did not share in the overly publicized economic revolution. As matters stood it was to prove extremely abrasive.

The celebrations spread over a four-week period in October 1968. Estimated expenditures for the festivities are put at 150 million rupees ($30 million). The seeming interminable repetition of slogans and grandiloquent speeches were more than the dissident urban population, particularly the students, could tolerate and toward the end of the month the disturbances began.

Once the students expressed their displeasure, opposition politicians began holding public meetings to condemn the government for its lavish spending. The administration answered with the imposition of Section 144, making it unlawful to congregate in public places. But the politicians would not be silenced and actually were encouraged to press their criticism when the former chief of the Pakistani Air Force, Mohammad Asghar Khan, joined their growing ranks. The chorus of dissent reached a new pitch as members of the bar, journalists, teachers, doctors, and the knowledgeable urban lower middle class joined in.

When representatives of the ulema took up the tune it was only a matter of time before the factory workers chimed in. The student population stood in the vanguard, however, and it was not until their lines had been attacked and bloodied that the real rebellion got under way. The chant was deafening and in unison and it reverberated throughout West Pakistan: "Ayub Must Go!"

What followed was not very different from the disorder that overtook France some months before. Unlike de Gaulle, however, Ayub was ill equipped to cope with the situation and his political supporters began deserting him. Meanwhile, the civil service and the military questioned how long they could afford to bolster their unpopular leader. In de Gaulle's case the political initiative remained in his hands down to the loss of the May 1969 referendum. Ayub Khan, however, had to suffer the humiliation that comes with the collapse of personal prestige.

THE AGARTALA CONSPIRACY

The regime's weakness was demonstrated in the so-called Agartala Conspiracy. In December 1967 and January 1968 the government accused a number of East Pakistanis of a secessionist plot. In all, some forty-six persons were alleged to have been involved. Thirty-five were later formally charged and eleven pardoned when they promised to assist the prosecution. According to the government the plan involved an armed revolt with weapons supplied by India. Those detained were reported to have planned the establishment of an independent government with India's protection and recognition of a new state of East Bengal. The supply of arms supposedly had been discussed at Agartala across the East Pakistan frontier on July 12, 1967. Hence the designation given the conspiracy.

Apprehended were a number of nondescript Bengalis, mostly from the Pakistan Armed Forces. But the list of accused did include three CSP officers, Navy Lieutenant Commander Moazzam Hussain, assigned to the Inland Water Transit Administration (IWTA), and Awami League leader Sheikh Mujibur Rahman. Of the CSP officers, one was K. M. Shamsur Rahman, the 1965 director of the Rural Academy at Comilla and a brother of a former Chief Minister of East Pakistan. Another was M. R. Quddus, who had been recently appointed vice principal at the Administrative Staff College. Ahmad Fazlur Rahman, who was reported on leave from duty since January 26, 1966, was the third CSP officer to be charged. The 1967 CSP Gradation List rated them 126, 98, and 94, respectively. Sheikh Mujibur Rahman was already in prison, having been detained almost a year and a half before the allegations and arrests in this particular case. The appearance of Manzur Qadir, the President's intimate associate, as a leading prosecution counsel underlined Ayub's intention to get a swift conviction. That he would be thwarted in this effort was not apparent when the trial got under way.

The government complaint read on June 19, 1968, specified how Army units in East Pakistan were to be paralyzed.[10] The plan supposedly called for: (1) the enlisting of recruits; (2) securing arms; (3) creating civil disturbances; and (4) setting dates for the seizure of strategic points throughout the province. The conspiracy was said to have had its roots in September 1964 when Sheikh Mujibur Rahman attended a meeting convened by Lieutenant Commander Moazzam Hussain. Sheikh Mujibur Rahman was alleged to have agreed with the plans for organizing a revolutionary council and securing the necessary funds.

According to the government, at another meeting held in August 1965 Sheikh Mujibur Rahman obtained money from India which he gave to the conspirators. After Mujib's arrest on May 6, 1966, the meetings continued in his absence and were attended by the First Secretary of the Indian High Commission, P. N. Ojha. Ojha was declared *persona non grata* and forced to leave the country when the administration moved against the alleged conspirators in January 1968. Upon hearing the charges, all the accused insisted on their innocence. In pleading not guilty Sheikh Mujibur Rahman noted that there certainly was a conspiracy underway, however. "It is a conspiracy against me," he was reported as saying.

The Agartala trial was a severe test of the Ayub regime in East Pakistan. Involved in the proceedings was an all-out effort to discredit and silence the man who at this date seemed to best typify Bengali sentiment. If the government could prove its case, Mujibur Rahman might well be written off as a leader of the political opposition in East Pakistan. But he had already spent five of the ten Ayub years in prison and had long ago earned his martyr's status. The trial therefore could only reinforce his power and creditability. Mujib claimed a large following in the perennially dissatisfied eastern wing and his 1966 Six Point Program was a rallying ground for the disenchanted, just as the Twenty-one Point Program had been in 1953–54. In point of fact, the Twenty-One Point Program of the East Pakistan Awami League was the first to insist on regional autonomy (19th point) and all later opposition programs were merely shorter versions of this seminal document. Hence the defense counsel's assertion that Mujib and his co-defendants had been falsely charged in order "to sabotage the just demands of East Pakistan" was greeted with convinced enthusiasm.

Tension mounted in the province when the news was later circulated that prosecution witnesses had been brutally tortured and threatened with death if they did not testify in support of the government charges. As the trial dragged on through the fall and into the winter of 1969 it became apparent that the government's case could not be substantiated. Despite the calling of 251 witnesses the state was unable to establish a winning case. Also, by this time East Pakistan was experiencing widespread student and labor disorder and West Pakistan was verging on anarchy. East and West Pakistan shared little in common, but their combined protests eroded the will of the regime to resist.

THE RIOTS BEGIN

In West Pakistan the main issue was Ayub Khan. The principal thrust of the student demonstrators lay in dramatizing the tyranny of the Ayub regime. Repressive government tactics bore out the general complaint that the country's youth was being punished in order to protect a privileged elite. While the public was being asked to be patient, to practice austerity, and generally sacrifice for national development, a prosperous minority was free to stuff their larders. To correct this situation Ayub had to be unseated.

In East Pakistan the issues could not be reduced to an attack on Ayub Khan, however. There, the "great leader" mentality was practically nonexistent, and social issues overshadowed the actions of individual personalities. Believing that they had been systematically deprived of their birthright the East Pakistanis demanded nothing less than a new political system. No government after Mohammad Ali Jinnah's death in 1948 could be said to have represented their interests. Their abject poverty, the superior attitude of the West Pakistanis, the failure to provide economic and military parity, and the continuing political dominance of the West wing gave credence to Mujib's demands and also explains their over-all support.

When Ayub under pressure declared on February 21, 1969, that he would retire after the expiration of his term, the East Bengali response was predictable. Ayub's withdrawal was merely one step to a larger end. Hence the increased fury and frequency of the disturbances. It can be generalized that West wing politicians were reasonably content with Ayub's announcement, but for the Bengalis the battle had only been joined. Now was the moment to insist on a new political arrangement, or so it seemed at the time. There appeared to be little sense in replacing Ayub with another personality so long as the East Pakistan–West Pakistan relationship remained unaltered.

Several days prior to the President's announced retirement plans the authorities shot and killed one of the defendants in the Agartala Conspiracy trial. It was alleged that he tried to escape from custody. His funeral on the following day precipitated a clash with the police which quickly escalated into large-scale rioting, arson, and looting. Residences of government ministers and administration buildings were beseiged. Ironically, the mayhem reached a pitch of intensity on the eve of the President's proclamation bringing an end to the state of emergency that had been in force since the opening hours of the India-Pakistan War in September 1965. The formal end of the emergency brought the suspension of the Defence of Pakistan Rules which had been used to justify the imprisonment of hundreds of political dissidents.

Ayub was now forced to meet with the politicians. No longer in effective control, the President extended invitations to his opponents and requested that they meet with him in a round-table conference in Rawalpindi. The Agartala Conspiracy trial was ordered closed and the accused released. Mujibur Rahman and his followers had been vindicated and Ayub unceremoniously humiliated. Moreover, Ayub's ever-diminishing power was now apparent. Government administrators now began looking for neutral ground and more and more disassociated themselves from Ayub's policies. In this situation the opposition politicians were not to be stampeded into accepting the President's invitation. The Agartala fiasco symbolized Ayub's weakness. Now the politicians insisted that before agreeing to talk, the presidential system had to be scrapped and a new parliamentary and federal structure substituted for it.

THE BHUTTO CHALLENGE

In February 1968 Ayub was felled by an attack of virus pneumonia which was later complicated by a blood clot on the lung. His physical disability coming on the heels of the Agartala incident produced the first genuine signs of instability. The President took a long time recuperating from his illness, and rumors circulated suggesting he had suffered a stroke and was partially paralyzed. His extended period of seclusion naturally led many to believe he would be unable to perform the tasks of the presidency and thus would be forced to name a successor. Unlike the civil service, whose over-all reaction could be described as guarded but hopeful that Ayub would resume his normal functions, political leaders thought otherwise.

Three months passed before the President could hold a cabinet meeting. His first public appearance did not come until mid-April when he greeted the Soviet Union's Premier Aleksei N. Kosygin. Although appearing to be in good health there were signs that his extended illness had taken a toll of his stamina. Some reports stated he had already decided not to seek another term and would eventually step aside for a younger, more durable personality. But he had also indicated that he could not trust Pakistan's future to Bhutto or Mujibur Rahman. But if not these figures, who from among the country's civilian leaders would be acceptable? At this point both advertised and unadvertised aspirants began jockeying for position.

Bhutto clearly did not count himself out of the running. Bhutto had left the President's cabinet a disillusioned young man. Initially he maintained strict silence. Later, however, he voiced his opinion on various political issues. Looking at Ayub's Muslim League party in 1966 he thought it could be revitalized only if a "Forward Bloc" were created within the organization. The Bloc would comprise those individuals possessing revolutionary ideas and willing to initiate unorthodox programs. The "Forward Bloc" was not a new device in subcontinent politics. Usually employed by disenchanted elements within the dominant party it historically heralds the breaking away from the parent organization. Such was the case with Subhas Chandra Bose and the Congress Party in the period immediately following India's involvement in World War II. Bhutto, like Bose earlier, insisted on a more radical course in the government's policies. His call for a "Forward Bloc" was nothing less than an attack upon President Ayub, however. Although first insisting that he stood with his old leader, he later changed his position and remarked that it was only Ayub's Election Manifesto (which he very likely had helped to draft) and the welfare state idea that he really supported.

In a visit to East Pakistan in November 1966 Bhutto had openly attacked Ayub's policies and expressed his support of the Six Point Program of Sheikh Mujibur Rahman. Only a few months before, as Foreign Minister, the same Zulfikar Ali Bhutto had condemned Mujib and volunteered to debate the Six Point Program with him. But soon after throwing this challenge, Bhutto excused himself saying he had more pressing matters to attend to. Now, however, he was no longer a member of the President's cabinet. Bhutto thus publicly defied Ayub by coming out in support of a program which the President had labeled parochial, divisive, and aimed at the destruction of Pakistan. Returning to West Pakistan Bhutto declared he would reserve the option to join another party or form a new one if the Muslim League failed to fulfill its pledge to the people. He noted, however, that there was still scope for a "Forward Bloc."

On December 10, Malik Khuda Bakhsh Bucha, then president of the West Pakistan Muslim League took note of Bhutto's demand. (Bucha was soon to be replaced as president of the West Pakistan Muslim League by Ahmad Said Kirmani, a lawyer and newly appointed Minister in Governor Mohammad Musa's West Pakistan government.) *The Pakistan Times* (December 11, 1966) recorded Bucha as declaring emphatically that "there was no place for any 'forward' or 'backward' bloc in the Muslim League." Taking cognizance of Bhutto's defection, Bucha said that "fissiparous tendencies in the Muslim League were noticeable at certain places" and they had the effect of dissipating party vigor and strength. He called upon the discontented to close ranks and offered his good offices in an effort to resolve outstanding differences. The party could not be dominated by any particular individual or group of personalities. Moreover, the Muslim League, said Bucha, refused to engage in political sloganeering. "Gone are the days when a political party was meant only for electioneering and seeking votes." Now the most urgent political work involved the social and economic betterment of the people. Bhutto was put on his guard. Either accept the view that the Muslim League party was an instrument for mobilizing the masses for development work or quit the organization.

In the spring of 1967 Bhutto toured West Pakistan speaking out against the government on both domestic and international matters. It is interesting to note that a number of EBDO'ed politicians celebrated the termination of their restrictions at a lavish dinner in Karachi's Hotel Intercontinental on the evening of December 31, 1966. Although Bhutto was in the dining room, few of the politicians felt it wise to spend too much time at his table. While he failed in his attempt to form a Forward Bloc within the Pakistan Muslim League, Bhutto was not prevented from organizing his People's Party, however. Prior to this event in July 1967, the government sought to discredit him by publishing documents which purported to show that the former Foreign Minister considered himself a citizen of India at least up to the year 1958. As has already been noted, the Bhutto family at one time possessed land which after partition was located in India. Bhutto, like so many other Pakistanis, registered applications with the Indian Government in connection with the eventual restitution of this property. The legal transactions were handled through the office of the Custodian of Evacuee Property. In this proceeding, however, it was alleged that Bhutto declared he had always been an Indian citizen. Moreover, it was only in 1958 after he became Ayub's Minister of Commerce that he filed a petition with the Supreme Court of India withdrawing his appeal against the Custodian's decision.

The question of Bhutto's citizenship became a heated issue and the opposition asked why, if this information was known in 1965, Bhutto had been allowed to remain in office for still another year. To this the Central Government's Information Minister Khwaja Shahabuddin responded that the details were not clearly known at that time. When prodded by the opposition to debate the matter with Bhutto personally, and also to agree to the holding of an inquiry into the antecedents of other ministers, Shahabuddin backed away.

Bhutto later denied the principal allegation, but admitted he had traveled to the United States on an Indian passport in 1947. He added that a Pakistani passport was issued to him in Karachi on July 12, 1949. Bhutto also verified he had laid claim to ancestral holdings in India. He emphatically rejected the allegation that he did so as an Indian citizen, however. Furthermore, he reported, the Pakistan Government had been kept informed of the negotiations. Later, under advice from his lawyer, he withdraw his case altogether.

The entire affair was reminiscent of the Suhrawardy episode in 1947–48. Suhrawardy, the last Chief Minister of Undivided Bengal and a loyal Muslim Leaguer, had been elected to Pakistan's First Constituent Assembly only to be denied his seat on the grounds that he was still an Indian citizen. In later years Suhrawardy developed a formidable opposition party, the Awami League, and eventually succeeded in challenging and defeating his former Muslim League colleagues. The tactics to deny Suhrawardy a place in Pakistan's political structure backfired, and it was doubtful that they could succeed in Bhutto's case. All that was gained was the heightened opprobrium of the attentive public for those in authority.

It was three months after Bhutto's exchange with the administration that he chose to create his People's Party. With a political organization in tow Bhutto began looking for recruits over and above his eager student supporters. At a press conference in Karachi in October 1967 he said he intended to develop a program which would look like a socialist manifesto. Its main plank would be the nationalization of banks, insurance companies, heavy industry, and all public utilities. In the field of foreign policy Bhutto said his party would be independent and hence could insist on Pakistan's withdrawal from both SEATO and CENTO. Moreover, closer links would be forged with Afro-Asia, but especially with other Muslim states.

According to Bhutto, none of the existing opposition parties measured up to his criteria in leadership or programs. With elections scheduled for late 1969 and early 1970 there was little time to get his new organization in high gear, but he expected students and professionals to assist him in cultivating the opposition. With the divisions in the Awami League and National Awami Party, the inability of Mian Mumtaz Daultana to increase the membership of the Council Muslim League, or Choudhri Mohammad Ali's Nizam-i-Islam to influence the peasants, only the Jamaat-i-Islami of Maulana Maudoodi presented an organized front. Unfortunately, however, the latter's program had little appeal for the Pakistani masses. Even the Pakistan Democratic Movement compromising the Council Muslim League, Jamaat-i-Islami, Awami League, and Nizam-i-Islam had goals which in Bhutto's estimation were far too limited.

Even were these diverse parties capable of working together for a time, their basic differences would impede the building of a coherent political base. And without a stable foundation the restructuring of Pakistani society was impossible. Hence Bhutto's decision to go ahead with an entirely new party and his determination to face Ayub at the ballot box.

Bhutto's challenge could not be taken lightly. In an oblique reference to the former Foreign Minister, Central Communications Minister Khan A. Sobur rejected Bhutto's call for a socialist state. According to Sobur, socialism had failed to develop India and it was unrealistic to assume it could work in Pakistan. Noting that Bhutto had a fertile mind and intimating he was a charlatan and opportunist, he reminded his East Pakistani brethren that this was the same man who had condemned the Six Point Program, suggested that Pakistan should be a one-party state, and assisted in making operational the 1962 Constitution. Over and again, Ayub, his cabinet ministers, and party officials reminded their listeners that dissidents like Bhutto concealed nefarious motives and that such men preached the cult of parochialism, provincialism, and division and were to be rejected lest the country be torn apart. Interestingly, the localisms to which Bhutto and others like him appealed were not considered dangerous by the public, and the more the government sought to undermine their attractivness the greater their strength grew.

CRITICISM AND COUNTER-CRITICISM

In an effort to sidetrack government criticism the president of the West Pakistan Democratic Movement (PDM), K. M. Safdar, declared that the opposition would never contemplate dismembering Pakistan. The key to the PDM's eight-point program was the restoration of the 1956 Constitution. The PDM supported the integration of East and West Pakistan and recognized the necessity for a strong center, but felt that the Central Government must be more representative of the country's diversity and that this was only possible within a federal framework and under a parliamentary system. While not joining the PDM, Bhutto voiced virtually identical views. He held that the government could not be stripped of all but its defense and foreign affairs functions as Mujibur Rahman had proposed. He did not hesitate to add that the Central Government needed the power to deal with emergencies. But apart from answering governmental critics, these responses also demonstrated the gap still separating the various opposition groups.

For all intents and purposes the opposition remained neutralized. With the exception of the Agartala trial the Ayub adminstration, even with the added problem of the President's illness, seemed to be in no special danger. In the autumn, however, the celebrations marking the development decade commenced. What were only rumblings in the distance now merged into a tumultuous crescendo. The government was celebrating its own, not the country's good fortune. The enormous sum of money spent for propaganda aroused the student community in West Pakistan first. Once more it was the students who represented national opinion; there being no other outlet for their emotions, they took to the streets.

A report of the Pakistan Planning Commission cited in *The New York Times* on December 1, 1968, provided additional fuel for the alienated and frustrated young people. Despite the claims of foreign and domestic experts, economic development was not judged co-equal with social change. A salient if understated comment on the report read as follows: "The conflict between economic dynamism and social justice has become fairly sharp." In Karachi, Lahore, and Rawalpindi one could observe all the symbols of new wealth—new cars, luxury hotels, and ostentatious housing for the privileged few. But for the impoverished multitudes and the unrewarded lower middle class there was only envy and bitterness. Although industrial production had risen by approximately 160 percent in eight years, the laboring class had yet to realize any significant advantage.

Similarly advances in agricultural production were confined to those with sizable holdings in West Pakistan. The 23 percent jump in grain production in 1968 did not in any way benefit the peasant masses. Government projections aimed at a 7 percent increase in economic growth. At the same time, revenues allocated for the Armed Forces were estimated in excess of two and a half billion rupees ($500 million). With such an expenditure the material life of the masses could not be improved and educational and welfare services remained static.

The larger question raised by the Commission study involved the possibility of deliberately slowing down economic growth. Only then, it was felt, could the human dilemma be tackled. The contention that statistical growth was not enough was also the main argument of Ayub's antagonists. Now that a respected agency of the higher bureaucracy found itself in agreement and suggested reevaluating government priorities, the opposition could not be expected to reduce their attack.

Student rioting increased in tempo, and the toll on human life and property escalated accordingly. Ayub pleaded again and again for calm and restraint. His words fell on deaf ears, however. On November 10, 1968, while Ayub was waiting to address a Peshawar meeting a young man standing approximately thirty yards from the speaker's platform fired several shots in the direction of the President but missed his mark. The assailant was seized on the spot and Ayub proceeded to make his appeal for order, but his young countrymen were in no mood to listen.

Zulfikar Ali Bhutto shared responsibility for the student disorders. Not only had he refused to aid the government in restoring law and order, but he had urged his young supporters to continue the fight until Ayub was forced from office. His standard reply to those wanting an end to the turbulence was "How can I do that when they are fighting against tyranny." It is possible that Bhutto wanted the government to arrest him. He had been unsuccessful in uniting the political factions opposing Ayub and in the present anomic situation a stint in jail might provide him with needed leverage. What the government lost in the way of prestige, Bhutto gained. Furthermore, the greater the degree of repression the larger the confirmation that the struggle was one in which *good* was pitted against *evil.*

Nonetheless, arrests multiplied. By November 15th some forty-five politicians were incarcerated. Unlike 1966, those seized represented Pakistan's leftist parties, particularly the People's Party and the National Awami Party. According to the government these groups pursued policies detrimental to the unity of the country. The NAP, for example, had resurrected its old demand that West Pakistan be broken up into its pre-1955 administrative units. With many of the prominent politicians in government custody a new personality now entered the arena.

On November 17, 1968, the former chief of the Pakistan Air Force, Air Marshal Mohammad Asghar Khan, announced he would actively campaign for the support of the political opposition. Charging the Ayub regime with corruption, nepotism, graft, and administrative incompetence the airman said he would begin a nation-wide tour "to mobilize public opinion for the solution of problems facing the country." Although long in retirement, even though only forty-nine, Asghar Khan was the highest ranking military officer ever to come out in opposition to the President.

Asghar condemned the suppression of press and speech freedoms generally. And he noted that the administration could remain in power only so long as it enjoyed the capacity to coerce. Obliquely he called upon his brother officers to recognize the plight of the country, the unpopularity of Ayub Khan and the need for them to remain neutral in this propitious moment. There could be no mistaking his strategy. In the circumstances, Ayub could not govern without the direct support of the military.

With Asghar Khan in the field, the student ranks were swelled by other groups previously uncommitted but sympathetic. The jailing of political leaders was a last desperate act of a quickly declining administration. Pakistan's multi-party political system is an amorphous congeries. Although the organizations have identifiable leaders they have always operated on a more or less headless basis. Hence the detention of the leaders did more to accelerate the movement than slow it down. Rebellious youth was in no need of leadership, for its objective was the destruction of the old system. What would follow did not seem to matter. With the national figures removed from the scene the crowds became more, not less, truculent.

The Political Demise of Ayub Khan

In the agony of a country no longer governable it is impossible to distinguish the guilty from the innocent. They usually perish together. Throughout Pakistan property lay in ruins and the semblance of civilized order was rapidly deteriorating. The rampaging throngs were unrelenting, however. While the Pakistan Democratic Movement was considering a boycott of the 1969–70 elections in order to dramatize their dissatisfaction with the government's repressive tactics, Pakistani society appeared to be coming apart. No one led the urban crowds and certainly no one controlled them. Hence no one could really speak for them either. The explosive fury of the people had reached a point of spontaneous destruction.

Some preferred to interpret the chaos in a favorable light: the country was passing through a catharsis; after the storm a new beginning could be anticipated. It is possible that this view was what compelled S. M. Murshed, a former Chief Justice of the East Pakistan Supreme Court, to enter the political scene. East Pakistan needed political representation in this uncertain period. Murshed reflected the pious belief that the prevailing anarchy would somehow cleanse Pakistani society. Pontificatingly he declared that the time was at hand for the creation of "a truly advanced society." [11] Political amateurs like Asghar Khan and Murshed kept opposition hopes alive, but like their predecessors they refused to come to grips with the realities of the nation's life-style.

Ayub made some low-key attempts to put his house in order. Early in December he offered the olive branch to the rampaging students. Major concessions were announced in an effort to redress grievances of long-standing. A seven-year-old ordinance which permitted the government to withdraw college degrees from students engaged in actions determined to be anti-administration was repealed. Minimal qualification grades were lowered and students in the lowest academic ranking were to be given another chance to improve their standing. At the same time, Ayub defended the government's prerogative to arrest anyone performing an unlawful act. This, he reiterated, meant politicians who directly or indirectly inflame public passions. In reference to the accusations that his regime was corrupt and undemocratic, he called the former "an incurable disease" and said the latter charge was completely unfounded. "Political parties are free to present their programs to the people. There is only one condition: these political differences should not assume the shape of lawlessness, violence, force and terrorism." [12]

Ayub's sense of frustration was at its peak. He was convinced that Pakistan had made considerable progress during his ten years in office, and it was impossible for him to understand the depth of popular dissatisfaction.

> If in the face of evidence anyone shuts his eyes and says that he sees no progress at all; that no development has taken place; that, in fact, conditions are worsening, then there is no cure for the malady.[13]

Ayub pulled out all the stops. He made references to the external threat and how Pakistan's enemies can make capital of Pakistan's disunity. But he was unconvincing. Even the President's defiant response that he would not stand idly by and watch the efforts of the last ten years destroyed sounded hollow.

In December the demonstrations which at first were confined to West Pakistan spread to the eastern province. Precipitated to an extent by the appearance of Asghar Khan, they were soon exploited by NAP and NDF members. Speaking in Dacca's central mosque Asghar Khan called upon Ayub to resign and his audience responded with wild cries of "Down with Ayub." But the East Pakistani politicians did not want Asghar Khan leading their movement. This was clear from the outset. Neither he nor Bhutto were acceptable substitutes for Ayub Khan. They shared a common determination but the relationship was ephemeral. After all, Asghar Khan was a West Pakistani and a military figure. These were both attributes that the East Pakistanis had to weigh carefully. Asghar Khan afforded them an opportunity to gain leverage with dissident groups within the bureaucracy and Armed Forces, and this was to their advantage, but too much success could undermine East Pakistan's separate goals. Certainly it would make it less possible for Bengalis like Nurul Amin, S. M. Murshed, and Sheikh Mujibur Rahman to compete for high office. Thus the decision was made to take advantage of but not directly support Asghar Khan's campaign.

Ayub was in East Pakistan at this time. He seldom ventured forth from Government House, however, and there were rumors that he was seriously contemplating retirement. His problem essentially revolved about the choice of a successor. Ayub trusted no one in the opposition camp. All, he concluded, would sabotage his ten-year effort at the first opportunity. Furthermore, his contempt for the politicians was undiminished. Their activities in the last few months confirmed his worst fears concerning their destructive propensities. The more he pondered the consequences of his retirement the more his mind turned toward a military solution.

The violence that erupted in West Pakistan in late October continued into 1969. In mid-January it spread and intensified. Student demonstrations resulted in numerous deaths in Dacca and a general strike paralyzed the city. Angry young people dominated the streets; their battle cry demanded Ayub's resignation. In the tumult newspaper offices belonging to the government's National Press Trust were burned, government installations were attacked, and the National Assembly (which was in session at the time) was surrounded. In Karachi, Lahore,

Rawalpindi, Chittagong, and elsewhere the story was the same. Crowds were running excitedly through the streets, taunting, burning, and looting. Effigies of Ayub were burned in dozens of places in both wings of the country. The fires that blazed in the battered cities and towns were often fed by gleeful students who took special delight in destroying the President's newly published autobiography, *Friends Not Masters.*

Curfews were imposed in the major metropolitan areas in an effort to stem the rising tide of death and destruction. But to no avail. By this time law enforcement was on the verge of collapsing. The administrators and police sensed that the government had lost control of the situation and they began retreating from the scene of the disorders in a desperate effort to preserve themselves. In some ways the failure of local officials to face up to their responsibilities resembled the situation immediately preceding and following independence. Then the bureaucrats and police deserted their posts, leaving the vengeful mobs unrestrained. The result was incredible carnage. Although the magnitude of this latest series of riots was on a decidedly lower scale the pattern was familiar and the end was not yet in sight.

President Ayub dispatched his personal confidant and adviser, Fida Hasan, to East Pakistan to investigate the continuing strife. He was also charged with the futile task of trying to rally the demoralized and beleaguered civil and police services. A career officer, it was thought he could inspire the administrators and possibly help in restoring their confidence. Fida Hasan explained that the President had decided to make new concessions, the reforms to be in keeping with the demands of the rebellious public. But the situation was beyond recall. Rebellion, not reform, was the order of the day. Disillusioned government officers found themselves sympathizing with the opposition. Asghar Khan reflected their position when he declared: "In his person, President Ayub Khan rightly or wrongly symbolizes in the eyes of the people all that is evil in our society." Nothing less than Ayub's total surrender could possibly restore even a modicum of tranquility.

Toward the end of January elements of the Pakistan Army moved into Karachi, Lahore, Peshawar, Dacca, and Khulna—scenes of the more serious disturbances. More newspaper offices had been damaged and foreign installations assaulted. The authorities by this time had arrested thousands of individuals. And while no accurate figure could be given for the number of dead, the estimated toll ranged in the hundreds. The mobs had turned on Ayub's supporters with the Muslim League offices being prime targets. A number of party workers were slain and others seriously wounded. Thus virtual martial law was put into effect in the heavily populated regions. Not since October 1958 had the military been asked to pacify so many areas at the same time.

With the rioting unabated the opposition organized an *ad hoc* coalition called the Democratic Action Committee, comprising eight parties. The DAC quickly drafted a program of joint demands and presented them to President Ayub. Only Mujibur Rahman's East Pakistan Awami League and the NAP declined to cooperate with DAC, but even these parties did not disagree with the purpose of the program. Above all, the DAC insisted on the restitution of the federal parliamentary system and direct adult franchise. Under pressure from his advisers Ayub agreed, if reluctantly, to examine the Committee's proposals. His reply, however, was indirect and came in the form of an editorial in *The Pakistan Times*. In it Ayub said he was willing to meet with the politicians but hedged where the specific proposals were concerned. Pakistan required a stable political system and to Ayub Khan anything less than a strong presidency would mean anarchy, not democracy. The DAC had no need to compromise, however. They had already announced publicly that their demands were non-negotiable. Hence the President's apparent willingness to discuss "constitutional issues" was interpreted as a tactic to buy time and possibly get the opposition leaders to reduce the level of hostility. But they certainly had no intention of playing into Ayub's hands and repeated their all-or-nothing proposals.

The newfound semi-unity and determination of the opposition paid quick dividends. In another broadcast to the nation on February 1st, Ayub stated he would put aside his "personal pride" and meet with his political detractors on their terms. He said: "I have on previous occasions expressed my views on amending the constitution. The constitution is not the word of God. It can be changed." Commenting on the necessity of holding consultations with the representatives of "responsible political parties" he added: "We shall have no hesitation in agreeing to any settlement that is arrived at through mutual discussions." A letter sent to Nawabzada Nasrullah Khan, convenor of the DAC, at the same time invited all political leaders to a meeting to be held in Rawalpindi on February 17th. The tone of this letter was in sharp contrast to Ayub's earlier remarks condemning the same individuals for their antisocial and antistate activities. Now, he acknowledged, he would be "happy" if they would "stay in Rawalpindi as my guests during the conference." The mighty had indeed fallen!

As a precondition for the talks the opposition now insisted that the state of emergency be lifted and all political leaders released from custody. This was necessary in order to clear the atmosphere, to make it more conducive to what was expected to be hard bargaining. At this point Ayub again pulled up short. He was convinced that many of those detained were guilty of criminal acts. In disgust he exclaimed: "How can you release them in a hurry?" But there was also little reason to believe he could long refuse to satisfy these demands.

With the invitations extended, Ayub flew to East Pakistan for a meeting of his Muslim League party. Seeking to restore confidence and calm the fears of the membership he said he would not remove himself from the political wars—and thus allowed himself to be reelected for another term as president of the organization. It was a last symbolic gesture at maintaining the solidarity of his political following and it appeared to be ample proof that he had not yet decided to step down. Many Muslim Leaguers were unimpressed with Ayub's performance, however. Defections mounted with each new disturbance. In the absence of bureaucratic and military support Ayub's politicians could only think of running. The situation was now critical.

On February 18th the Ayub government capitulated and lifted the three-year-old state of emergency. The announcement came one hour before Zulfikar Ali Bhutto was scheduled to begin a hunger strike in protest against the same regulation. With the termination of the emergency, a ludicrous act in view of the turmoil that was opening society at the seams, Bhutto and other political detainees were set free. It was hoped these leaders, especially Bhutto, would now take advantage of the President's invitation for a round-table conference.

But even these developments did not end the civil disobedience. The Hyderabad bazaar was set afire, demonstrators were tear-gassed and beaten in Lahore, and Karachi was a virtual no man's land. In East Pakistan two more newspapers were put to the torch and labor strife began in earnest. Business and public transportation were at a standstill in both provinces and total paralysis was beginning to set in. The period was one of uncontrolled passion. Bhutto's return to the political arena spurred his supporters to expand their activities. Thousands assembled in Larkana to celebrate their leader's freedom and vindication. Some days later, while riding in a triumphal motorcade through Karachi, Bhutto was implored not to negotiate with the President. When elements loyal to the government tried to disrupt the festivities a melee followed. Undaunted, Bhutto proceeded to the Jinnah Tomb where he made another of his emotionally charged speeches. If the President thought Bhutto would sit down and discuss their differences he was badly misinformed. The former Foreign Minister made it clear he would not accommodate his once-revered leader.

In Lahore Bhutto's wife led one of the two large processions which again reminded the politicians that they should not be trapped into talking with Ayub. All the while the President remained secluded in his residence in Rawalpindi awaiting an official response from the DAC. When it finally came it was decidedly less than what he had hoped for. The DAC, with some members pushing for and others opposing the conference, was forced to compromise. It was finally agreed that only Nasrullah Khan would attend. As for Bhutto, he and six other opposition leaders declared they wanted no part of any negotiations and would boycott the talks. Bhutto was quoted as saying Ayub could not be trusted. He was playing "a yes-and-no game, a cat-and-mouse game." Bhutto refused to give the President the satisfaction of having outfoxed his antagonists. Nothing was to be done which would enable Ayub to regain his respectability. Ayub was still a power to be reckoned with, and only by sustaining societal turmoil would the opposition politicians be in a position to loosen his grip.

Bhutto knew exactly what he wanted. Once committed to demolishing Ayub he could not relent. Reforms were totally unacceptable. In this he shared a common bond with the demonstrators who had already gone beyond the point of no return.

On February 21st the first significant impact of the disturbances rolled over a dazed Pakistani nation. Ayub Khan dramatically and without prior warning spoke to his disenchanted and frightened people. In a calm voice but betraying anguish he declared: "I shall not be a candidate in the next election. This decision is final and irrevocable." But he obviously was not yet about to bow out of the picture. Again the President was attempting to buy time. Alluding to the reluctance of the opposition to accept his invitation for a round-table conference, he offered the thought that "I shall have only one course open to me and that will be to place before you my constitutional proposals. . . . As required by the Constitution these proposals would then go to the National Assembly for approval." He concluded his speech with a flourish, exclaiming "offices and power are things transient. Pakistan will hold forever."

THE OPPOSITION REORGANIZES

The President's decision to retire with the expiration of his term in January 1970 galvanized the opposition into feverish activity. It was now agreed that nothing would be lost by meeting with Ayub. Not only had the President agreed to step aside in the forthcoming elections but he had also ordered the release of Sheikh Mujibur Rahman and the other defendants in the Agartala trial. The release of Mujib added another dimension to the political confusion, however. While the rioting in the streets continued, the leading politicians scurried around trying to shore up their ruptured organizations. None among them commanded a national following. Each suspected the other of deviousness. Hence an acceptable replacement for Ayub would not be a simple matter.

Nasrullah Khan was a colorless personality with minimum support in West Pakistan and none in East Bengal. Daultana, Choudhri Mohammad Ali, and Maulana Maudoodi though different had something in common. Each had passed that moment in time when they could have commanded a wide following. None were acceptable to the Bengalis. While Bhutto and Asghar Khan attracted much public attention, and perhaps were instrumental in forcing Ayub to retire, their capacity for leading a coalition government was questionable. Among the East Pakistani politicians, Bhashani was too old and certainly too radical for the more orthodox leaders. This left only Mujibur Rahman, and his protestations down through the years made his name anathema in many circles. To say that Ayub had filled and was now about to leave a political vacuum heightens the emphasis given to vice-regal politics in Pakistan. It also explains why the military-bureaucratic nexus succeeded in perpetuating itself. And why this arrangement usually proves acceptable to the Pakistani people.

Sheikh Mujibur Rahman's first public address upon being released emphasized East Pakistan's desire for proportionate representation and genuine autonomy. There was no question but that most articulate East Pakistanis felt this was the ideal moment to press their major objectives. There is also little doubt that this is exactly what the rioting students and workers wanted their leaders to do. Ayub's power may have eroded but there was still no indication that West Pakistan's hold on East Bengal had weakened. If East Pakistan tempered its demands West Pakistan would refuse to make concessions. The Bengalis wanted one of their own to succeed Ayub. Hence the new importance given Mujib's possible candidacy.

The postponed round-table talks were finally held in Rawalpindi toward the end of February. After four days of deliberation Ayub capitulated and agreed to dispense with the indirect elections (the electoral college of Basic Democrats). Direct election based on universal franchise was to be written into law and put into practice in the forthcoming campaign. Moreover, the presidential system would be modified and the parliamentary institution resurrected. Mujibur Rahman expressed dissatisfaction with the outcome of the talks, however. The question of autonomy for East Pakistan remained unanswered. Furthermore, the new federal structure failed to spell out the fate of the One Unit. Was West Pakistan to remain a single administrative province or was it to be divided into its pre-1955 components? Sheikh Mujibur Rahman made it clear where he stood while the West Pakistani leadership vacillated. As a result Mujib announced he was removing his party from the DAC and made another of his celebrated withdrawals.

Asghar Khan was reasonably satisfied with the decisions taken at the meeting and sensing that the moment had arrived to become actively committed to the political struggles revealed that he would create a new political organization which would be "truly national in character." It would be called the Justice Party.

Bhutto had boycotted the talks. When they were terminated he lost no time in registering his displeasure. Apparently in an effort to woo the East Pakistanis he called upon Ayub to submit his resignation and allow for the immediate formation of a National Caretaker Government. The Caretaker Government would arrange to hold the elections and also guide the elected representatives in the drafting of a new constitution. As he envisioned the new political system, East Pakistan would be given its autonomy within a federal structure. The federal structure, he noted, would also necessitate relative autonomy for the newly reconstituted provinces of Sind, Baluchistan, the North West Frontier, and the Punjab. Bhutto's plan reserved a place for an elected President but, given the emphasis on federalism and parliamentary government, executive authority had to be shared. The Prime Minister would be responsible to the parliament but must be an East Pakistani if the President was from the west, or *vice versa*. The central legislature would be bicameral with each province having the same number of representatives in the upper chamber. The lower house, it was assumed, would be organized on the basis of population. Although the Bhutto plan reflected the objectives sought by East Pakistanis in the period 1947-56 it was greeted with considerable suspicion. In West Pakistan there was apprehension.

Maulana Bhashani also absented himself from the Rawalpindi discussions. He indicated relative satisfaction but cautioned that "political freedom is meaningless without economic independence." The NAP still wanted an end to alliance commitments and the nationalization of all private business, both foreign and domestic. Islamic socialism was to be insisted upon; the demand was non-negotiable. No compromise was possible.

As for Ayub, after years of toil he was now being forced to dismantle his once proud and seemingly impregnable edifice. The only solace Ayub received was in the comments of Nasrullah Khan and Choudhri Mohammad Ali. The President was cited for his "courageous and realistic" decisions. The latter declared: "History would record the height of the statesmanship Mr. Ayub Khan has shown."

THE MILITARY SOLUTION

Ayub had concealed his distress in his public remarks. While accepting direct adult suffrage he brooded over the future design of the federal system. As in 1958, he feared East Pakistani secessionist tendencies and he worried about the influence of the new movement to dismember West Pakistan. Whereas he was reconciled to removing himself from the political contest, he did not want Churchill-like to preside over the dissolution of the Pakistan nation. Soon after the conference adjourned Ayub called his advisors together. Spelling out his misgivings he urged the imposition of martial law. While there was general agreement in the military high command that drastic action was in order lest East Pakistan become another Biafra, decisive steps were possible only if the generals were not hobbled by an unpopular and repudiated leader. Just as Iskander Mirza got in Ayub's way in 1958, so Ayub was an obstacle now.

Ayub was left with two bitter alternatives: (1) remain and observe his erstwhile enemies fight over the carcass of his defunct system, or (2) resign and give the military a free hand. Only the latter option promised a return to stable rule. It was also the only way to provide for continuity and preserve a semblance of the old order. Enervated and disillusioned, Ayub opted for the latter alternative, but even at this moment hesitated to commit himself.

The Democratic Action Committee was dissolved with the conclusion of the round-table conference. Nasrullah Khan, Nurul Amin, Mian Mumtaz Daultana, Choudhri Mohammad Ali, Maulana Maudoodi, Khwaja Khairuddin, and Hamidul Huq Chowdhury met with the President before returning to their homes. Representing the moderates and determined to bring peace to their ruptured country they believed Ayub when he told them every effort would be made to hold the elections on schedule. Ayub noted that once the new parliament had been organized the remaining outstanding demands could be thrashed out. While these politicians appeared satisfied with the President's assurance they were apprehensive over the intransigence shown by Sheikh Mujibur Rahman,

Bhutto, and Bhashani. The situation in East Pakistan was deteriorating steadily and none of these politicos seemed concerned with the consequences. The moderate politicians wanted to consolidate their newfound gains and this meant restoring the social order. If they did not concentrate on the latter they knew the military would have to. But the extremists were blinded by their success and their attitude remained defiant.

The All-Pakistan Student Action Committee meeting in Dacca endorsed a demand calling for a general strike. Maulana Bhashani announced he would convene a convention of his party on March 30th. He explained that the President's declaration was insufficient and the peasants and workers of the Krishak Samity should be afforded the opportunity to express their views concerning the future course of action. In the meantime, Mujibur Rahman, who would listen to no one (including Bhutto and Asghar Khan), presented his own draft of constitutional reforms to Ayub. In it he was alleged to have rejected any form of incrementalism. Thus East Pakistani affairs were in sharp contrast with those of West Pakistan. In the latter the turbulence had subsided appreciably. In the former the storm continued to rage.

All of West Pakistan was the enemy of the eastern province. "Awake Bengal, Arise Bengal" became a war cry. Ayub's collapse, it was hoped, heralded the end of West Pakistan domination. In the districts of Dinajpur, Dacca, Mymensingh, and Bogra the the police were in retreat. And as the law enforcement agency crumbled Ayub's supporters were exposed to the fury of the mob. A miniature civil war spread in the rural areas of these districts but the human toll was only guessed at. Doubtless, the extent of the carnage will never be known, but no one could deny that indiscriminate killing had occurred.

On March 21st in a surprise maneuver Ayub replaced General Musa with Yusuf Haroon as Governor of West Pakistan. Almost simultaneously he selected M. N. Huda to succeed Monem Khan, who fled to the more friendly confines of Rawalpindi. Haroon, a leading industrialist and Huda, a professor of economics and East Pakistan Minister of Finance, represented different philosophies and backgrounds and in a more settled time might have made successful administrators in their respective provinces. In the present circumstances, however, neither had a chance—nor were they to be given one. Their selection at this late hour merely stands as evidence of Ayub's desire to cling to power.

East Pakistan was now in chaos. Train service in Chittagong, Khulna, Mymensingh, and Dacca districts was suspended as a result of a continuing strike. Student delegations beseiged the provincial government with demands. Gazetted and non-gazetted staff of the East Pakistan

Cooperative Directorate left their posts to march in the streets. Mujahids organized as a militia were in armed revolt, and rumors circulated that they had linked forces with the National Awami Party. Factory workers had seized their managerial staffs and in numerous instances forced them to increase their salaries. One of Pakistan's leading industrialists, G. M. Adamjee, was coerced into increasing the wages of mill workers by a total of approximately six million rupees after his executive officer had been threatened with bodily harm. As a consequence of the strike, jute production was cut almost in half and industry throughout the province was coming to a standstill.

Still another dimension of the struggle in East Pakistan lay in the conflict between the NAP and the Jamaat-i-Islami. With the future uncertain, the Jamaat feared a Communist take-over in East Pakistan. Processions taken out in Kushtia, Barisal, Jessore, Chittagong, and several rural areas by the Jamaat attempted to warn the populace about the threat. "Down with the Communists," "Long Live Religion," and "Make Pakistan an Islamic State" were typical slogans. The leader of the Jamaat-i-Islami, Maulana Maudoodi, was reported in an Indian newspaper as saying the "tongues of those who speak of communism will be torn out." In reply, Bhashani is supposed to have said: "The house of religious fanatics would be burned." [14] In this conflict Mujibur Rahman was cast in the role of a moderate. Though outwardly neutral he appeared to favor the Jamaat to the NAP. Maudoodi was no threat and with the NAP in difficulty, Mujib's Awami League could be expected to carry the field. But Mujib had misread Ayub's intentions.

Ayub had studied the Awami Leaguer's draft of amendments to reform the Constitution and was convinced that he should not be given an opportunity to gain political office. He concluded that Mujib would eventually win control of the province and with such leverage perhaps the country as well. Mujib wanted to shift the capital to East Bengal, give East Pakistan a majority of the parliament, and establish a separate and independent budget. Denied these changes he might well be inclined to mobilize East Bengali sentiment behind a movement to create an independent state.

The disorder that swept over rural East Pakistan was in some ways reminiscent of South Viet Nam. The indiscriminate slaughter of lower government functionaries, particularly those affiliated with the Basic Democracies and the President's party, was cause for exceptional concern. Ayub did not hide the fact that "mob rule is the order of the day," and declared that he dare not hesitate in bringing it under control. Public executions began to mount and rural police officials, tax collectors, and Basic Democrats were the principal victims. The general intimidation of local officials was emphasized when student dissidents demanded the resignation of all those associated with the Basic Democracies. Nor were the killings confined to administration supporters. Attacks on authority were a convenient cover for local feuds which now escalated into violent acts of individual, premeditated murder. While the enlarging death toll was of immediate concern, the frenzied destruction of crops and property could not go unnoticed either.

The outnumbered, poorly trained and equipped police detachments were in no position to restore equilibrium. In most instances they chose not to interfere and desertions were commonplace. Left to defend themselves from known and unknown enemies, many preferred flight to self-defense. Others whose lives were spared were brought before "people's courts" and summarily forced to sacrifice their property.

In the cities the story was the same. Governor Monem Khan remained secluded in his residence until March 19th when he flew secretly to West Pakistan. With the government's power gone, strikes paralyzed the economy, murder and arson went unchecked, prices for scarce foodstuffs soared, and administrative services were at a standstill. East Pakistan had been brought to the brink of anarchy. Even the events of 1958 were eclipsed by those now convulsing the province.

On March 25, 1969, Ayub Khan, frustrated by the politicians, abandoned by the bureaucrats and police, and no longer commanding the loyalty of the Armed Forces, resigned the office he had held for ten years and five months.

Army Chief of Staff General Agha Mohammad Yahya Khan took up the reins and immediately reimposed martial law throughout the country. As in 1958 the Constitution was abrogated, the national and provincial legislatures dissolved, and all political parties banned. Members of the President's cabinet and the two newly appointed provincial governors ceased to hold their offices under the proclamation. General Yahya Khan announced that his first objective was the restoration of "sanity" in the country. The air would be cleansed, authority reestablished, and political stability guaranteed before making any attempt to redress societal grievances.

In the circumstances, it is remarkable how smoothly the transfer of power was accomplished. Ayub had justified his rule on the need for political stability. When it became clear he could no longer perform his task he was compelled to pass his responsibility to those who could. From his vantage point, the politicians were in no position to govern the country. In his last address to the nation he commented that to accept the opposition programs would spell "the liquidation of Pakistan."

> I have always told you that Pakistan's salvation lay in a strong center. I accepted the parliamentary system because in this way also there was a possibility of preserving a strong center.
>
> But now it is being said that the country be divided into two parts. The center should be rendered ineffective and a powerless institution. The defense services should be crippled and the political entity of West Pakistan be done away with.
>
> It is impossible for me to preside over the destruction of our country.
>
> . . . It hurts me deeply to say that the situation now is no longer under the control of the Government. All government institutions have become victims of coercion, fear and intimidation.
>
> . . . Except for the Armed Forces there is no constitutional and effective way to meet the situation.[15]

In a letter to General Yahya Khan, Ayub expressed his contempt for the politicians who in his judgment had placed their individual desire for power above the national interest.

> It is most tragic that while we were well on our way to a happy and prosperous future, we were plunged into an abyss of senseless agitation. Whatever name may have been used to glorify it, time will show that this turmoil was deliberately created. . . . I have exhausted all possible civil and constitutional means to resolve the present crisis. I offered to meet all those regarded as the leaders of the people. Many of them came to a conference recently but only after I had fulfilled all preconditions. Some declined to come for reasons best known to them. I asked these people to evolve an agreed formula.
>
> They failed to do so in spite of days of deliberations.[16]

Having provided the politicians with what he considered ample opportunity to cooperate with him in restructuring the political system, Ayub's patience had evaporated. Humiliated by the politicians he now took his revenge. Ayub transferred authority to his brother in arms and the politicians once more scattered to their individual retreats. The demonstrations and rioting, which for more than four months had rocked the foundations of the state, suddenly ceased. Once more an artificial calm covered the land.

Chapter 6

The Bureaucratic Legacy

IN 1953, Rowland Egger, a consultant to the Pakistan Government, submitted a document entitled: *The Improvement of Public Administration in Pakistan.* The treatise contained some important and cogent insights. Confining himself to administrative shortcomings, Egger suggested that deficiencies did not stem from any lack of intelligence but rather from the perpetuation of a dysfunctional system. Egger cited the acute shortage of technical personnel and the unusually large burden carried by a few public officials. Preoccupation with daily routine kept senior officers from appraising their operations, let alone initiating necessary reforms. Still another problem isolated by the author was what he called the inadequate development of Pakistan's political-administrative traditions. Egger noted that this may explain why politicians and administrators are often at odds over whose authority prevails in specific instances. "Pakistan's shortage of politicians skilled in political and administrative management is even more serious than its shortage of administrative officials qualified for top posts." [1]

His opinion was that political leaders needed training in the principles of administration before they could understand their connection with the bureaucracy. Egger identified two essential areas of deficiency. First, the bureaucracy was antiquated. And second, the bureaucracy's relationship with the political parties suffered from a serious gap in communication which left respective roles ambiguous. The answer to the double dilemma appeared to reside in the establishment of a new political-administrative structure. Only then could clear lines of authority be demarcated, officials properly trained, and specific functions institutionalized. Egger's recommendations could not be transformed into policy with the stroke of a pen, however; nor were they well received by the elite branch of Pakistan's bureaucracy, the Civil Service of Pakistan (CSP). Furthermore, subsequent events made serious consideration of reforms impossible.

When Egger submitted his report Pakistan was entering a phase of political instability. In 1953 the Nazimuddin government was dismissed without a vote of confidence. The dissolution of the First Constituent Assembly followed in 1954. This latter event was preceded by the nullification of the East Bengal elections and the imposition of Governor's Rule. The disintegration of the Muslim League in 1954–55 and the proliferation of quasi-viable political parties coincided with the installation of the Second Constituent Assembly.

When some anti-Muslim League opposition leaders voted against accepting the amalgamation of the provinces of West Pakistan and the constitution, the nation's political life was complicated further. There was also the unsurprising opportunism of politicians who repeatedly compromised their party affiliations. The quixotic shifting of political forces and fortunes is described in detail by Keith Callard.[2] Finally, political altercations and civil unrest hastened the declaration of martial law in 1958. With it, all hopes for reforming the political-administrative system along lines suggested by Egger were dashed. The advent of martial law created new opportunities for reform, but instead of the politicians dominating the administration it was Pakistan's elite administrators who displayed a fascination with and aptitude for politics. The civil servant invaded the domain of the politician, noted Keith Callard, "but the politician has never usurped the role of the civil servant. The politician's hold on power has often been brief and insecure: the civil servant is there for life." [3]

OBSTACLES TO REFORM

The CSP is composed of professionals whose training, experience, and loyalty to service are unequaled by any other group—with the possible exception of the military. Ironically, however, the CSP has been farthest removed from the fundamental social realities obtaining in the country and their aloofness has been the subject of much public criticism. "Closing the gap" between the administration and the public is an overused cliche. Attempts to get the administrators and the politicians to cooperate verge on the farcical. The omnipresence of the bureaucracy inhibits the development of political organizations. Masihuzzaman, a high-ranking member of the CSP and also something of a social reformer writes:

[The] Muslim League and Awami League were political parties of some size. In terms of sheer membership they could easily outrival the bureaucracy. But in competence, education, wealth and power they were no match for the latter. It was natural for the government organizations to resent the growth of the political organizations. These organizations had started demanding a share in the power, privilege, and patronage of the government servants. At lower levels they wanted to break the monopoly of the petty government servant over bribery and corruption. Through creating One Unit, while the country took an important step towards integration, it should not be forgotten that it removed the politicians further away from the locus of power, that is, the district.[4]

Administrators and politicians are participants in the same societal matrix. It would seem that each group is essential to the progressive development of the other, while both are inextricably linked with nation-building. Nevertheless, they live in compartmentalized worlds. In Egger's view, the CSP lives in the past—its practices and policies are obsolete.

> This is not to question the loyalty or impugn the patriotism of the members of the service. It would be difficult to discover a group more fiercely loyal to the ideal of Pakistan than those dedicated men. Indeed, part of the source of their myopia is the fact that almost every one of them has a comprehensive, exclusive, and self-sufficient formula for Pakistan's salvation . . . despite their loyalty, dedication and efficiency they are somewhat apart from the community which they serve.[5]

Nowhere is this problem more alarming than in the CSP's dealings with the politicians, however. Given their own aversion to politics and the contempt in which they hold all politicians it is not difficult to understand the lack of rapport between them.[6] It might be asked how this attitude developed, and insights might be found in the pre-independence relationship of the administrator to the politician.

Representative institutions were introduced in British India after the second decade of the twentieth century and did not really become significant until the fourth decade was almost over. Up to this time administrators had few contacts with politicians. They also represented different interests. The administrator's duty lay in serving his superiors; his calling required him to support authority irrespective of personal preferences or feelings. Hence, the administrator, whether he be British or Indian, was engaged in the maintenance of public order. This often meant suppressing political movements and imprisoning indigenous politicians.[7]

In the case of those Indian politicians who eventually assumed positions of responsibility in the central or provincial governments, their association was normally with the senior administrators in the secretariats and virtually all of these were British. It should be noted that those Indian civil servants who opted for Pakistan were by and large holding junior positions at the time and only a small number had secretariat experience. As Egger explains, "The attitude of civil servants who did not have contact with political leaders, moreover, reflects rather faithfully the attitude of their British superiors, who in general accepted the necessity of representative institutions without developing any particular sympathy for the representatives." [8]

Pakistan's need to reconstruct its political-administrative system has been recognized from the inception of the state. But the argument quickly gained acceptance that it would be foolhardy to tamper with a system which not only enabled the state to survive but was vital for economic progress. In the subcontinent the British established institutions especially designed to achieve the objectives of colonial power. And if they were successful it was because they made a serious attempt to fathom the sociopolitical environment.[9] They also learned something about the psychology of the people. The employment of indigenous intermediaries enhanced the British position—but it also granted special opportunities and privileges to those so favored.

Although the present environment differs only slightly, the objectives of government are supposed to have changed. The overriding requirement in colonial administration was the maintenance of civil order. While still a key to successful government, it now shares a place with economic development and social change. In these latter activities the participation of organized public groups is essential. It also means utilizing resources normally beyond the range of bureaucratic concern. Both administrators and politicians are expected to devote maximum attention to national goals. In Egger's opinion this cannot be done by relying on the outmoded instruments of bureaucratic rule.[10] Political reform must accompany administrative reform.

In 1955 Bernard L. Gladieux, another American consultant, submitted a report to the Pakistan Government through Zahid Hussain, then chairman of the Pakistan Planning Board. Gladieux proved to be a more severe critic of Pakistani administration than Egger. This was perhaps due to the unpleasantness that Gladieux encountered while conducting his research.[11] In the wake of the Egger report enough residual hard feeling remained among elite Pakistani administrators to frustrate his efforts. Gladieux's findings were contained in a lengthy document which touches the more sensitive aspects of Pakistani administration. His principal target was the CSP, which he characterized as inept and unworthy of commanding the governmental heights:

> Theirs must be the chief responsibility for the general lack of a simplified and expeditious system of administrative management, for the perpetuation of tortuous secretariat procedures, for the failure to work out a reasonable system of delegations of authority, for under-utilization of personnel, for restrictive public services policies, for the cloak of official secrecy which surrounds so much of the public business, and finally for the general failure to convert government to development objectives. By their aloof attitude toward day to day administration they have neglected to take vigorous steps needed to clean up management, including the exaggerated pay rolls of government. The present corps of administrative leaders must also bear the onus for failure to implement or even take very seriously the many reforms and improvements recommended by various official commissions over the years.[12]

Gladieux assaulted the heretofore sacrosanct edifice of District Administration and suggested a reorganized pattern which would strip the Deputy Commissioner of his important magisterial powers. Applying the concept of the separation of the judiciary from the executive, he insisted that "good government" requires placing emphasis on those activities which eventually allow the people to govern through their elected representatives.[13] So long as the Deputy Commissioner is primarily interested in maintaining law and order he must neglect the developmental and educational requirements of the people living within the district. And where this is the case, self-government is impossible.

The CSP cannot justify its domination of local affairs by using the argument that the people are easy prey for unscrupulous politicians. Gladieux shatters this myth with the sweeping comment that people can only learn the art of self-government by experiencing it. Mistakes will naturally result but they must be tolerated, for they are essential to the learning process. The American consultant did not mince words when he accused the bureaucracy of impeding Pakistan's modernization programs for purely personal and selfish motives: "At the root of the problem lies the fact that the public service system is self-regulating and self-perpetuating in that those who control the system are at once its beneficiaries." [14]

It is little wonder that Gladieux's report failed to produce an immediate response; or that it went unpublished and thus failed to attract a wide audience. Professor Albert Gorvine has analyzed the Egger and

Gladieux documents and comments that as foreign advisers the two men were somewhat over-zealous, spent far too little time in Pakistan and, although experts in their own country, were totally unfamiliar with the sociopolitical system prevailing in the subcontinent. The projection of their American experiences in a land with absolutely different cultural traditions and institutions "doomed" their efforts before they began.[15] Irrespective of their shortcomings, however, both Egger and Gladieux succeeded in identifying the sorry relationship obtaining between politicians and administrators.

PROSPECTS FOR CHANGE

In his Manifesto announcing the 1962 Constitution, President Mohammad Ayub Khan identified the course that Pakistan would follow in the ensuing years:

> Fortunately, our people are endowed with all the qualities which go to make a sound and sensible nation. All that they require is suitably adjusted institutions to release their creative energies effectively. Much, therefore, depends on the shape of politics in the country. The past has many bitter lessons. We cannot afford to repeat our mistakes. We have to go off the beaten track and find a way which shows us the straight path, in the light of our temperament and circumstances.[16]

The 1958 revolution brought Pakistan's political realities abreast of its political theory. The new Constitution legitimated a condition of centralized rule by endowing the President with over-all powers. It was Ayub's opinion that politicians, not the administrators, threatened the nation with ruin. Thus his reference to "suitably adjusted institutions" reinforced the authority of the latter over the former. Where the CSP was concerned there would be no movement away from "the beaten track." Ayub's treatment of the political parties all but eliminated their capacity to impede executive decision-making.

High on Ayub's agenda were: (1) the need to socialize the population; (2) to create a national consciousness and civil loyalty; and (3) to prepare the people for limited roles in the political-administrative system. What the country needed above all else, however, was political stability. And President Ayub believed this could be accomplished without the encumbrances of partisan exchanges. Hence the exaggerated importance given the bureaucracy. Thus the disaffection of the urban intelligentsia. *Ayub urged his countrymen not to repeat the mistakes of the past but was himself guilty of such repetitions.*

THE INSULATED BUREAUCRACY

The civil service was exempt from contemplated reforms. The bureaucracy was not to be divested of its antiquated colonial perceptions. The British legacy identified the civil service so closely with that of the state that it consciously equated the state with its own organization. In 1931 L. S. S. O'Malley wrote:

> The Indian Civil Service is, in fact, more in the public eye than the English Civil Service. . . . They [the latter] are regarded as outside politics and, as a rule, are free from attack and hostile criticism, though there may be a general grumble about bureaucratic methods. The Indian Civil Service, however, is very much in the limelight. Its personnel is well known: a Civil List showing its members, their length of service, their appointments and their pay, is published quarterly and can be bought by anyone. It is exposed to constant criticism, largely no doubt because, having long helped to direct as well as execute policy, it has been identified with the government of the country.[17]

Pride of service is also part of the heritage and, perhaps as much as security tended to shape the Pakistani bureaucrat. That pride was made of the stuff which Lord Dufferin, Viceroy from 1884 to 1888, described in this manner:

> You asked me to tell you the plain truth regarding the skill, experience, and, in more general terms, the moral worth of the officials of our Indian Civil Service. I reply without hesitation: *There is no Service like it in the world.* For ingenuity, courage, right judgement, disinterested devotion to duty, endurance, open-heartedness, and, at the same time, loyalty to one another and their chiefs, they are, to my knowledge, superior to any other class of Englishmen. They are absolutely free from any taint of venality, or corruption. Naturally, they are not of equal worth, and so I am merely speaking of them as a whole. And moreover, if the Indian Civil Service were not what I have described it, how could the government of the country go on so smoothly.[18]

O'Malley and Lord Dufferin may be allowed their high regard for colonial administration, but what about the impact of their bureaucratic tradition on the indigenous officers who succeeded them? When the British passed their duties on to the Indian and Pakistani members of the Indian Civil Service (ICS) the *raison d'être* of the bureaucracy was already indelible in ICS minds. *In Pakistan the CSP was preoccupied with its own survival.* The organization's goals therefore were made the nation's goals. This distorted perspective of their importance resulted in the obsession that only the CSP knew what was good for the nation. Thus nothing stood in the way of the CSP's self-sustaining dominance. Instead of Ayub's policies politicizing the country, bureaucratization was more complete.

Etzioni identifies two bureaucratic models, the "survival" model and the "effectiveness" model. Although recognizing that in reality no two distinct models exist, it is his contention that bureaucracies tend to fit one or the other. If this is correct, then perhaps Pakistan's bureaucracy typifies the survival model in that it "only asks whether the basic requirements of the organzation are being met." [19] It cannot be associated with the effectiveness model for it still refuses to evaluate the changes occurring inside and outside the organization or understand how such changes affects its capacity to attain specific national goals.

Pakistani society has been conditioned to accept the administrator as the custodian of national life. No effort or expenditure of time need be made by the citizenry, and it is rare to find those who do not follow custom in this matter. The government proposes and disposes. The perception of an all-pervasive government is the natural consequence of a tradition which places virtually unlimited power in the hands of bureaucrats. In short, totalistic control is often paternalistic and society adjusts to it. Who can fault the politicians for their amateurism? In such an atmosphere they have had precious few opportunities to develop their organizations or polish their techniques. Is it any wonder that their performance is so easily discredited? Politics may be an art, but it cannot be perfected in the absence of practical experience.

POLITICAL-BUREAUCRATIC RELATIONSHIPS

In some respects the British were favorably disposed toward democratic institutions and given the pressure exerted by indigenous politicians they slowly, if reluctantly, began relinquishing some of their powers. However, this devolution of authority was uneven at best. In point of fact, only the urban scene was affected and the lives of people in the villages were largely untouched. Politicians seldom ventured into the countryside where the bureaucratic system was most ubiquitous. While the British ruled India few programs were aimed at inducting the rural population into the political process. Strategies therefore were devised to apply maximum pressure in areas promising rapid gains.[20]

Organizing tens of thousands of villages required resources the politicians did not have. Moreover, a struggle in the countryside might have prolonged the British presence. It should also be emphasized that many of the politicians who wanted to oust the British were absentee landlords. Their interests did not lie in awakening the cultivators. But whatever the explanations, bureaucrats and landlords governed vast agrarian areas without a struggle. Thus when the British finally abandoned the subcontinent the feudal-administrative structure was relatively unaffected; a notable situation, given the publicized development of a new political system based on popular consent and concretized in the parliamentary institution.

The indigenous administrators, imbued with the values of their former superiors, posed a problem—but government was unthinkable without them. The juxtaposition of the ruling politicians and the "ruling" administrators was another consequence of partition and independence. The politicians were ill equipped and too loosely organized to control the administrators, let alone the country. And the more powers they delegated to the bureaucracy, the greater the bureaucrat's contempt for them. Generally speaking, "good government" meant more to the bureaucrats than any incipient form of self-government and it was not unusual to find bureaucrats and politicians in open conflict. This state of affairs could not go on indefinitely, however, and indeed it was short-lived.

Although the implications were not grasped at the time, Ghulam Mohammad's rise to the office of the Governor General in 1951 restored the civil service to its preeminent position.

> The rot in our politics really set in during Ghulam Mohammad's regime. He was responsible for dealing the first deadly blow to whatever democracy there was in the country.[21]

From that time forward the vice-regal tradition, not the parliamentary experiment, proved dominant. Iskander Mirza, who succeeded Ghulam Mohammad in 1955, and Ayub Khan, who followed Mirza in 1958, only perpetuated the rule of the elite bureaucracy.[22]

British India was divided into territorial units and sub-units and within these territories the administrators were politically as well as administratively supreme. Training was on the job and objectives were relatively simple. The generalist administrator who was hardly less than an absolute ruler in his assigned domain was also a substitute for local self-governing institutions.[23] Furthermore, the maintenance of the status quo during the Ayub era conflicts with the lip service about making the people masters of their own destiny. It also explains the failure of the Basic Democracies scheme. The once confidential Pay and Services Commission Report of 1962 (it was released by the Yahya Khan government in 1969) discussed the matter in the following fashion:

> The tradition of colonial rule is to reserve the highest remuneration for the "power-symbols," namely, those to whom the administration of conquered territory on the civil side is entrusted, and these have hitherto in the subcontinent been non-specialist officers, whose success lay in their capacity to constitute and operate a "governing corporation" or "board of directors." An independent country, if it values its independence, has to discard such an incubus.[24]

Keeping in view the need for administrative expertise the Commission did not suggest the liquidation of the bureaucracy, only modifications to meet the needs of a modern, independent nation-state. The Report anticipated that specialist administrators would replace the political generalists, however. The new bureaucrats were to be made functionally responsible to the people's representatives and the latter given every opportunity to manage local administrative-political activities.[25] Ayub Khan chose not to heed the recommendations of the Commission, however, and his programs suffered accordingly.

PAKISTAN'S CSP

The Civil Service of Pakistan (CSP) is an outgrowth of the Indian Civil Service (ICS). With independence the ICS fragmented. The British officers left the subcontinent in large numbers and only a relatively small contingent of those remaining assisted in organizing the new Muslim state.[26] They, along with their indigenous counterparts, comprised the nucleus for the newly designated CSP. In all, the ICS in Pakistan totalled 158 members at partition. This was considerably less than the 244 "policy-making" posts reserved for it. Although the ICS played an important role in stabilizing the new state it would be unfair to say that it singlehandedly saved Pakistan in those perilous first hours. The organization of a new government, administering to millions of refugees, and quelling communal riots, presented problems of such magnitude that a small elite—no matter how able—could never have done the job alone. As has been noted in the Pay and Services Commission Report:

. . . the task involved a scale of effort and performance which required many times the number of ICS. Tasks at high levels were undertaken by men in all ranks of the Services, including the clerical branches, which were far above those belonging to their real status. Were it not for the loyalty and ability shown by the entire body of men who constituted the administration, the few top-officers, with all their experience in the field of prestige-rule, could never have staved off the danger of general administrative chaos that hung over the scene, if they had kept all responsibility to themselves.[27]

In 1950 the CSP was established officially. By that date its ranks had been swelled by the inclusion of officers drawn from other services and by direct recruitment. Interestingly, the CSP never increased in numbers to fill all the posts reserved for it,[28] thereby arousing the ire of members from other services who were denied these choice positions.[29]

Members of the CSP enjoy opportunities and privileges of a unique character. Their promotions are more or less guaranteed, given the reservation of posts; this means they attain the highest offices in government while those in other services, with perhaps as much or more experience, can do little more than meekly acquiesce to the situation. In the days of British rule, ICS officials were not nearly as fortunate as are the present members of the CSP. In most cases careers terminated at the level of deputy commissioner. In fact, it was not until World War II demanded an expansion in the ranks of the bureaucracy that members of the ICS were given greater access to higher posts. But even then the number of posts at the higher levels were far fewer than the number of persons capable of competing for them.

In the pre-independence period only the very best administrators could satisfy their personal ambitions. Moreover, the stiff competition caused the establishment of even higher administrative standards. Such standards were maintained so long as promotion was based on merit and competition maintained. But whereas the CSP accepted the values of the ICS, the competitive aspect disappeared. Similarly, the CSP not only has never come up to the strength reserved for it but its selection process must take into account provincial and territorial representation (at the expense of the merit principle). This naturally reduced its quality to that of an ordinary service. It is not surprising, therefore, that the Pay and Services Commission should characterize the CSP as a "mediocrity." [30]

It needs no saying that when superior posts open to the CSP exceed the total number of members of the service, the struggle to secure them loses all its intensity, and promotion becomes not only automatic, but exceedingly rapid as well. A conflict appears between the condition, as it affects these officers, and as it affects the public interests. The more rosy the prospect of these officers, the more bleak the outlook becomes for the public interest. And any comfort which the public could possibly derive from the contemplation of the good fortune which follows this favoured section is eliminated when consideration is paid to the small extent to which they have deserved it by intellectual or other superiority.[31]

In point of fact, there is little if any difference in the intellectual capacities of the generalist services. The CSP and its leading antagonist, the Provincial Civil Service (PCS), are composed of men with similar talents, drawn from identical backgrounds and subject to the same customs, mores, and general experience. PCS officers in the provincial governments of East and West Pakistan perform tasks much as do the officers from the CSP. The CSP officer, however, can be posted anywhere in the country and is destined for the highest policy-making posts once he has attained his seniority.

Officers belonging to the CSP argue that they are superior. They assert that PCS officers hold positions in the districts only because there are not enough CSP officers to man these stations. Observers are supposed to believe that PCS officers are 'inferior alternatives." Taking issue with this smug attitude, the Pay and Services Commission praises the PCS officers:

. . . [the] work has been carried on for years and is being successfully carried on, by a class of men who despite the proof they have given of their adequacy for this work are denied the recognition which is their due, and is the due of the Service to which they belong.[32]

THE PAY AND SERVICES COMMISSION REPORT

The Pay and Services Commission saw no constructive purpose in sustaining the elite bureaucratic hierarchy, and gave President Ayub a golden opportunity to modernize Pakistani society when it called for the integration of the various services and the creation of one national civil service. Special privileges, they stressed, had to be abandoned. The new integrated service, which they named the Civil Executive Service (CES), would cover all offices between district-level and divisional-level appointments other than that of the Divisional Commissioner.[33] In this way, the Deputy Inspector General of Police, Deputy Director of Health Services, Deputy Director of Education, and Superintending Engineer, could all fill top posts in the Civil Executive Service. In calling for this new arrangement the Commissioners obviously hoped to unify the services, but their ultimate goal lay in rallying the nation behind an administrative system it could readily support. Its immediate impact, however, would be on the bureaucracy itself. Uniformity in levels of performance could be striven for, standards raised, and only the best officers selected "for entry into the directory ranks." [34]

These CES officers would then be attached to the Pakistan Administrative Service (PAS). The PAS would consist of posts carrying salaries rising in excess of Rs. 2,000 and would encompass Secretaries to the provincial governments, Inspectors General and Additional Inspectors General of Police, Directors of (Provincial) Health Service, Joint Secretaries and Secretaries in the Central Secretariat, etc. Although the PAS would consist of a number of specific posts drawing graded salaries, it was not to be encadred because the officers would fill top positions in many different departments. Seniority was considered unacceptable as a principal criterion for selection to the PAS, and tenure in office had to be fixed to avoid the long-term dominance of a department by a particular officer. The Commission set the maximum time an officer could be included in the PAS at nine years.

Tenure in any one post would not be extended beyond three years. Perhaps the crowning feature of the Commission's recommendations was that appointments to all posts would be made on the basis of the officer's expertise in handling the work of the department to which he was assigned. In other words, where possible the officer would continue in that line of work for which he had special knowledge.[35]

A Selection Board, chaired by the President, would admit officers to the PAS. In the Commission's view, the PAS would be a more unified and national service than the present CSP.

> Their cohesion would not be the result of encadrement, and being drawn from all branches of the service, they would be unlikely to develop monopolistic tendencies, or the attitudes of a ruling class. The aspect of personal prestige or privilege would be excluded, and men would hold their places, on an equal footing, namely, that of proved merit and efficiency.[36]

It was hoped that esprit de corps in the PAS would develop from the individual's association in the career-managed CES and the knowledge that he had been selected for this higher responsibility on the basis of recognized achievement. Officers selected in this manner who remained with the central career-managed service until their retirement, who would make no distinction between the work of the center and of the provinces, could be expected to cultivate an "All-Pakistan attitude." Thus the Commission envisioned a significant change in the work and behavior of the elite officer. In their judgment, the changes would have a beneficial effect on subordinates and through them on the country at large.

While deliberating on the problem of the service structure the Commission could not avoid the need for greater national integration. The CSP's aloofness from the people and their sentiments put it in a poor position to counteract divisive tendencies. The CES, it was argued, would not suffer from this colonial legacy. On the contrary, it would have the ability to act "as a deterrent to any parochial tendencies," [37]

It would be of a totally different order from any that the present system of Central management, from start to finish, of the careers of officers of the CSP and the PSP [Police Service of Pakistan] can possibly produce. The ICS and the Indian Police were the "steel frame" of foreign rule from Whitehall, by which a grip was maintained over the subject people. It was then thought that by keeping a firm hold on the administration of law-and-order and security, through Police agency, the continuance of that rule could be ensured, irrespective of the extent to which the beneficial and developmental services were allowed to get into the hands of the Indians themselves. The entire state of things has now disappeared. The question is no longer one of imposition of rule from outside. Law-and-order and public security must take, in Pakistan, the same position among the public affairs of the country as they occupy in other free countries, that is to say, not unimportant, but at the same time, not of supereminent importance, so as to confer the status of rulers upon their officers. Something of that supereminence lingers on by the exclusive recognition of those two Services as All Pakistan Services. The scheme we proposed corrects this imbalance, and we hope that at the same time, it will bring about a true balance among all the public services, by raising personnel into high directory positions, in proportion to the relative importance and utility of the service to which they belong.[38]

Undermining the Bureaucratic Legacy

The Pay and Services Commission gave special attention to the subject of general administration and it is important to note their findings. By "general administration" the Commission referred to field administration centering round the Commissioners, Deputy Commissioners, and their subordinate officers. Traditionally, general administration has not only been concerned with law and order and gathering taxes, but has enjoyed over-all control of branch services. In the British period, general administration posts were the monopoly of the ICS. The same group which staffed the secretariats had exclusive right of appointment to membership on the Provincial Executive Councils, Provincial Governorships (except in the presidencies), and to practically all the seats on the Viceroy's Executive Council. While the British ruled India the ICS was so powerful that all the other central services, i.e., Education, Health, Engineering, etc., were forced to accept inferior status.

When the general administrative chores of the ICS increased to a point where they could no longer adequately cope with them the PCS was formed. Demonstrating the contrast in opportunity, a member of the ICS would move rapidly into the post of Deputy Commissioner but a PCS officer could expect to complete his career in the same post he entered as a recruit. Few PCS officers in those early days moved beyond the posts of Assistant Collectors or Magistrates to Additional Collectors or Additional District Magistrates.

It was not until the twentieth century that posts long reserved for the ICS were opened to a small number of PCS officers at the district level. These were the famous "Listed Posts." The exclusive British club that was the ICS began to break down, and 1922 marks the year when Indian recruitment into the ICS commenced in earnest. On the eve of partition the key administrative posts were still in the hands of the British, but scattered in their ranks were also a number of Indians from the ICS and PCS. Anticipations ran high that once independence was achieved the indigenous civil servants manning these key posts would discard their British-imposed designations and unite in a common service. But although this may have been the expectation it did not come to pass. Indigenous CSP officers jealously guarded their privileged position.

It has already been mentioned that no sensible person believed the new nation could organize and run a government without the services of professional, seasoned administrators. Why Ayub Khan permitted the

CSP to maintain its pre-independence superiority may be a somewhat puzzling question. Necessity may be one explanation. Certainly the state desperately needed trained administrators—and the CSP already filled the significant posts. It was felt they could not be dislodged without seriously weakening the whole governmental edifice. This is to cite the obvious.[39] What may not be apparent, however, was the commitment to the rule of law. The CSP had been established on the basis of rational-legal doctrines and Pakistan's leaders were disinclined to tamper with this legal heritage.

Statutes, special codes, and custom governed the performance of the ICS and when Pakistan emerged as an independent state it did not sever these conventional legal connections. The number of nineteenth-century statutes that are still in force in the country is testimony of this reverence for the continuity of law.[40] Hence the ICS, and now the CSP, were guaranteed their privileges; if they were disregarded, the sanctity of the entire legal institution would be seriously jeopardized. By contrast, law did not protect the political heritage and there is a curious reluctance to link legal commitments with political institutions. The latter, therefore, have been violated at will and with increasing frequency.

Still another aspect of the elite services analyzed by the Pay and Services Commission was that of personal rule. The CSP, like the ICS, is a prestige service. It employs a method of administration which is significantly paternalistic. People were generally powerless to alter a decision of the bureaucracy, and there were few tests of strength; once resigned to bureaucratic rule, whatever initiative may have existed soon evaporated. Unable to influence their bureaucratic masters, the peasantry did what was expected of it. Normally this involved keeping the general decorum and paying taxes. In the words of the Pay and Services Commission Report:

> The temper of the people had been greatly affected by this attitude. They are accustomed to accept oppression without complaining, except where some political issue might possibly be raised. The tendency to perverse use of law by the Government Agent breeds imitation by the whole body of public servants working under his supervision or control, and the evil is spread until it becomes a permanent epidemic. Out of the demoralisation thus bred, affecting the officers as much as the people whom they are supposed to serve, came many and great evils, of which the worst is corruption, and a good second is retardation of local self-government.[41]

Today, there is "no scope, as there was until some 20 years before the close of British rule, for the rulers to decide what was best for the people, and in case of opposition, to enforce their view by all powers in their possession, being secure in their conviction of the benevolence of their motive." [42] According to the Commission the rule of law must prevail but the elite administrator, no matter how compassionate and beneficent his techniques and intentions, must be transformed. Toward this goal the Commission suggested a radical change in the traditional character of general administration.

In part this meant separating the Deputy Commissioners and Commissioners from many of their powers, especially where they interfered with the work of the specialized agencies. Eventually, the posts of Commissioner and Deputy Commissioner were to be thrown open to members of the newly conceived Civil Executive Service, thus making it possible for the specialists to enter those positions. In the Commission's judgment this was necessary because the role of the DC was to guide development, not rule, and who could better coordinate the development work of the district than someone who had the specialized training to go along with his office?

> The recommendation we have to make is that the reservation of posts of District Heads for CSP and PCS officers should now be replaced by reservation in favour of officers in the pre-PAS grade.[43]

After dismissing all the arguments in favor of maintaining generalists in the field posts, the Commission discussed the specialist's capacity for such work. "How can a Veterinary Doctor be a Deputy Commissioner?" The Commission rhetorically responded:

> . . . our idea is that the sixty-two District Coordinators or Commissioners whom we envisage as replacing the present Deputy Commissioners, may be found by making a careful selection from among administratively-trained officers of all the Services, on the basis of high achievement, initiative, resource, public spirit and other such qualities, is by no means so revolutionary as it may seem, at first sight. *It is revolutionary only in its impact upon entrenched privilege.*[44] (Italics added.)

DEPOLITICIZING THE BUREAUCRATS

The Commission also considered whether the "generalist" administrator should be permitted to continue interfering with the operation of the main departments of government by exerting his conventional policy controls in the Secretariat. With stress on departments run by specialists drawn from the CES, the Commission offered the view that there would no longer be a dependence on the CSP. Similarly, CSP advice need not be solicited by central or provincial government politician-ministers. If the ministers were in need of guidance this could be sought from the specialists in the executive departments. In their opinion, no CSP generalist could match the contribution of the specialists. Where politician-ministers are completely unable to understand the details of technical schemes they should be replaced, added the Commission.

On the other hand, if generalist secretaries continue making decisions for politician-ministers the fundamental purpose of any constitution is violated. Moreover, the status of the secretary should always be lower than that of the minister. This being the case, it is in the interest of the nation to find administrators who enjoy their work more than they do their positions. "The country is in need of practical men, capable of carrying out the large scale development plans, which are on the *tapis*. It will not fail to find them, if it gives them preference over those who prefer the comforts of Secretariat life." [45]

The Pay and Services Commission Report is clearly a revolutionary document. It marshals facts, organizes them into significant arguments, and thrusts home recommendations in language free of equivocation. It is a remarkably brave presentation and there can be no mistaking the objective; the complete and utter destruction of the CSP along with the virtual elimination of the traditional generalist administrator. Given these drastic goals, it is not surprising that the Pay and Services Commission Report was not released during Ayub's tenure. Two notes of dissent were appended to the document, and one of them was sufficiently strong to have the entire document marked as highly confidential and unsuitable for publication. Furthermore, its recommendations were never discussed in public. Only Ayub Khan could have given substance to the Commission's recommendations, but the President chose to sustain the status quo. Ayub gambled that in a moment of crisis the bureaucracy was indispensable.

REACTION TO THE RECOMMENDATIONS OF THE PAY AND SERVICES COMMISSION

The two members of the Pay and Services Commission who dissented from the majority report were G. Mueenuddin and Ali Asghar.

At the time of the report's presentation they were the only members of the Commission to be drawn from the ranks of the CSP.[46] The dissenters disagreed "with the basic and fundamental features of the proposed service structure and reorganisation." [47] They did, however, affirm their acceptance of those chapters relating to specialized subjects. For this reason they did not divorce themselves from the entire document. Their signatures are affixed to it with the reservation that their note of dissent be included. The CSP officers complained they did not have sufficient time to peruse the report, having received it only a few days before its formal presentation to the President. Such statements cannot conceal the differences within the Commission and the frank comments of the dissenters exposes the concern and even anger that the report aroused among the elite CSP.

G. Mueenuddin and Ali Asghar cite the words of the then Chief Justice A. R. Cornelius, the chairman of the Commission and undoubtedly the man responsible for drafting the document, to the effect that the report's proposals envisioned "the most drastic changes introduced anywhere in the world." Such changes, they felt—in agreement with Aziz Ahmad, a leading CSP officer whose words they chose to quote—would precipitate a "psychological upheaval" within the services and "for many years to come the country and administration would be busy settling the problems introduced by these drastic changes and the drive for development would lose momentum and be neglected." [48] With this introduction the CSP members note that:

> . . . *The present system, which has stood the test of time, not only during the British regime but also during the tumultuous and important years since independence, should be permitted to continue with such change as experience has shown to be necessary.*[49]
> (Italics added.)

The reason for the ban on the report's publication is given by the dissenters. In their view, the document discredits the CSP and can only sow seeds of discord and discouragement among the various services, hence undermining their effectiveness. "These remarks would supply lethal ammunition to those who are interested in bringing the administration into contempt." [50] Furthermore, disparities and injustices in the pay structure of the services could be rectified without abolishing the CSP. The dissenters also took issue with the description of the district officer as a power symbol. Deputy Commissioners performed vital functions and therefore had to be endowed with "a good deal of power." [51] Such exercise of power is not what it was during the period of British rule. As an instrument of government the Deputy Commissioner's power today is highly institutionalized. Countering the argument that the country could discard the conventional Deputy Commissioner and replace him with a "General Manager," the CSP members declare:

> In the peculiar socio-psychological conditions prevailing in the country, particularly in the rural areas, the handler of men and situations is indispensable for development projects and plans.[52]

After calling for the continuance of the present administrative structure, Mueenuddin and Ali Ashgar defend their elite service. The patriotism of the CSP and its adherence to the ideology of Pakistan is given special attention. So, too, is its over-all honesty. While accepting the view that some new CSP recruits may fail to reflect the highest standards of intellectual attainment, the dissenters cite the limitations imposed by the regional quota system which gives preference to certain backward areas. All the same, they argue, the large majority of CSP officers have not faltered when confronted with difficult challenges.

Another telling remark is contained in a paragraph stressing the need in most countries for an elite service. "It would not be too much to claim that in Pakistan also the continued progress and development of the country during the years of political instability owe a great deal to the soundness of the administrative system and the devotion of the officers." [53] Finally, the dissenters defend the CSP generalist. The generalist administrator does not interfere with the work of the specialist but simply applies to the technical field decisions of public policy which are well beyond the "competence and responsibility of the technician." [54]

On this point there is a noticeable difference of opinion. An editorial in an issue of *The Pakistan Student* published by the Pakistan Student's Association of America made the following comment concerning the generalist-specialist controversy:

> The fact that notwithstanding this situation, hundreds of our most talented people are living in exile, leads us to a more fundamental point. While the hallmark of the cultural lag in many advanced nations is the situation brought about by the so called cybernetic revolution, we are experiencing what might be termed as the "structural lag" or the "administrative lag." While a large number of our citizens are equipping themselves to become the instruments of a rapid national progress, corresponding administrative changes are not being made to accommodate, assimilate and utilize these people. The Ph.D.s are still being made to work "under"

section officers, the scientists are being classified as I, II, III class officers and put into the water-tight compartments, and the intelligentsia is still at the mercy of the whims of the bureaucracy. While the cult of the C.S.P. has become a monster, the intellectuals have been denied the freedom of expression. Persons are hired and fired not according to the needs of the society but according to the availability of "positions" on the paper. In other words, the creed and the practices of the bureaucracy stand in diametrical opposition to the aspirations of the intelligentsia.[55]

It can only be conjectured what might have resulted had Ayub implemented the recommendations of the Pay and Services Commission. Their continued relevance cannot be ignored by future Pakistani leaders, however.

The Yazdani Malik Episode: A Case Study

The Yazdani Malik affair in December 1966 adds credence to the view that administrative attitudes, as well as the relationship between bureaucrats and politicians, are in desperate need of reform. Ghulam Yazdani Malik, a high-ranking member of the CSP, a former Commissioner in Bahawalpur Division and at the time of the incident, Secretary in the West Pakistan Home Ministry, exposed himself to bitter condemnation. His alleged act undermined his service and the government, and reinforced the critical views that Pakistanis hold regarding their administrators.

While Commissioner of Bahawalpur, G. Yazdani Malik made a number of enemies who were determined to get their revenge. Allegations were made against the former Commissioner, now Home Secretary, and a statement of charges was drawn up in the form of a pamphlet under the heading: "The Black Deeds of G. Yazdani Malik During his Tenure as Commissioner of Bahawalpur." The pamphlet described Yazdani Malik as a corrupt, self-aggrandizing official who used the power of his office to extort money and goods.

When the West Pakistan Legislative Assembly met in Lahore for its regular winter session the pamphlet was introduced in the House. The leader of the opposition, Khwaja Mohammad Safdar, on reading the charges listed in the pamphlet published in the name of the "People" of Bahawalpur, tabled an adjournment motion in order to discuss the contents of the document. The motion was rejected, however, and the pamphlet was not discussed.

Several days later the affair came to a head. The records state that Yazdani Malik allegedly entered the lobby of the provincial legislature and in a moment of indiscretion seized and manhandled a member, one Makhdoom Shamsuddin Gilani. The Home Secretary was also alleged to have employed abusive language. The incident was allegedly witnessed by Sahibzadi Mahmooda Begum, another opposition member of the legislature. It was reported that when Yazdani Malik left the building, Mahmooda Begum rushed to the assistance of her colleague. Both then entered the House chamber, seemingly visibly upset. Gilani was reportedly in tears and trembling. Mahmooda Begum was described as on the verge of breaking down. In a voice "choked with emotion" she told the House what she had supposedly witnessed in the lobby. In a moment the legislature was up in arms.

Members rose to their feet, angrily condemned the act, and demanded that the government take immediate and "drastic" action against Yazdani Malik. Some members insisted on staging a walkout in protest, allegedly "against the high-handedness of a Government servant." They noted that the very prestige of the House was at stake. Legislators began filing from the House even while these statements were being made. Observing this, Malik Khuda Bakhsh Bucha, then leader of the government party, stood up and expressed his "profound shock and regret over the unhappy incident." He notified the House that the act would not go unpunished and that "suitable action would be taken against Mr. Yazdani Malik for his indecent conduct."

The House was then adjourned for what was to be a fifteen-minute recess. However, there was so much activity in the corridors that when the members reassembled only twenty MPA's occupied their places. Makhdoom Shamsuddin Gilani was one of them. He then introduced a motion seeking to discuss a breach of privilege of the House. After relating the story he offered the view that the Home Secretary's alleged act was an example of bureaucratic behavior "which had no parallel in the history of any legislature." The Acting Speaker ruled the motion in order, which meant a debate would follow, but before the House could take it up Malik Khuda Bakhsh rose again to make a statement. While noting that everyone "was pained by the most unhappy and shameful act" he thought the House should adjourn and take the matter up at the next session. His plea was accepted in the midst of mounting excitement.[56]

Governor Musa was in Karachi at the time of the incident and a frantic telephone call forced him to return to Lahore that evening. After discussing the affair with his staff he ordered Yazdani Malik's immediate removal as Secretary of the Home Ministry. The Governor also called upon the Deputy Inspector of Police to conduct an inquiry and to submit his report to the Governor's Secretariat in two or three days. The next day the Muslim League Parliamentary Party in the National Assembly condemned the alleged "outrageous indignity" perpetrated by a public official on a member of the provincial legislature. The meeting recommended immediate action against Yazdani Malik. "Exemplary punishment of dismissal from service" was the only penalty that could remedy such a callous act was said to be their conclusion.[57]

When the West Pakistan Provincial Assembly met again a Standing Committee was set up to look into the motion of Makhdoom Shamsuddin Gilani. The Committee held its own inquiry and Yazdani Malik was summoned to appear before it on December 5, 1966. When the former Home Secretary asked that the hearing be opened to the public so that he might "vindicate his honour," the Committee rejected the request and the proceedings were held *in camera*. A request by Begum Yazdani Malik to appear before the Committee was also rejected.[58]

On being questioned Yazdani Malik denied having been in the legislature on the day when the incident reportedly occurred, and declared that the whole affair had been contrived by a group of politicians in Bahawalpur who were bent on discrediting and destroying him. His antagonists, on the other hand, accused the CSP officer of threatening them with bodily harm unless they disowned their signatures which were affixed to the pamphlet containing the charges. As the hearing drew to a close Yazdani Malik reportedly asked the Committee to "forget" his earlier testimony, and indicated his gratitude for their having heard him with "patience and deference." This was interpreted as a sudden *volte face* for a man who had all along insisted on his innocence.

When the Standing Committee submitted its report on December 9, 1966, they declared that great damage had been done to the prestige and sanctity of the Assembly.

> The Committee takes a serious view of the matter that a very responsible officer should have the audacity to flout the dignity of the House and should have acted in a manner unworthy of a good public servant and particularly of the rank of Home Secretary of a province. His acts were deliberate and intentional.[59]

The Committee could see no reason for recommending leniency in this case and therefore called upon the House to recommend to the Central Government that G. Yazdani Malik be dismissed from the service because of "gross misconduct." [60]

The Yazdani Malik hearing dragged on for an additional year. Eventually the charges against the CSP officer were withdrawn, however, and Yazdani Malik was returned to duty. If nothing more, the affair again highlighted the deep animosities existing between politicians and administrators.

LIMITED REFORM

Although the pattern of bureaucratic rule is unchanged there have been alterations in administrative organization and procedure. Many of these changes followed the 1958 revolution. One of the principal concerns of the Ayub government lay in decentralizing government activity in order to involve more persons in the task of national reconstruction. The Pay and Services Commission, therefore, was only one of a number of constituted bodies directed to study ways in which the administrative system could be popularized and reorganized. Another important body was the Provincial Administration Commission.[61]

The recommendations of the Provincial Administration Commission led to the establishment of the Committee on Provincial Reorganization which was set up on August 4, 1961. The government directive to the committee took note of the basic soundness of the new divisional arrangement in the provinces (notably the work of this commission), but cautioned that not enough delegation of powers had taken place with respect to duties of the Commissioners and Deputy Commissioners. The committee was asked to consider the possibility of (1) further decentralization; (2) determining the scope of financial and legal delegations; (3) the feasibility of reducing the provincial secretariat staff; (4) exploring measures for improving recruitment procedures; and (5) to suggest how the disparity in pay scales between officers of different services could be reduced. The task was formidable and the committee began by establishing two provincial subcommittees, one for East and another for West Pakistan.

The main problem facing the investigators was how to make the administration more responsible to the public. It was accepted that the existing administrative organization suffered from over-centralization, the almost total absence of coordination between departments, agencies, and other organizations of government, antiquated methods and procedures of work, and excessive delays and duplications of effort, as well as a general inability to adjust to changes in the socioeconomic environment. Answers to these recurring dilemmas, although not necessarily found in the magic of decentralization, could at least be sought in wide-ranging inquiry.

Pressures exerted by the emphasis on development imposed even greater strains on the provincial administrations, and some measures had already been introduced to relieve the tension. In addition to devising a more rational divisional and district set-up, changes had also taken place in the directorates and field organizations, in the training of district officers, and in the delegation of financial and administrative powers, by the introduction of the section-officers system in the provincial secretariats and in the appointment of financial advisers in various administrative departments. However, since the introduction of these reforms a new constitution had been promulgated which called for changes of a more popular nature.

> The new constitutional provisions envisage the devolution of much greater executive authority to the provinces than has been the case so far. Except for the subjects included in the Third Schedule of the Constitution and matters of national importance like planning or interprovincial coordination, the executive authority of the provinces will extend to all other matters, including many subjects which were on the Concurrent List under the late Constitution, such as Labour, Civil and Criminal Law (except for offences against laws with respect to subjects in the Third Schedule), and so on. The new Constitution also provides for the transfer of railways to the provinces by the 1st July 1962, and some other major decisions, like the bifurcation of the PIDC into two provincial corporations, have also been taken by the Government.[62]

With more responsibility devolving on the provincial authorities the question remained as to how to institute changes insuring the achievement of development targets. The recommendations of the two subcommittees were lengthy and detailed but they followed parallel lines and might be adumbrated in this fashion:

(a) The existing administrative arrangements, namely, the secretariat, departmental directorates, divisions, districts, etc., be retained except in a few isolated cases.

(b) Departments were to be headed by more senior officers and regrouped for their homogeneity and functional relationships.

(c) Each administrative tier should have its functions spelled out to avoid overlapping and duplication of effort as well as to insure the proper decentralization of authority.

(d) Functional decentralization was to be supplemented with a maximum delegation of powers to the divisional, district, subdivisional, and Tehsil/Thana levels in the legal, executive, financial, and administrative fields.

(e) Basic Democracies were to be given more powers related to development and local government.

(f) The existing practices and procedures in vogue in the government were to be reexamined so that those found to be dysfunctional could be replaced.

While taking note of the Central Government's desire to share its power with the provinces it is instructive to see how the authorities visualized the impact on themselves. In 1962, under a directive from the President, the Standing Organization Committee was ordered to study the matter. The Committee was instructed to define the role of the Central Government under the new Constitution. The new Constitution provided a central list of subjects but did not identify a concurrent or provincial list. Hence it was assumed that those subjects not found in the Third Schedule of the Constitution were *ipso facto* the responsibility of the provincial governments.

The National Assembly, however, was given the power under Article 131 (2) to make laws with respect to any matter not specified in the Third Schedule required by the national interest of Pakistan in relation to: (a) national security (including economic and financial stability); (b) planning or coordination; or (c) the achievement of uniformity in respect of any matter in different parts of Pakistan. The Assembly was also granted power to make laws under Item 2 of the Third Schedule in the field of foreign affairs and trade. Significantly, the Central Government could also intervene in provincial matters by allowing the President to issue orders to the Governor under Article 66 (2). Similarly, under Article 30 (a) the President could declare a state of emergency if Pakistan was threatened from without or where the security or economic life of the nation was put in jeopardy by internal forces. Under Article 135 (b) the Central Government could also assume executive authority if so provided by a law under Article 131 (2), even in matters falling within the purview of the provincial governments.

Observing these powers, the Standing Committee voiced the opinion that the Central Government would have to carefully guide the decentralization program. Though provincializing subjects like education, health, food and agriculture, labor, social welfare, railways, industries, and fuel and power, it was still considered necessary to maintain similar but small administrative units in the Central Government. These small units were not to discourage provincial responsibility but would "keep in touch with the conduct of affairs in the Provinces in their respective fields—specially in regard to broad policy and planning—in order to assess the need for Central legislation or Presidential intervention." [63] It is important to note that after conceding the need for watchdog units in the Central Government, the Committee emphasized that every possible device should be employed to see that these units do not interfere with the executive and operational fields "which should remain the exclusive domain of the Provincial Governments." [64]

The statement clarifying this latter point is of such vital importance that it seems appropriate to quote it in full:

> As many of the Ministries had construed articles 131 (2) and 135 as a charter for the Center's intervention in the Provincial sphere and the consequent need for having a suitable machinery for doing so, the Committee felt it necessary to remove this misunderstanding which was due to an incorrect interpretation of these articles. During the course of their discussions with the Secretaries to the Central Government, the Committee took the opportunity of explaining to them the role of the Central Government under these articles and the philosophy of the new relationship between the Centre and the Provinces. In particular, it emphasises that although the Presidential form of Government envisaged a strong Central Government, this did not mean that the Centre should extend its authority to the Provinces in areas which were clearly the Provincial responsibility. *The shift in the constitution towards decentralisation should be translated into practice and the Centre should only control broad national policy, and not enter into executive and operational fields.*[65] (Italics added.)

Summary

Reforms such as those anticipated above may have "liberalized" the administrative system, and, in some instances, improved its efficiency; but when contrasted with the need to evolve a more popular political system they obviously had only token value. The central issue to which the Pay and Services Commission addressed itself remains in limbo. President Ayub Khan was ill advised in this matter and merely postponed the day when another government must come to grips with the real questions of the country's political development.

Sympathetic observers may read in Ayub's performance the sincere desire to politicize the elite bureaucracy. In short, to socialize them into new patterns of a political nature, reducing their power and special privilege. Objective studies of the Pakistan scene show how dismally he failed, however. The bureaucratic status quo remains intact. The political system has in fact been bureaucratized. Braibanti's conclusion that Pakistan is an "administrative state" [66] is wholly justified.

The paternalism of Pakistan's elite bureaucracy obviously cannot be examined in a vacuum. It must be observed against a historical background and related to Pakistan's political and social culture. Even the devices effecting decentralization of administrative and political authority must be seen in this larger context. Life in the rural areas, for example, continues to be based on older patterns of socioeconomic and caste structures. Decentralization is therefore hardly a panacea, and is even likely to strengthen existing patterns of power relationships.[67]

Chapter 7

Power, Politics, and the Rural Scene

AGRARIAN and urban life-styles stand out in vivid contrast. The differences involve cultural values and hence affect fundamental perceptions of the two groups. Disparate structural patterns are observed in family organization, group associations, class, caste, and the employment of political power. Moreover, these variations determine behavior, attitude, and general environmental response. Pakistan's urban and rural populations would seem to share little in common.

Exceptions may perhaps be found in "test areas," however, such as the Comilla Thana where the East Pakistan Academy for Rural Development has been experimenting with a number of new approaches to development.[1] One study published under the sponsorship of the Academy recorded the following:

> Education is highly valued by the people in the [test] village. Their desire to send children to school is intense. In general, their attitude towards improved practices and innovations is favourable. A small number of people in Gaolgaon show characteristics of the more outside-world-oriented people of a city. They read a newspaper and keep themselves informed about the political developments of the country and the world. They reside in the village but in many ways resemble the educated people living in the cities.[2]

This may be the appropriate place to note two factors which also make the East and West Pakistan scenes different. First, Bengalis (not considered one of the martial peoples of India) have been more receptive to education and hence more literate. The 1961 census shows 17.6 percent literacy in East Pakistan and 13.6 percent in West Pakistan. Second, the pressure of people on the land in East Pakistan is enormous. East Pakistan is approximately one-sixth as large as West Pakistan but contains 55 percent of the total population. Statistically, more than 1,000 persons inhabit each square mile of East Pakistan whereas in the West the figure is under 200. An average landholder in East Pakistan possesses less than 3.5 acres. In West Pakistan the average is approximately four times this figure. Similarly, only 5.2 percent of the East Pakistanis live in urban locales as compared with 22.5 percent in West Pakistan.

Employment opportunities in West Pakistan are better and migration to the cities has been fairly permanent; those leaving the village seldom return. On the other hand, many East Pakistanis who move to metropolitan centers are more likely to return to their villages. Generally speaking, conditions in East Pakistan are more fluid and it is not always possible to disentangle rural-urban patterns. The principal cities in East Pakistan appear to blend into the countryside. In West Pakistan, however, the rural and urban worlds are quite separate, and this chapter seeks to analyze the implications of this situation.[3]

THE IMPORTANCE OF LANDED INTERESTS

Despite indications of accelerated urbanization, Pakistan is still very much land-oriented.[4] The rural masses continue to live under the influence of local leaders of personal wealth and power. In West Pakistan the zamindars maintain positions of authority in spite of the introduction of land reforms in 1959. In East Pakistan the elite landlords lost their equivalent importance after the flight of the prosperous Hindus in 1947 and the subsequent land reforms of 1950–51. Landlordism, however, is still a respected and influential institution. Villagers in need often look to the landlord for support, advice, and sustenance, and in times of crisis the rural masses lean heavily on them.[5] In periods of extreme difficulty as well as in relatively normal situations it is the landlords, not the government, who are appealed to for assistance.

In the Comilla study mentioned above, two lineages or castes were especially influential, the Syeds and the Khondkars. The two castes represented different factions. each vying for control of the village, with the more influential Syeds losing ground to the Khondkars. Both factions possess land, the Syeds owning more than the Khondkars; but the creation of a Village Cooperative Society which elected a Khondkar to the chairmanship seemingly reduced Syed power. The reduction, however, was deceptive in that the Syeds still dominated the Basic Democracies Union Council. Real influence was obviously still with the Syeds, who had more direct contacts with government officials, and it is this connection which ultimately is the essential indicator.

Another aspect of the study concerned the villagers' attitude toward their more influential landlords. It is interesting to note that both the

Syed and Khondkar leaders were considered clever and practical persons, but their honesty was questioned. The Khondkar was "accused of taking loans and not repaying, boasting of his connections with the government officers, dressing and behaving like a city-man. He was described as an aggressive, ambitious and articulate person." The Syed, who was also a local commander of the Ansars, was said to be corrupt and active in smuggling. "He was described as a man of few words and many actions . . . outwardly polite and gentle but selfish and expert in intriguing." [6] But regardless of how the villagers thought of the dominant landlords, they were still dependent. In addition to meeting basic needs, zamindars are indispensable for interpreting rules and regulations, obtaining necessary government services and facilities, and securing official favors.

It was noted in another study conducted under the auspices of the Comilla Academy concerning factors associated with the limited growth of village cooperatives that peasants generally believe membership in a cooperative is the exclusive option of the landlords. Cooperative societies are viewed as assisting landlords in increasing yields. A landless person is not likely to perceive personal benefits derived from membership in a cooperative, even if he were permitted to join. A typical response from a tenant farmer quoted in the study was that "no one takes care of the person without land." [7]

By and large, only those with landholdings normally expect to gain from participating in cooperatives. Landless peasants are largely leaderless and unorganized. Moreover, the prevailing socioeconomic and political structure dulls ambition. It is only reporting the obvious to state that Pakistan's villagers retain their traditional caste differentiation and social status. The landlord's grip remains strong and, irrespective of signs that the older order is being challenged, there is not enough evidence to prove that changes of a fundamental nature are occuring. Where socioeconomic mobility is restricted, political power remains a monopoly of vested interests.[8]

THE RURAL SCENE: PERCEPTIONS AND REALITIES

In a series of five articles collected and reprinted under the title *Perspectives in the Rural Power Structure in West Pakistan,* Inayatullah, a former instructor at the Academy for Rural Development in Peshawar, West Pakistan, described and analyzed the continuing importance of the landlord castes. In describing life in a Punjabi village he notes that there are two broad caste categories, the zamindars and kammis. The zamindars are the most influential sub-caste within their category and it is customary for them to control the political life of the community. All non-agricultural sub-castes, the artisans and simple laborers, for example, are included in the kammi caste. Each kammi has a particular social and/or economic function in the village, and the sub-castes within this general grouping are ranked in order of status as are those in the zamindar caste. This emphasis on caste will be found throughout Pakistan, apparently a residual influence of Hindu society on the Muslim way of life.

Although Islam stresses equality, the observance of the caste system —which is absolutely opposed to this tenet—can be attributed in part to the general need for sociopolitical stability.[9] Moreover, a point needing emphasis is that caste has an important place in the life of rural Pakistanis. Inayatullah reports that:

> The first question to be asked from a visitor [to a village] is about his caste, as this information decides whether he is to be given a cot to sit on or if he is to seat himself on the ground. . . . A Jat [zamindar] in dirty rags will be seated on a cot, while a clean, even fashionable kammi is to sit on the ground.[10]

Village societies are not always integrated and harmonious working units. Members of the village community are suspicious of each other and all guard themselves against the incursions of outsiders. Factions linking different sub-castes and cutting across major caste groupings are omnipresent. When the village peace is broken it is usually over the disposition of land, the allocation of water, or the molestation of women. Family and factional feuds sometimes bring the government into the village and usually it is the local police officer who is charged with the restoration of tranquility. Nonetheless, village affairs are organized by the dominant landlord. And it is not unusual to observe more influential zamindars controlling both the revenue collectors (lambardars and patwaris) and the local police.

In the Punjab, the concept of *"izzat"*—respect, honor, superiority— in the village shapes the behavior of the more powerful landlords. Their ability to command the allegiance of different groups marks them as successful leaders. "This goal ['izzat'] which the zamindar cherishes, stirs him to act so as to get wealth and hold power over other persons and a sharp conflict is precipitated which sometimes gains more or less a permanent character." [11] Most villagers are submissive and will readily acknowledge the power of the landlord. It is widely believed that the landlord is strong and successful because God has ordained it. Nothing can happen without God's permission. "God has guaranteed man his *rizq* (his daily food, etc.) but this guarantee is conditioned by the initiative and efforts of man: 'You work and I will bless it,' says God according to a common saying." [12]

Oriental fatalism is clearly not the only, or even the most significant factor for any lack of achievement-orientation in Pakistani society. Nor should the piety of the great majority of the population be equated with the absence of intellectual insight. A more plausible explanation for the average villager's ascribing all his misfortunes to God, and his reluctance to improve his condition, is his sense of powerlessness and insignificance. The villagers believe good deeds and hard work make it possible for some men to improve their condition; but the village power structure is so oppressive that most choose passivity. While they despair at changing the sociopolitical order, they turn to God. It is only God who can make everything right.

> This belief in the inevitability of external forces has given an inexhaustible patience to the villager. He can silently suffer the worst catastrophies without even questioning the worth of life.[13]

Thus the average villager learns little of formal government. He has virtually no connection with the administrative system, and political parties seldom cater to his needs or seek his support. The only ties the villagers have to the formal political structure is through powerful leaders in the village who control revenue collection and in whose behalf order is preserved. It is the more influential landlord who deals with the bureaucracy; he alone is concerned with activities beyond the village.

By and large, villagers visualize the distant government as monarchial in form. Government, in order to perform the supreme function of safe-guarding the traditional mode of life, must wield absolute power—and this only a king can conceivably do. Monarchial government implies the power to issue decrees which may well mean life or death, the seizing of property, or the exiling of those who do not comply with commands. The maximum ruler is often viewed as standing above the law which emanates from his authority. The villagers imagine their king surrounded by advisers and administrators who carry out his directives. The chief administrator is cast in the image of the vizeer of Moghul tradition and the king delegates authority to his officers through him. Above all, the monarch demands obedience and respect. Local administrators, on the other hand, are generally despised. Inayatullah points out that the ad-ministrative system developed by the British is still equated by the

villagers with Moghul rule. The villager ". . . could not always understand the British administrative system. He would call its machinery as
Sarkar, which again, is autocratic, despotic and irresponsible." [14]

Traditional government bestowed no rights on rural citizens. It also
left them without significant duties. The fact that soldiers were recruited
from among them or that they were called upon to pay their taxes were
not viewed as duties but merely levies for what little protection they
received. In Pakistan, as in India, "the foreign conqueror, the landlord,
and the money lender" took far more than they gave. "Hence economic
stagnation continued through the British era and indeed into the present
day." [15] Of course the villagers were aware that they were to keep the
peace of the village, that an offence could mean swift punishment.
Similarly, they were supposed to be ready to entertain and nourish officers who from time to time came to visit. It is difficult to discern, however, whether the tradition of hospitality or fear dominated the exercise.
Moore summarizes the traditional features of Indian society as: "a
sovereign who ruled, an army that supported the throne, and a peasantry
that paid for both." [16]

THE PERENNIAL VILLAGER

It might be asked what the villager really expected from the government, the Sarkar. Reference has been made to preserving traditions; but
what did this involve? Simply stated, it meant leaving the villager to live
his own life. The village political system was supreme and only occa-
sionally did the Sarkar truly make its presence felt. In these special
instances the Sarkar was looked to for some act of benevolence, such as
the return or cancellation of land revenues when the rains failed.

Most of what is perceived of government beyond the village is drawn
from folk stories and the villagers' personal experience with local officials
and influential landlords. Lack of socioeconomic mobility and illiteracy,
coupled with the perpetuation of a feudal village political system, rele-
gates the peasants to an almost stagnant situation. They have little if any
connection with large urban communities, and migration to the cities has
still to register a significant impact on old habits and beliefs. One ob-
serves little feedback to the villages from those who had left for the
cities. Moreover, the villagers feel the city is an unhealthy and wicked
place. Those peasants who settle in the cities seldom, if ever, return to
their villages with the idea of changing its structure or outlook. The impression is gained that no appreciable change has taken place in rural
life since Moghul times.

It matters little to the average villager what form government takes. Insofar as he is concerned the power of the ruler is the historic power of the "Badshah" and there can be no check to his authority, either from a council of elders (a legislature) or the legal community (the courts). In an enlightening study the Rudolphs argue that the villagers saw the anglicization of Indian law as another form of despotism.[17] Furthermore, with the possible exception of the elections to the Basic Democracies in 1959–60 and again in 1964, the villager was usually oblivious of his participation in any decision-making process. Provincial elections were held in the Punjab, Sind, Baluchistan, the N.W.F.P., and East Bengal between 1951 and 1954, but the experience was new to the mass of rural voters and the people for whom they voted too remote. It is doubtful that they learned very much from the elections in light of the events leading to the declarations of martial law in October 1958 and March 1969. The concept of "nation" continues to elude the Pakistani peasant.

The personalized political activity reflected in the Basic Democracies elections was one of the system's chief defects. At the same time, President Ayub considered it an all-important asset. He insisted: "The vast majority of our people live in villages. They are illiterate and uneducated. They can exercise their right of vote judiciously only at the village level or mohalla level in towns where personal contact, the immediacy, urgency of individual and community interests make it practical and possible for them to judge people and elect only those in whom they have full confidence based on personal knowledge of the candidate's background, temperament and behaviour towards other people and past performance in general."[18] The people elected to the union councils in the villages more and more represented the traditional power structure in the rural areas, however.[19]

The villager could not expunge the feeling that those who ran for office in the Basic Democracies did so for only one reason: to maintain their status in the community. Most unsophisticated villagers found it difficult to believe that the Basic Democrats were expected to be their representatives and that through them they could seek redress for their grievances. The possibility of the Basic Democrats forming themselves into articulate aggregations for the benefit of the poor tillers and artisans scarcely entered their consciousness. Although some political experience has undoubtedly been gained from the Basic Democracies, the negative aspect of village politics is still too real to be minimized.[20]

Village politics remain at a level where votes can be freely bought and sold.[21] Community issues are secondary; personal gain and prestige are primary. Elections for the union councils were full of awkward incidents but it was in the indirect elections for the President, the National Assembly, and the provincial legislatures that corruption was especially serious. A personal letter to the author describes the experience of one Basic Democrat who sought to obtain a seat in the West Pakistan Provincial Assembly in 1965. It read in part:

> I received your letter when I was in the thickest of the election battle. The campaign was so hard that it left me no time even to sleep well. The number of B.D. votes for the seat I was contesting was only 339 but the number of candidates was seven. From the top to the bottom all forces combined to defeat me and I am now a defeated candidate. Bargainers jumped in and the vote became a commodity in the market. A Rasputin and a Rascal rushed to the opposite camp and helped attack me—the leading candidate among them all. I am not sorry for the defeat—but I am trying to realize why I was selected for the attack.[22]

The reason why this particular Basic Democrat was "selected for the attack" was that he represented modern aspirations. For many years he lived away from the village. He played an important role in the independence movement, was well educated, had traveled extensively and taught in a leading American university. When he returned to the village he had left as a young man (he was now in his seventies) he could not avoid the political wars. A devout and pious Muslim, a man of intellect, integrity, and broad experience, he genuinely wished to serve the village folk.[23] He proved he could win a seat on the Union Council; nonetheless, the rural power structure prevented him from capitalizing on this success.

In a way, this episode demonstrates why there is so little feedback from the sophisticated to the inarticulate, depressed rural masses. It may also be an explanation for the failure of some community development programs. Above all it addresses itself to the absence of political change.

VILLAGE AGGREGATIONS AND OBLIGATIONS

The zamindars and their families and managers live in an entirely different setting from that of the impoverished peasants. Landowners do not believe in self-exertion, which is for menials only. As Inayatullah notes: "In agricultural castes the ideal life would be of a Choudhury, who sits in the dera the whole day, gossiping and settling disputes of the villagers or roams in the villages, free from work." [24] The fact that the landlords have perpetuated their authority cannot be minimized. The villagers accept them unquestioningly, and actually assist in sustaining their influence. To defy the customs and mores of the village is to commit an unpardonable sin and punishment is often swift and severe. He who does not work for the landlord as a tenant farmer or serve the community as a kammi simply does not survive. And those few who seek to make trouble can be expected to receive no mercy. Often they are ostracized from the village altogether.

In a confidential note to Ayub the then governor of West Pakistan Malik Amir Mohammad Khan, a significantly powerful landlord, noted that the villagers are traditionally inclined to help one another, "however, as one rises above the village level, this spirit tends to disappear and people act in an individualistic manner and are subservient to party factions and interests. The identity of the village is recognized traditionally and there is a certain sanctity attached to it." [25] The Governor cited a number of cases in support of his presentation. The custom of "maang" (voluntary help) is found in many areas of West Pakistan during the harvest season, especially in Mianwali. The equivalent of the word "maang" is found in other dialects in West Pakistan. In Campbellpur it becomes "maangali." On the Frontier it is "blandaror." In Hazara it is called "hashari." In other words, an unwritten code calls upon neighbors to assist one another in the harvest season and only in the rarest circumstances are people known to refuse their aid.

In Mianwali, Dera Ismail Khan, and Dera Ghazi Khan, small dams for diverting water running off the hills are fashioned by people working together on a quasi-voluntary basis. The common term for the custom is "kumara." In this latter activity it is generally the government which supervises the activity through a low-ranking official. It is the official's task to rally the village folk, and absence from this form of labor is usually punished by means of a fine realized as arrears of land revenues.

The socioeconomic structure of the village family also preserves the old order. The family patriarch has unlimited power and is entitled to the greatest respect. It is this family relationship which when broadened encompasses all those coming under the landlord's influence, both tenants and kammis. In effect, village society prevents the exercise of individual freedom.

> In fact, the real individual in the sense of Western urban society does not exist in the village. He is an inalienable part of multiple groups which completely overshadow his individuality. He is not master of his own will and architect of his own fate.[26]

Important decision-making groups in West Pakistan, especially in the Punjab, can be identified in the following order: the family, which sets the life pattern of the individual; the "baradari," or all the families in a village extending from a common ancestor. For a kammi, caste status in even more pronounced. Kammi castes are groups making up all the village families in a particular profession, e.g., barbers, carpenters, shoe repairmen, etc. The baradari is unified vis-à-vis other baradaris but weak internally, especially when it comes to the division of lands. Next in order are the caste groups which bring together a number of baradaris in different villages who all share a common ancestor. Caste becomes significant, especially in the selection of a spouse, but caste and baradari groups usually parallel each other; the importance of zamindar and kammi groups have already been discussed. It is enough to say that the kammi who lives on a particular zamindar's land comes under the influence of that zamindar. His allegiance is to his zamindar in disputes involving other kammis. Hence it is clear the kammi tends to lose his independence.

When decisions must be made, the dominant group or groups make them and they are seldom subject to challenge. A villager who disagrees with a decision generally has no other recourse but to submit and accept the consequences. Again this is not oriental fatalism. It is a pragmatic response to superior power; and it is sufficient to deter retaliatory action. The only real "individuals" in the village are the "leaders" or "headmen." And it is customary for them to align themselves with others in their category who are even more influential. This alignment continues until a point is reached where the leadership in the smallest village is linked with a leader who has access to high officials in government, or in some instances with a particular political party which is supposed to represent the interest of that village at the national level. No formal arrangement institutionalizing this latter type of political structure obtains in Pakistan despite all the efforts of Ayub Khan.

In a particular village there can be and often is more than one leader or headman. As has been noted, factions develop from among competing leaders and they in turn attract family, baradari, caste, and dependent castes. At this juncture competition is keen, but because it is unsophisticated and disorganized very little is achieved. If Pakistan developed grassroot political parties these traditional political factions might lose their relevance and perhaps a more modern political structure could be constructed. Huntington's observation that "the process of party development usually evolves through four phases: factionalism, polarization, expansion and institutionalization," is salient.[27] Although family and caste groups will undoubtedly continue to operate for socioeconomic reasons, the baradari may well break down under the influence of a more sophisticated political system. Should this happen it could foreshadow the first major breakthrough in the village power structure.

Speculation should not obscure reality, however. The highly effective rural power structure remains intact. National events, like general elections, are influenced by traditional alignments and votes are cast by groups, not individuals. Before Basic Democracies were introduced the prevailing system made it easy for politicians to campaign in villages without ever visiting them. A politician simply arranged "an understanding" with the leader of a particular group or faction and all the votes within that faction were delivered in his behalf. Inayatullah reports that villagers look down upon an individual who takes money for a vote but do not object if the money is bestowed upon the group. Hence "the candidate would give the money to a family and say that this was for the expenditure they would make in his behalf." [28] Ayub hoped to obliterate this method of campaigning after seizing power in 1958.

Political parties up to the time of Ayub's "revolution" adapted themselves to the existing village power structure. They did practically nothing to change it. Ayub viewed the parliamentary system as merely perpetuating conventional attitudes and customs. The politicians were responsible to the leaders of various factions, not to the people at large; hence participation was circumscribed and political education virtually impossible. Petty economic and social pressures in the village sapped the vitality of the peasant masses and candidates were "forced" upon them. Above all, social factionalism thrived at the expense of national unity and political consciousness.

The Basic Democracies system was meant to correct this situation. The village folk were called upon to elect those whom they knew to represent them. It is important to reiterate that when Ayub launched the Basic Democracies he had no thought of reinstating political parties. Unfortunately, not even Ayub could breach the rural political power structure. Conventional village life was reinforced, not altered, by his "new" system of local self-government. The one slight difference between pre-1958 and post-1958 rural politics was the increasing remoteness of the political parties in the latter period. Even Ayub's belated endeavor to build a national party came to nothing. Open competition between political parties was impossible in the elections of 1959, given the existence of martial law; in 1964 it was feeble at best. It remains to be seen how they will fare in the elections forecast for the autumn of 1970.

Not surprisingly, it is the bureaucracy which links the villages with the national government. Where political parties are neutralized, the bureaucracy is in a position to fill a vacuum. Ayub Khan justified this bureaucratic role. While interested in changing village life he was primarily concerned with raising economic standards. He has been criticized and even condemned for putting the villagers at the mercy of the bureaucrats. However, he had long convinced himself that only the administrators could produce positive results. Intuitively, Ayub was compelled to go with the group that personified modernity, education, and national orientation. He thought an association of bureaucrats and rural folk could produce a desirable and healthy metamorphosis. The President counted on the villagers gaining maturity and self-reliance; and as education spread and economic opportunities broadened their horizons the prevailing political structure could wither away.[29] When that happened the bureaucrats were supposed to relinquish their power. Ayub said he wanted the people to "run their own police, they will run their own revenue system, they will run every thing. I would like to see them progress in that direction . . . I would not be surprised if in ten to fifteen years time a situation may arise when the officials are only there to guide and assist and not to function as administrators and rulers." [30]

AN APPRAISAL OF BASIC DEMOCRACIES

Enough evidence exists to show that the President expected his Basic Democracies system to progress more rapidly than it actually did. In East Pakistan the Rural Works Program helped in a small way to improve the lot of the poor masses. After a limited experimental success in the Comilla Kotwali Thana by the Academy of Rural Development during 1961–62, the government allocated 100,000,000 rupees ($20,000,000) for a province-wide program. By May 1963 Ayub was recorded as saying: "You would be surprised how much happiness it [the Rural Works Program in East Pakistan] has given the people of East Pakistan . . . and how much they really feel thankful to the Government. . . . Wherever you go you get the spontaneous word of thanks from even the ordinary villager. . . . We are going to continue the system." [31] To underline Ayub's enthusiasm the government released the following figures:

> Comparative study of the physical achievements of the Works Programme during 1962–63 and 1963–64 reveals that larger percentages of allocations was devoted in 1963–64 to complex . . .

works. . . . . The Municipal Committees and Town Committees built 363 culverts and bridges, 28,250 miles of pucca [hard-top] roads and 163 drains and canals in 1963–64; the corresponding figure for 1962–63 were 112 bridges and culverts, 336 miles of roads and 84 miles of drains and canals. Of 27,818 miles of roads built during 1963–64 in rural areas 487 miles were pucca construction as against 20,926 miles of roads during 1962–63 . . . 856 miles of embankments were raised or repaired and 1,315 miles of canals were excavated or reexacavated during 1963–64 as against 248 miles of embankments and 902 miles of canals during 1962–63.[32]

The relative success of the Rural Works Program is cited as a major factor in Ayub's carrying of East Pakistan in the 1965 presidential election despite the loss of the principal cities of Dacca and Chittagong. Nevertheless, progress was exceedingly slow despite official euphoria.

Early in 1964 the President publicized his distress and although recognizing that "a good start" had been made suggested that far more could be done. It was at this time that Ayub had become interested in the Yugoslavian and Chinese Communist experiences. The mobilization, organization, and motivation of the rural population in those two countries he thought might hold a clue for Pakistan's own problems.[33] But after a prestigious committee met to study the operations in these two countries they found protracted deliberations unnecessary. The key variable in Yugoslavia and China, they noted, was the one-party system. Ruling out the one-party state as unsuited to Pakistan's conditions, the committee concluded by noting that only a satisfactory blend of authoritarian and libertarian activities would work in Pakistan.[34]

The President stoically accepted this judgment, but it meant more or less maintaining the status quo and he was not pleased. Hence in April 1965 he issued a minute calling for further decentralization of the Basic Democracies. Ayub wanted to reach as many people as the system would allow and thus called for the establishment of a sub-tier below that of the Union Council which he termed the "ward." Wards already existed for purposes of elections, but now they were to be used for administrative and development work as well. The ward was to reach into each village, no matter how remote. It would also allow for the delegation of more authority to individual Basic Democrats and, hopefully, dilute the growing power of Union Council chairmen.

The President urged individual Basic Democrats to enlist the support of skilled private persons in their wards and with their assistance to organize village cooperatives. The principal idea behind the plan was to involve every village in reconstruction and to link up local projects with area-wide development schemes. In all of these activities, Ayub noted, the government would have to play a key role. "Since the community cannot, under our conditions, pool its resources for common projects the advantages of working jointly can best be shown by providing common facilities with government funds." [35]

The President did not hesitate to point out that compulsion as well as rewards might have to be built into the plan in order to break the vicious circle of inactivity and petty rivalries.[36] Ayub was convinced that there were only two methods whereby the rural population could be freed from its own torment. Both required sacrifices. One was the Communist technique of rigidly enforced rules and procedures. The other was the voluntary cooperative where government and people pooled their resources. The President sidestepped the first alternative, but in calling for the adoption of the second he was frank to admit that the "voluntary" aspect of the cooperative would have to be "coerced." Time being an important factor, it was obvious the country's problems would not wait for the people to become duly motivated.

Village cooperatives are not new to Pakistan. Such societies existed in pre-independence India but enjoyed few successes. Later they were abolished by the Pakistan Government and Union Multipurpose Cooperative Societies organized in their place. These larger societies were deemed to be more economically viable; however, there was never any real test of the creditability of one against the other. What was overlooked in this change was the simple fact that the larger cooperatives did not have the support of the villagers.

Only the relatively enlightened are interested in union cooperatives; the average villager is aware of little but his own needs and refuses to participate in such organizations. The villagers, as has been shown, are jealous guardians of their property and are naturally suspicious of those who would entice them to accept what for them are ambiguous arrangements.[37] In essence, they fear losing their meager possessions to the "crafty" townspeople who tend to dominate the multipurpose cooperatives. It was only after Akhter Hameed Khan reintroduced the village cooperative in East Pakistan that the institution again began receiving some support from the simple rural folk.

Akhter Hameed's idea involved building strong village units and combining them in a federation at the thana level of the Basic Democracies. Akhter Hameed's rationale was that the village was the nearest equivalent to a true community in the subcontinent.

The village is the smallest administrative unit where people live together, know each other, face many obstacles such as flood, cyclone, drought, etc. At the relaxing moments, the villagers gather under the shade of a large tree or in a central place of the village, and discuss topics of common interest as they smoke *hookah*. Among them, many would be farmers, some would be craftsmen, others would be artisans like weavers, carpenters, blacksmiths, small traders, etc. Village life is a community life. In festivals one shares the happiness of others and similarly in funerals one suffers the sorrows of one's neighbour.[38]

Akhter Hameed Khan was President Ayub's closest adviser on village affairs and rural development. Their channels of communication were as informal as the two men themselves. It may well be that the director of the Comilla Academy influenced Ayub to draft the memorandum calling for the establishment of wards in the Basic Democracies. Experiments and tests at Comilla proved over and again that development must begin at the lowest organized level, and in Pakistan this could only mean the village. The fact that union councils often ignored the needs of certain villages within their jurisdiction weakened the whole edifice of Basic Democracies. The Comilla Academy's thana development scheme, with its central focus on the cooperative, and Ayub's insistence on the creation of ward committees seemed to point to a way out of the dilemma.

RURAL REFORM

Pakistan's Third Five Year Plan called for the establishment of Thana/Tehsil Development Training Centers in both East and West Pakistan.[39] In the thana/tehsil center village cooperatives assisted by wards and the Union Councils could federate without limiting their autonomy. The center was to maintain a staff of trained administrators expert in agriculture, health, education, cooperation, and other nation-building activities. The administrators were to act in their customary roles but also double as teachers in the thana training center located in the same installation. It was this scheme which the President admired and sought to have implemented on a nationwide basis.

The multipurpose cooperative societies never went beyond the supply of credit to farmers. The cooperative federation or central cooperative located at the thana now sought to assist all cooperatives, agricultural and non-agricultural, i.e., kammis (rickshaw pullers, artisans), etc. The central cooperative would also make available mechanical devices, set up demonstration farms, help village cooperatives in the purchase of needed equipment, seeds, fertilizer, etc., carry on intensive educational programs for adult literacy and modern farming, and assist in school works projects and family planning programs. The central cooperative also stressed saving for future investment in cooperative ventures, for joint buying and marketing of produce. An essential feature of the Thana Development and Training Center was the training of villagers through their own organizers whom the Comilla Academy called model farmers.[40]

The establishment of the wards was the first step. They would provide a foundation for the Basic Democracies by revivifying village activity and, it was hoped, the village cooperative as well. Other ward propects were to be coordinated at the Union Council level, i.e., involving the Rural Works Program. The over-all union development program, however, was to be serviced at the Tehsil/Thana Development and Training Center.

The Works Program launched in East Pakistan in 1961 became an all-Pakistan activity in 1963. The Basic Democracies system was given full responsibility for its implementation, thus giving it special stature. Between 1963 and mid-1964 some progress was made in decentralizing administration and providing local leaders with a share in the decision-making process. Large numbers of people were mobilized for minor development projects in their immediate environs as mentioned above in regard to East Pakistan. However, sustaining, let alone accelerating the program proved to be impossible once the election campaign gained momentum in the late summer and fall of 1964. The following table illustrates the losing battle in trying to keep the Rural Works Program vibrant.[41]

REGRESSION

In November 1964 general elections were held for the second generation of Basic Democrats. In January 1965 the new Basic Democrats formed themselves into an electoral college for the election of the President, and in March and May of 1965 they again were called upon to decide who should sit in the national and provincial legislatures. Thus from the summer of 1964 through the spring of 1965 the Basic Democrats were deluged by campaign oratory and their attention diverted from development projects. Political activity left few moments for the Basic Democrats to play the leadership role in their communities.

SECTORAL BREAKDOWN OF EXPENDITURE UNDER THE RURAL WORKS PROGRAMME

SECTORS	1963–1964		1964–1965		1965–1966		TOTAL	
	EXPENDITURE IN RS. '000	% OF TOTAL	EXPENDITURE IN RS. '000	% OF TOTAL	EXPENDITURE IN RS. '000	% OF TOTAL	EXPENDITURE IN RS. '000	% OF TOTAL
Social Welfare	9,418	12.6	5,250	5.8	5,760	6.7	19,168	8.3
Agriculture	2,632	3.5	4,856	5.4	2,580	3.0	9,518	4.1
Education	20,751	27.7	17,657	19.6	14,360	16.7	49,658	21.3
Communication	15,855	21.2	34,628	38.3	43,000	50.0	84,083	36.1
Irrigation	6,006	8.0	4,505	4.9	6,110	7.1	15,311	6.6
Health and Sanitation	15,083	20.2	15,910	17.6	12,900	15.0	41,163	17.7
Other Projects	5,101	6.8	7,613	8.4	1,290	1.5	13,754	5.9
TOTAL	74,846	100.0	90,419	100.0	86,000	100.0	232,655	100.0

Subsequently, development projects were retarded or curtailed and the rural population lost whatever drive it had achieved earlier.

There can be no denying the physical gains produced by the Rural Works Program.[42] Psychological progress is more difficult to estimate, however. Figures can be cited detailing the miles of embankments erected in East Pakistan, the number of schools constructed in West Pakistan, and the like, but these developments in no way describe their impact on popular attitudes.

With some of the old Basic Democrats defeated and new ones still to take office, few people applied themselves to community tasks. In the meantime projects lay incomplete and money earmarked for new schemes went unused. In addition, the reputation the Basic Democrats had earned for their earlier leadership was sullied as many engaged in illicit or corrupt election activities. Hence it became increasingly difficult for the rural people to accept the Basic Democrats as genuine leaders and many refused to contribute either their labor, land, or money to community projects.

It should be noted that the Indo-Pakistani War in September 1965 also affected the Basic Democracies. The elections which brought the new provincial legislatures into being in May 1965 were not the last elections for the Basic Democrats. The first generation of B.D.'s remained more or less suspended until such time as the new bodies could meet and elect their chairmen. This proved to be a difficult task, as the chairman was usually an influential member and the only salaried person on the council. Furthermore, there was a considerable amount of controversy as to the delineation of constituencies, and in East Pakistan a case was before the High Court which sought to declare the whole Basic Democracies system unconstitutional.

Despite these difficulties the government plodded ahead but found it essential to postpone the elections of the chairmen until such time as the wards were established officially. It was then that the Indo-Pakistani War broke out. While the conflict raged on the borders of West Pakistan, the East Pakistan government sanctioned the creation of the ward committees; the West Pakistan government did not follow suit until well after the cease-fire. But once this was accomplished the elections of the chairmen were pressed with even greater vigor; the fear persisted that the entire Basic Democracies system was becoming moribund.

After the Tashkent Agreement in January 1966 many Basic Democrats, especially in the urban areas of West Pakistan, gave serious thought to resigning their posts as a protest against President Ayub's decision to withdraw the Pakistan Army from the Indian frontier and

Kashmir. Nonetheless, early in 1966 the elections were held and the chairmen finally inaugurated. Almost two years had passed since the Basic Democrats had laid aside their development responsibilities, and both the Basic Democracies and Rural Works Program had paid a high price. Rural development was virtually at a standstill and neither the sincere intentions of the President nor the efforts of the administrators could transform what was into what should have been.

By April 1967, the Rural Works Program was in the process of being scrapped altogether in West Pakistan. The Annual Development Program was under consideration by a committee of the Planning and Development Department. As Shahid Javed Burki reveals, the committee recommended the transfer of executive responsibility for small projects—rural schools, dispensaries, water supply schemes, roads, etc.—to the nation-building departments. "The projects transferred by the Committee to the new sector would have cost Rs. 11.0 million to execute in 1967–1968. This was an ingenious suggestion; *it would have killed the Rural Works Program without taking 'rural works' out of the provincial development plan.* The Committee's suggestion was not accepted largely because of the pressure of the central government." [43] (Italics added.)

EAST PAKISTAN'S BASIC DEMOCRACIES

Compared with East Pakistan, West Pakistan lagged far behind in a number of areas. Critics in East Pakistan insisted from the outset that Basic Democracies brought little that was new to their province. Their experience with union and district boards were given as cases in point. Many argued that the Basic Democracies were really fashioned for West Pakistan, where the landlords dominated the scene and the people never had the opportunity to govern themselves. The more politically conscious people of East Pakistan were and remained the severest critics of Basic Democracies. Nevertheless, they proved they could manage with the innovation even if it did not give them what they desired in the way of political responsibilities.

East Pakistan introduced the Rural Works Program and achieved some remarkable successes. It was also in the East wing that local government in a number of instances absorbed or replaced the bureaucracy; it was the first province to introduce the ward committees, the first to elect the second generation of Union Council chairman and again the first to develop organizations in the municipalities which harmonized with traditional administration and popular government.

Political party activity within the Basic Democracies of East Pakistan was also on a more sophisticated level than in the West. Certainly it would be unfair to ignore the Rural Academy at Comilla and what it meant to the province's development. Rural administration reform; the training of officials and non-officials, Basic Democrats, and simple farmers; experimentation with training and development centers, cooperatives and the utilization of thana-level administration for the coordination of all nation-building activities; the research and publications and the essential encouragement given to persons in all walks of life—these are only some of the accomplishments of the Academy.

The Comilla Academy's living spirit and mentor, Akhter Hameed Khan, deserves full credit for the sharp contrast ·between the achievements of this institution and those of its sister academy in Peshawar. Perhaps the most noteworthy experiment at Comilla is in the realm of cooperatives. Akhter Hameed feels that voluntary cooperatives are the key to Pakistan's future. Should they fail, the only answer to the nation's ever increasing dilemmas will be some form of rigid authoritarianism. Akhter Hameed does not mince words when he says that this will probably mean the spread of communism. Opening a dialogue with the people, communicating ideas and techniques, and getting them to adopt policies and methods beyond the range of their immediate comprehension are prime tasks of the Comilla Academy. However, the Academy is an expensive undertaking; similar institutions cannot be established all over the country.[44] Moreover, men with the charismatic qualities of an Akhter Hameed Khan are not easily duplicated.

Finally, where should the government look for those scholars of rural life who would sacrifice their time, energy, and comfort to take up residence in a remote and often dreary environment? Clearly the Comilla approach is not a panacea. Candor demands recognition that neither the Comilla nor Peshawar Academies can move the rural population into the twentieth century—but they certainly can assist in that endeavor. Under the prevailing arrangement the principal agent of change remains the field administrator, and it is his attitude and industry which will determine how far and how fast the rural population progresses.

THE ADMINISTRATOR AND RURAL PROBLEMS

Senior administrators expect to be given positions of power and subsequently resist attempts to place them in such activities as social welfare, for example. The Social Welfare Department is supposed to sponsor community development projects. The department in West Pakistan (it is a provincial subject) has failed to evoke support from members of the elite bureaucracy, and a posting to the Social Welfare Department is usually considered a demotion in the service hierarchy. When an officer is assigned to an underrated station, his time is usually consumed in trying to gain his release, and it is no surprise that social welfare projects are poorly managed or that money allocated for such purposes often goes unspent. A West Pakistani Director of the Social Welfare Directorate noted that 14.60, 27.17, and 80 million rupees were allocated for social welfare in the First, Second, and Third Five Year Plans, respectively. In the First, only 4.4 million was spent. In the Second it was 7.57 million. Something like 40 million was spent in the Third Plan.[45]

Another department the administrator tries to avoid is Cooperatives. Few officials take this department very seriously. It is still perceived as a place for the inefficient or those in need of chastising. In defense of departments concerned with social welfare and cooperatives, it should also be mentioned that many officers have served with dedication and distinction. It can also be said that many bureaucrats are ill equipped for such responsibilities. This unofficial intra-service grading of departments and positions inevitably undermines local development projects, and in part explains the failure of Ayub's decentralization programs. In the absence of genuine cooperation between nation-building departments and the traditional field administrators, village development is impossible.

It has been recounted how the practitioners of general administration jealously guard their time-honored prestige and tend to stifle the innovations introduced by nation-building agencies. Undoubtedly this was a principal reason for establishing such training institutes as the Rural Academies. It may also be why it was found necessary to open other training schools for middle-level managers and senior administrators. The National Institutes of Public Administration at Karachi, Lahore, and Dacca are responsible for the former whereas the Pakistan Administrative Staff College trains the latter.[46]

Development administration and economics are the themes around which the courses are organized and although the NIPA's attempt to impart skills, the main objective of the PASC is to awaken ranking officers to their roles as development officials. One illustration will suffice. At the PASC participant members come from all over Pakistan. They represent the central and provincial governments, the autonomous corporations, and the private sector. They are also drawn from a cross-section of the services (e.g., CSP, PSP, PCS, etc.), and most of the departments and agencies in Pakistan. Each participant must have at least twelve years of experience. The Staff College tries to ignore the participant's service, seniority, or anything which might seem to bestow an advantage over other trainees.

During the three months in residence at the College the participants not only work and dine together but organize their own recreational activities. Great pains are taken to provide the trainees (who are always referred to as members, not students, in view of their senior status) with experiences that enable them to work toward common goals. Emphasis is on the pooling of scarce resources and overcoming service and departmental rivalries.

A majority of the senior administrators attending the PASC have had little if any contact with grassroots development programs and a major segment of their studies focuses on the weaknesses in district administration. Although these senior administrators are reluctant to leave their posts for such in-service training, on completion of the course they usually concur that the experience has utility. While recognizing that many of their comments are platitudinous, that in-service training has yet to register an impact on administrative attitudes or workways, the existence and persistence of the training institutes offers the hope that improvement can still be expected.

GRASSROOTS BUREAUCRACY

The image of government remains cast in the form of bureaucratic despotism. Village officials, such as lambardars, patwaris, chowkidars, and police are the visible representatives of government on a day-to-day basis. They normally have linkages with powerful village leaders such as the landlords, retired government officers and religious teachers. The lambardar collects government revenue from the villages and receives a percentage of the collections as compensation for his efforts. Legal summonses and subpoenas are usually served through this same officer. The village patwari maintains an up-to-date record of rural properties and assesses revenue on a biannual basis. The village chowkidar in addition to being a watchman reports all conflicts, deaths, and births to the nearest police station or concerned agency.

The chairman of the Union Council was supposed to provide the link between these officers and the people. All disputes developing in the village were to be channeled through the Basic Democracies, their power to resolve conflict being granted in the Conciliation Courts Ordinance and the Muslim Family Laws Ordinance of 1961.[47] Intentions and prescriptions aside, lower ranking government officials continued to harass the villagers as in the past, however.

Government officers at the grassroots level are underpaid and generally only semiliterate. The patwari, for example, is synonymous with corruption and no one believes he performs his work honestly or efficiently. Together with the lambardars they squeeze the poor farmers on the one side while stealing from the government on the other. Patwaris are often exposed and publicly humiliated but this apparently does not deter them. The same is true of the local police and chowkidars.

None of these officers earns more than Rs. 100 per month (approximately $20) and many far less. While they bear significant responsibility for maintaining the village peace, the temptations combined with the indifference shown by higher authority perpetuates their sorry performance. No wonder, then, that the stereotype of government remains frozen in its more grotesque form; that government's grandiose schemes for rural development are so often stillborn. In a fine study of a frontier village, Inayatullah and Shafi discuss this serious condition:

> Unfortunately the negative image of the public servant did not entirely emerge from a distorted perception . . . the experiences of the villagers with the public servants help in the formation of such an image which was then continuously reinforced and strengthened. . . . In any matter affecting village development, the villagers have to depend on the lower bureaucratic machinery. . . . However villagers would not have been as much handicapped if lower bureaucracy had no contact with them. Contact with lower bureaucracy created negative conditions for the villagers which in turn sapped much of their initiative and detracted their attention from self-improvement. In the present village [under study] some of the land owners have been charged land revenue for nearly six years for land whose occupation had been taken by the government . . . to this may be added . . . bribery. When Academy staff [from Peshawar] were able to persuade twelve villagers to get loans from the Agriculture Bank, they went to the Patwari to get records of their land to support their applications. The Patwari charged each person Rs. 10.00 while his usual fee was not more than Rs. 00.25. Later these applicants were not able to secure the loans. One can imagine the state of mind of a villager who trying to get loans instead lost Rs. 10.00 from his own pocket.[48]

Government is not unmindful of the dysfunctional aspects of the patwaris. If a local self-government experiment could succeed, the lambardars, and their ilk could be dispensed with. As has been noted, the Basic Democracies scheme envisaged the police as eventually coming under the control of the union councils. At present this is questionable. Higher government officers are merely being encouraged and where necessary ordered to exert greater efforts in behalf of the villagers. The government is not yet contemplating the abolition of the patwari in West Pakistan (the institution does not exist in East Pakistan); rather, his salary has been increased and codes have been tightened. Moreover, visitation to the villages by higher authority is being pressed. The problem, however, remains—and the patwari seldom works alone. It is therefore incumbent on the more responsible senior administrators to devote more of their attention to the immediate needs of the villagers.

Ultimately, it is the Deputy Commissioner, the officer in charge of the entire district, who must ferret out corrupt officials. But in this activity the Deputy Commissioner is dependent on his subordinates. And simple delegation is not the answer. Even if his subordinates are ordered to work in the villages they are so few in number that they cannot do an adequate job. As Inayatullah and Shafi explain, Pakistan suffers from more than a "lack of personal commitment" to rural development among the officers of the professional services.

Below the district the next tier of administration is the thana/tehsil, which in West Pakistan usually oversees about 250 villages. "The number of officials in each tehsil level department is so limited that even if the officers are sufficiently interested in the work they could hardly find time to attend the problems of each village." The above-mentioned authors recall that when their study was being conducted there was only one agricultural assistant for the entire tehsil. He in turn was assisted by one field assistant for extension work. Similarly, members of the subinspector cooperative were responsible for seventy villages which they could not possibly visit even once in a year. The assistant inspector of schools, for example, is supposed to visit every school in his tehsil during the year. A hopeless task!

These examples could be multiplied in every sphere, but Inayatullah and Shafi emphasize another salient fact. These officers are without rapid transport and the difficulties of, for example, riding on horseback or simply proceeding on foot to remote locations deters them from taking any action at all. In addition to these handicaps the tehsil officers are often poorly trained and thus not equipped to serve the villagers. Delays in administration, either the result of ineptness or carelessness, and the ritualistic adherence of lower officials to written rules and procedures, most of which are archaic and dysfunctional in the present context, rounds out a somber picture of government at the grassroots.

> We have not been able to find an officer, with some rare exceptions, who could courageously and boldly initiate an action which he believes is conducive for national objectives, over the head of rules and regulations. The rules and regulations, unfortunately, serve as an excuse for inaction.[49]

Basic Democracies also sought to enlist the support of the village ulema. The villagers of Pakistan, East and West, maintain a high regard for the ulema.[50] If they can be brought into a political scheme, and motivated to accept government programs and willingly assist in community development projects, a real beginning could be made toward rural uplift. This would be especially important in the crucial area of population control where conservative religious elements continue to obstruct government efforts despite expenditures of energy and money.[51]

PEASANTS AND DEVELOPMENT

The rural development task is formidable in the extreme. National political consciousness in Pakistan's rural areas touches a select few. Hence the failure of community development programs can be attributed, in part, to the negative attitude of the population. Sociologists like M. I. Choudhury and M. A. Khan speak of a basic misconception about community development. While acknowledging the importance of physical improvements, they would stress non-material aspects.

A community development program, they observe, should bring the villagers together and inculcate in them a "spirit of self-help, responsibility, self-respect, initiative and confidence. It is necessary under this programme to cultivate among the masses the ability to understand their own problems or to solve them mostly with local resources." [52] Economic development is obviously impossible without considerable attitudinal change.

As this debate continues, the government endeavors to make the most of its scarce resources. In all development undertakings it is only too apparent that an agent of change is necessary to help in transforming the rural mentality as well as the physical surroundings. The villagers clearly cannot break out of their petrified shell without assistance. Either persons resident in the village or others who are familiar with its peculiar patterns and processes somehow must be motivated, trained, and equipped to carry the work forward. This is only the most fundamental requirement in a country as poor as Pakistan. The reinstatement of the multipurpose worker who evaporated with the abolition of the Village-AID program in 1961 is an absolute necessity; however, official recognition of this fact is not yet forthcoming.[53]

Pakistan is neither a democracy nor a totalitarian state. By the same subjective test it is still in the process of becoming a nation. Its fragmented population divided, subdivided, and cross-divided by geography, family, religion, caste, culture, language, education, tradition, bureaucratic hierarchies, political immaturity, and economic imbalance presents the observer with an amoeba-like entity; there is life, pulsing life, but little that lends itself to easy generalization. One need not conclude on a pessimistic note, however. Basic Democracies could not and should not have been expected to transform a society clinging so tenaciously to older, more familiar, and deeply rooted customs and institutions.

Basic Democracies was an essentially practicable and sensible device for instituting change, but patience and hard work along with personal sacrifice were also necessary. The system was structurally in harmony with known historic institutions; perhaps this was both its weakness and strength. It could be "understood" and worked—if traditional elites refrained from using it to maintain their privileged status. Basic Democracies was a rational, meaningful, and operable system and might still contribute to the laying of foundations of local self-government in Pakistan's rural area. However, success depends on the removal of impediments. Certainly the new martial law authorities are in an enviable position to put through the needed reforms. The crucial question seems to be whether they will perpetuate aspects of the system now that Ayub has left the center stage.

However, should the new regime decide to continue the system, more administrative power must be granted the Basic Democrats. Village officials like the patwaris and chowkidars must come under the direct control of the union councils, which should also be free from the overbearing restraints imposed by the controlling authority—the Deputy Commissioner. Similarly, the administrators charged with "servicing" the Basic Democracies should be upgraded. No distinction should be drawn between service in the Cooperative Department, Social Welfare Department, or any other administrative branch of government. In fact, only the very best, most senior and experienced officials should be assigned to work with the Basic Democracies.

Similarly, money will have to be made available to finance rural and local development. Although the union councils have taxing powers they have refrained from using them for fear they would lose favor with the more influential elements in the community. Subsequently, very little money has been generated in the villages. While recognizing that there are strict limits to what the villagers can contribute for community development projects, absolute dependence on government funds can only have deleterious effects. One approach would be for government to transfer some of its own taxing programs to the union councils where revenue could be used for reinvestment in local projects. Finally, training at all levels is essential. Pilot projects, school programs, adult education are all necessary to the successful development of local self-government.

Summarizing the Rural Scene

Speculating on the possible impact of the Basic Democracies on the rural power structure, Inayatullah believed it possible for a younger, more educated, and energetic leadership to emerge. He drew this conclusion on the basis of the psychological effects of land reforms. The rural folk, it was believed, would gradually understand that government no longer favored one group over another. He anticipated a diminution in the confidence of the landlords and a new assertiveness on the part of the cultivators. Reflecting optimism, he envisioned restrictions being imposed on the local police through the delegation of specific juridical power to the union councils. Furthermore, the development of the rural economy was supposed to bring about fundamental changes in the society. More traditional societal norms were expected to give way to functional ones. In political terms, these anticipated changes would reduce dependence on the zamindars and make it possible for the cultivators and artisans to elect their own representatives. The end result would be an achievement-oriented community, confident about its future and determined to improve its condition.

Surveying the Basic Democracies system ten years after it was introduced, it is not possible to discern the hoped-for impacts. True, some young people have emerged as leaders. In some regions skilled and dedicated people are struggling to change the rural life-style. In a number of instances tenant farmers have gained positions on union councils and kammi representation is a reality. These are only the exceptions, however. In the great majority of cases, the landlords reign supreme and the cultivators remain their subjects. Landlords still dominate the political system and in any future elections can be expected to "guide" their tenants.

The landlord class in West Pakistan, despite the land reforms, has not been displaced. In many respects the Ayub government revitalized its influence. The land reforms of 1958–59 were lenient and broke up only some of the very largest holdings. While the Ayub administration distributed some of the reacquired lands among the cultivators, in other instances the government retained control. Some of these lands, along with land reclaimed under the anti-waterlogging and desalinization pro-grams—as well as that land made cultivable with the development of new irrigation systems such as the Ghulam Mohammad Barrage—were set aside for cheap purchase by active and retired civil servants and members of the Armed Forces. In many cases these new landlords were much like their predecessors. They did not live or work upon the land themselves and in their absentee capacity hold their tenants at their mercy.

With the increasing emphasis on agriculture and agricultural pro-duction, landlords have become entrepreneurs. Today, the larger zamin-dars are more than just interested in the local importance that owner-ship gives them. Agriculture has become a profitable enterprise and the investment in tube-wells, fertilizer, new seed, and even mechanized equipment has produced the Green Revolution and made a number of landlords rich and hence politically prominent; this is true not only in the vicinity of their holdings but in the country at large.

The most cogent explanation for sustaining the big landlords in West Pakistan is economic rather than political, however. Ayub was warned that fragmentation of landholdings had already proceeded too far. The West Pakistan Land Reforms Commission Report (1959) revealed that from a total of 5.1 million landowners, 3.5 million had 5 acres or less and possess only 7.4 million acres of a total of 48.6 million. "In other words, about three-fifths of the cultivator families appear to be living on less than 2.5 acres. Not only is the holding small but it is scattered in a number of tiny plots situated at inconvenient distances one from another." A study made in the North West Frontier showed the follow-ing: "The average distance between each of the fragments and the largest fragment was 0.89 mile, whereas the maximum average distance from the largest fragment was 1.39 miles." These fragments "stand in the way of adopting modern techniques of agricultural production but also give the cultivator inadequate return for his labour, time and material investment." [54]

Drastic land reforms would only multiply the number of holdings on which farmers barely sustained their families. Marginal cultivation, it was argued, was not only uneconomic but dangerous. Pakistan depended on a productive agriculture, and the belief persisted that only when farms can be treated as business enterprises could the country hope to achieve its development goals. Ayub's advisers stressed keeping large holdings virtually intact while pressuring the landlords to reinvest profits toward the improvement of their properties. Hence, the landlords retained their holdings, proceeded to make them more productive and responded to the government's leniency by supporting official policies. Moreover, a minimum level was set for holdings generally; namely, 3 acres in East Pakistan and 12.5 acres of irrigated land in West Pakistan. Furthermore, the West Pakistan Land Reforms Commission emphasized the necessity of developing a province-wide program for consolidating fragmented holdings. The Consolidation of Holdings Ordinance (1960) was promulgated to prevent further subdivision of land despite the prevailing laws of Islamic inheritance.[55]

The West Pakistani land reforms leave the landlords in a dominant position and many social reformers have been angered by what they consider to be a sell-out to the prosperous elements. Lands of big zamindars are still cultivated by tenants-at-will or occupancy tenants. In East Pakistan large holdings are for all intents and purpose non-existent. But relatively speaking, even these smaller holdings give importance to the possessors. The relations between landlords and tenants in West Pakistan continue to be regulated by the Punjab Tenancy Act (1887), the North West Frontier Province Tenancy Act (1950), and the Sind Tenancy Act (1950). Other measures enacted in 1950 under the Punjab Protection and Restoration of Tenancy Rights are also in effect. All told, reforms safeguarding the interests of the tiller are meager and, in areas like Sind, barely discernible.[56]

Unquestionably there are two distinct political systems in Pakistan; the rural political system is separate from that prevailing in the municipalities and operates within the limits of a traditional socioeconomic framework. This does not mean that it exists in a vacuum. It has ties with the urban political system through the administrative instrument and the political parties but it is little affected by them. In other words, there appears to be very little feedback into the rural political system from either the urban intelligentsia or the national government. Little change can be observed in the traditional power structure, societal values or attitudes, and functions of the rural community.

Basic Democracies was established to rekindle the embers of self-reliance and personal confidence that might still flicker in the hearts and minds of some rural folk. But instead the status quo was maintained and older institutions which tended to nullify the efforts of the Basic Democrats were bolstered. It can be argued that the heavy hand of the landlord was necessary because the rural masses have not yet displayed the responsibility demanded of citizens in a modern nation. Some observers note that independence came too easily and too quickly to Pakistan and did not involve the rural population. And because those who became Pakistanis did not participate in achieving their freedom, little was learned from independence. As Hassan Habib has written:

> Our idealism was never tested in the furnace of self-sought adversity. The result was inevitable: we mistook the beginning for the end, the starting point for the destination.[57]

With Pakistan won, the leaders in the urban political system soon forgot their promises to the great majority of the population. The argument goes that those who should have done more for the people sensed only their own insecurity. Hence they proceeded to fashion what they could for themselves. Personal aggrandizement overshadowed patriotism. Social reformers like Hassan Habib have been appalled by the greed of some of their countrymen. He wrote:

> I have often had the lurking feeling that the popular phrase so frequently bandied about among not very popular circles—the phrase "raise the standard of living of the common man"—is an empty cliche which signifies nothing except contempt for the "common man"! As for "raising the standard of living" most of those who pretend to plan for doing so are really working mainly to raise still higher their already high standard, which is beyond all proportion to the average prevailing in the country. The growing chasm that divides the rich from the poor in our country, as in most of the countries of the Middle East and large parts of Asia, is too well know to bear repetition! [58]

Unable to break out of the political system which holds them fast, socioeconomic change is virtually impossible for the rural poor. Thus the tendency is to fall back on the time-tested institutions of family, caste, and other limited aggregational interests. The only way to break the vicious circle of parochialism and poverty in the villages is to alter the rural power structure. New leaders must emerge with creative and enlightened ideas and dedicated to toil; and this is possible only by bringing the urban political system into harmony with the rural. Innovations which are occurring in the cities and urban centers must filter down to the rural areas. The possible remedy for the stagnation of village life may be found in the cities and more will have to be done in the urban centers to influence development in the villages.

Chapter 8

End of an Era

MAN is intimately connected with his environment; influencing and being influenced by it. Hence consequent social and cultural patterns are usually the result of symbiotic relationships between the human species and the other creatures and things vying for a share of the earth's resources. In this complex web of life the dependence of one element on another cannot be overstressed. Human ecology narrows the field of study to man and his capacity to survive the vicissitudes of an environment which he only partially understands and hence only partially masters. Human ecology focuses on culture and the interdependence of human communities. Thus a study of political development in Pakistan must recognize the symbiotic relationship between its rural and urban political systems.

President Ayub's inability to exploit this rural-urban relationship frustrated his efforts at achieving ordered change. In spite of his intentions (and in some ways because of them) the compartmentalization of the rural and urban political systems was perpetuated. That this was also due to the machinations of elements within or associated with government to enhance and protect their privileged status has been surveyed in previous chapters. "Divide and rule" generally conjures up images of the British and their greed for empire; but it is just as much an instrument of other elites who are just as determined to cling to power despite their unpopularity.

The urban areas always presented the Ayub government with its stiffest opposition. Certainly the President's failure to carry Karachi and Dacca in the January 1965 election demonstrates the dissatisfaction of many city dwellers. It seemed to make little difference that the cities had made remarkable material progress. It may be considered something of a paradox that the areas having the least to show for the multiple efforts being made in expanding the nation's economy contained the staunchest supporters of the government.

172

ROOTS OF CONFLICT

The point need not be belabored that economic progress in a developing society's urban centers brings in its wake social dislocation, an expanding appetite for creature comforts, and heightened political consciousness. Concomitantly, greater literacy and a more attentive, aware, and involved public can cause a diminution in traditional values and modes of life. Along with a heightened desire to share the material product, there is the conscious feeling that authority should be less inhibiting and certainly more accepting of the principle of self-government. Even before the British departed from South Asia a popular stirring was in evidence.

Importantly, the British introduced political innovations in India's urban centers but confined them there.[1] When the British decided to "educate" some of their "subjects" in the art of self-government they must have known it would eventually mean their own downfall. How could they believe it possible to perpetuate their rule once a significant segment of the population had the will, determination, and knowledge to govern themselves! Moreover, given all the arguments that can be made to the contrary, the fact that they did or could do so little to resist the final push towards independence is indicative.

All the same, while the British ruled India political turbulence was seldom allowed to spill over into the countryside. There, the district administrators, zamindars, and their supporters reigned supreme. The political movements leading to the independence of India and Pakistan began and ended in the streets and bazaars of New Delhi, Calcutta, Bombay, Lahore, and Dacca. And while it is interesting to cite the British contribution to political socialization in South Asia, the Pakistanis, despite Basic Democracies, have yet to incorporate the rural areas. As David Apter remarks: "the socialization process becomes a tension-creating system."[2] But political tension must be controlled. The social fabric must be protected. Hence the reluctance to disturb rural society and the often severe restrictions imposed on the more animated groups in the cities.

Generally speaking, Pakistan's rulers are products of a military-bureaucratic tradition. Before independence they were functionally responsible for ensuring the security of the realm, maintaining internal order, and guaranteeing the efficient, economic administration of routine government activities. Led by British officers, indigenous members of the permanent services were inducted into elite aggregations and given

professional status. Imbued with an esprit de corps, they owed uncon-
ditional obedience to the British Raj. As members of the permanent
services they were insulated from the independence movements which
were dominated by the urban-based intelligentsia.

Thus the leaders of the independence movement came in direct
conflict with the military-bureaucratic institution. And the struggle for
independence was essentially aimed at wresting political power from the
bureaucrats. The intelligentsia, although confining their activities to the
cities, claimed widespread popular sanction and support. Motivated by a
conception of representative government and given the opportunity to
manage legislative institutions established under the Government of
India Act (1935) and the India Independence Act (1947), they felt
justified in arguing that they alone were politically responsive to the
masses. Compared with bureaucratic rule, there would appear to be no
denying their claim of popular legitimacy.

When the British transferred authority to the Congress Party in
India and the Muslim League in Pakistan they knew they were passing
political power to minority groups. However, while the Congress Party
was already an organized national political party, the same cannot be
said of the Muslim League. The Muslim League was, admittedly, unprepared to assume the responsibilities which were so abruptly forced
upon it. In spite of recent reorganization only the higher levels of the
party were affected. Clearly, only a semblance of grassroots organization
existed.

The clash of Muslim League leaders in Bengal, the uncertainty of
the outcome in the struggle for control of the North West Frontier, and
the arduous campaign in the Punjab where the Unionists sought to
maintain their control all betrayed the weakness of the party elite and
made efforts at organizing the peasant population impossible. Moreover,
it was only the dominant personality of Mohammad Ali Jinnah which
tempered the political in-fighting and calmed the passions of those who
were already impatient to harvest the fruits of independence. Jinnah
cautioned his followers to mind their manners and concentrate on the
desperate needs of the fledgling state. As Governor General and Head of
State he ordered his political associates to submerge their differences and
assist in the enormous task of national survival. Fully cognizant of the
politicians' weaknesses, Jinnah had no option but to turn to those members of the military and bureaucracy who had chosen Pakistan for their
homeland.

POLITICIZATION POSTPONED

The permanent services worked diligently to stabilize the nation. It was a task the politicians could not perform. The terrible bloodletting in the Punjab, the enormous influx of improverished Muslim refugees from India, the need to establish a new government from a fractured political edifice, the immediate threat to the security of the young state as a result of the Kashmir conflict, the petty political squabbling, and shortage of experienced administrators were only some of the more pressing matters facing the country's leaders in those first fateful months. It cannot be denied that it was the intellectual-politician who achieved the establishment of Pakistan, but it also cannot be repeated too often that it was the permanent services, "the steel frame," which sustained the infant state in its most trying hours.

National unity is a *sine qua non* for a nation-state. Despite the diversity of its history, ethnic composition, culture, and values, competing groups are expected to resolve differences before they undermine the country's stability. Although individuals instinctively identify themselves with family, tribe, caste, village, religion, etc., their supreme loyalty is owed the nation-state. In point of fact, however, national unity is problematical in nation-states suddenly gaining independent status. This is especially true in states where persons and groups have not personally experienced the struggle for national independence. If their loyalties have always been narrowly defined they cannot be expected to respond affirmatively to the dictates of a new order without first having been conditioned to understand their place in it.

With rare exceptions, government in the new nation-states brings together persons who have imbibed of the Western tradition and have assimilated, in ways peculiar to themselves, the ideas of the European world. This seems a valid judgment irrespective of the type of political system they choose to develop. What needs to be stressed is the relative similarity of the different nation-states insofar as rudimentary concepts and institutions are concerned.

The importance given to national boundaries and the peculiar character ascribed to persons living within them, the inviolability of the territory of the state, its legal equality with other states, and the right which it reserves to itself in settling domestic disputes are all features and characteristics of nation-states. Loosely interpreted, international law describes an independent state as a territorial unit wherein reside a people who are guided and protected by a government which can, if it so desires, enter into relationships with governments of other nation-states. This deliberate simplification explains how territorial units gain admission into the "family" of independent nation-states. Nevertheless, the standard for acceptability in the family of nations is something significantly different from one for establishing a stable and viable nation-state.

Nation-states of the European tradition (identified with the Western world) evolved through numerous historic stages, only the most recent bringing about the politicization of the general population. It is important to note that European peoples became organized into culturally identifiable units before they began insisting on political liberties. In many of the new nation-states a colonial dispensation has reversed this process. In Pakistan and India political independence preceded cultural fusion, and the diverse populations that inhabit these two countries are not altogether aware that they owe supreme loyalty to a superordinate authority.[3]

Pakistan, like other Asian and African states, emerged with startling suddenness and with no time to work out internal relationships. Where a myriad of linguistic, ethnic, and regional loyalties persist, where former colonial boundaries impose an arbitrary settlement on the drawing of frontiers, and where a grinding poverty saps the vitality of the majority, the question of how to establish nationhood is imposing. Pakistan's leaders have established as their primary task stability and national unity. This presents a colossal challenge but there are few clues as to how it is to be accomplished.

In the quest for national unity, fear is a conventional weapon. Persistent external threats are supposedly why vigilance cannot be relaxed, why the only "true" leaders are those presently in power, and why stern measures are needed to protect the nation. In sum, the nationalism reflected in the policies and pronouncements of new elites is constructed of fearful negativisms.[4] Herein also is the logic for permanent revolution; for it is the task of leaders to articulate the desires and aspirations of a people whose national goals are still on the horizon.

This is one explanation of why Pakistani officialdom is divided in its perception of the urban political system. While the urban system is intertwined with the national ethos, and the city folk are by and large cognizant of their identity as Pakistanis, there remain large questions concerning roles. There is little evidence that private persons in the municipalities would voluntarily contribute their time, energy, and/or wealth for the general development of the country. Similarly, the village is seldom entered by the more sophisticated urbanites. Nor do they show much inclination to do so despite the clamor about building grassroot political organizations. Communication with the rural population, therefore, is reserved for government officials. Of course the argument can also be proffered that the government does not want urban dwellers meddling in village affairs. The government, so the argument goes, wants a free hand in the villages in order to perpetuate administrative dominance. The point has already been made that government collaborates with the zamindars in order to control the cultivators. Neutralization of the rural scene frees resources needed for urban control.

THE URBAN RESPONSE

If the above is valid, then it certainly becomes necessary to cite the political grievances of the urban intelligentsia. The intelligentsia is comprised of professional people—teachers, lawyers, journalists, doctors, etc.—and also includes the student population and other less organized but no less important artists, musicians, and poets. In another category, but not to be overlooked in observing urban politics, are low-ranking government officers—clerks, typists, and personal assistants—who are often discreetly vocal and usually anti-establishment. Another group gaining in political assertiveness is that of the nascent labor unions. This is especially true in Karachi and to an increasing extent in East Pakistan. However, it should be noted that thus far the more important urban political leaders usually emanate from among retired civil servants, military officers, absentee landlords, the legal profession, or more sophisticated ulema. This is not to suggest that all these "articulate" aggregations are absolutely anti-government. But if a generalization is warranted, the great majority were decidedly against the political innovations of President Ayub Khan.

While political action necessitates the organization of coalitions, Pakistan's intelligentsia has failed to create disciplined, integrated, broad-based associations. Coalitions, it has been declared, are normally held together by the "glue of ambiguity" which enables people to perceive diverse goals as somewhat related. In Pakistan, however, coalitions have never held together long enough for assimilation or integration to take place. For example, members of the legal profession have joined on occasion with some of the leading ulema, and journalists have been known to plead the cause of the students, but the linkages between them remain weak and temporary at best.

The intelligentsia, whether it be representative of modernity or tradition, secularism or religious renewal, nationalism or cosmopolitanism, ultimately will agree on only one issue. They are characteristically dissatisfied with their rulers and eager to depose them.

The intelligentsia *never* accepted the Ayub Constitution of 1962 or the form of government it imposed on the country. Given opportunities, some joined political parties in order to voice their displeasure more effectively. But the overwhelming majority did not or could not take advantage of these organizations. Teachers are much like lower grade government officers and clerks and thus unable to participate in formal political activity. Only a few doctors are politically motivated; most are absorbed by their calling. Most journalists were under strict supervision and only those working for papers outside the government-controlled Press Trust dared get involved in politics. This left the lawyers, artists, retired civil servants and military officers, some absentee landlords, members of the ulema, the students, and representatives of the new commercial class to spearhead the political war against President Ayub.

The intelligentsia resented being governed by persons whom they considered no better than themselves and in many respects inferior. They were dismayed that the supreme power of the state could be used against them. While modernists among them looked upon Ayub's government as politically illegitimate, traditionalists judged it to be heretical. The special privileges and attitude of the bureaucratic class (especially the CSP) were principal targets, as has been shown in Chapter 6. A number of bureaucrats held positions of exceptional authority under alien rulers while the intelligentsia seemed to be risking everything. Having seized control of the state, these same administrators now sought to silence the people's "true" representatives.

Few members of the intelligentsia are prepared to accept the notion that the elite bureaucracy is apolitical, impartial, and only interested in serving the nation. Rather, the opinion is held that they are a chosen group who, in collaboration with the military on the one side and the landlords and certain entrepreneurial elements on the other, have succeeded in reinforcing their influential position—their prime concern being the enhancement of private interests. The conclusion drawn from this perception is simple: the propertied and privileged classes [5] assist one another in supporting the political status quo while they improve their personal and family economic positions.

Some urbanites view the Army as an unwitting partner in an insidious plot. Others insist the Army has always had ties with the landlords and now, through intermarriage, has also drawn closer to the bureaucratic and entrepreneurial classes. Thus the Army is not free of criticism. Conversely, the Army high command's perception of the intelligentsia is less than favorable. Were the Army to support rather than dominate the intelligentsia it could upset the relative national equilibrium, and there is genuine concern that the ensuing instability might lead to serious disorganization. Moreover, the fear that Pakistan's "aggressive" neighbor, India, might take advantage of the country's internal weakness is an important factor in gauging the solidarity of the Armed Forces.

SUCCESS OR FAILURE

Pakistan's economic successes have been summarized. The achievements under the Second Five Year Plan were widely applauded. In some instances the country has been held up as a model for other developing nations. Political stability, few restraints on free enterprise, reasonably efficient administration, and the effective use of foreign assistance have all helped to bolster a successful image. However, this progress did not ease the impoverishment of the overwhelming majority. The concentration of national wealth in few hands was abrasive. And only the intelligentsia could speak out against obvious displays of greed.

While insisting that Pakistan would become a welfare state, Ayub had no compunctions about the rich increasing their fortunes. Moreover, the President's explanation that profits were being reinvested in the nation's economic program did not quiet the critics. But by far the most dismal aspect of this scenario was Ayub's personal involvement. During the 1964–65 presidential campaign, the President, and particulaily his family, came under heavy fire. Ayub was accused of becoming the richest man in the country. He had in fact acquired large tracts of fertile farmland and certainly allowed his sons to build an extensive industrial empire. While ridiculing the allegation that he was the wealthiest person in the land, Ayub did not deny these allegations.[6] Undoubtedly the President would have developed some leverage with the intelligentsia had he relinquished his holdings and compelled his sons to retire from the business world. But the fact that he did neither flawed his administration beyond repair.

THE QUESTION OF IDEOLOGY [7]

The urban political system can be classified as leftist and radical. Although Ayub's policies and public statements were also cast in this spirit, in practice they were otherwise. President Ayub repeated over and again that the country's first need was political stability. Economic progress and social change would follow in that order. The President's formula for modernizing Pakistan was perhaps too simple. Real political stability implies popular satisfaction and a general acceptance of the prevailing governmental process. In Pakistan, however, an endless battle for political survival is being waged; political unity is undermined by regional issues and urban-rural divisions are no less exacerbating. If this were not enough, the struggle between modernizers and traditionalists complicates the situation further.

The conflict between those in power and those who want it defies ideological identification, despite the awareness that many of the conservative landlords and administrators are on one side while the intellectuals and emergent laboring class are often on the other. Ayub, a pacemaker where political innovation was concerned, was a pragmatist and showed little patience for philosophical and/or metaphysical reasoning. For an extended period he also proved to be a successful manager of men and issues. Certainly he was capable of manipulating people and events. Although lacking charisma, he was a realist who often gave full reign to his intuitive judgment. And it did not fail him until illness sapped his energy.

If realism is equated with conservatism then perhaps Ayub was ideologically identifiable; but there is something wrong with this synthesis. In all societies personal interest, more than ideological commitment, shapes political behavior. For example, bureaucrats are conservative only to the extent that their calling demands loyalty to government. However, while they support authority and obediently follow commands they have not necessarily accepted government policies. As public officials they are supposed to remain apolitical; personal convictions are never to be confused with professional functions.

What taints the bureaucracy is its heritage and this cannot be wished away. Theirs is not to reason why! There are bureaucrats who openly courted the President because it was in their interest to do so. There were others who supported his policies because they believed their calling demanded unquestioning obedience. There were still others who followed orders in grudging fashion. If a search of the records is made it will be difficult to find an officer who took the fateful decision to leave the service rather than enforce a directive he could not support. In other words, to label the bureaucracy as conservative seems to miss the point. A pervasive syndrome in Pakistani society is insecurity. With this in mind, it is doubtful that even the most critical bureaucrat would chance jeopardizing his personal status.

Similarly, in discussing ideological tendencies in the intelligentsia it is possible there are as many conservatives among them as radicals, and perhaps more. Again what remains paramount is the need for personal security. For example, members of the legal community who were overwhelmingly against Ayub feared the undermining of their affluence. The elimination of the parliament, the long period of martial law followed by the promulgation of the 1962 Constitution which they had practically no say in drafting, the clash over the justiciability of fundamental rights, and the emergence of the Basic Democrats with their formation into an electoral college and their power to hear and settle legal disputes under the Muslim Family Laws and Conciliation Courts Ordinance, all infuriated as well as frightened the legal fraternity. When Ayub chose members of the bar to advise him as he did with Manzur Qadir, S. M. Zafar, and S. S. Pirzada, there still was no appeasing the lawyers. They felt the President had betrayed them by devising a system which denied them their "day in court." Ideology certainly played an insignificant role in these disputes.

The President was gifted in the art of conciliation so long as ideological differences were absent. For example, on February 17, 1967, Ayub inaugurated the centenary celebrations of the West Pakistan High Court and after lauding the judges and lawyers turned to the matter of their dissatisfaction. The President told his audience that an appropriate reform body would be set up to examine the general body of laws and to suggest improvements.[8] He appealed to the judges and members of the Bar to submit suggestions for modifying or introducing new laws. In calling for this assistance the President was fully cognizant that only two months before a new West Pakistan Bar Council had been elected and every one of its members were critics of his administration.[9] It is noteworthy, however, that the majority of these members were not radicals in any ideological sense.

Before leaving the ideological argument, it should also be remembered that the more conservative members of Pakistani society are to be found in the ulema. All the same, the arch-conservative Maulana Maudoodi never supported the President and went to prison time and again for his outspoken criticisms. In early 1967 he was jailed again, this time because he urged a demonstration against the government's "radical behavior" in establishing a committee to declare when the Eid moon (ending the month of Ramadan and the long Muslim fast) had been sighted. In 1966 the old custom of permitting the ulema to announce the moon's sighting was followed—and as in previous years varying inaccuracies had led to much confusion.

By the end of the month of Ramadan tempers are short and people are eager to return to their normal ways. Thus when hopes are raised that the moon has been sighted, then dashed, then raised again, as in 1966, it can cause the government embarrassment. To avoid a repeat performance in 1967 the authorities pressed ahead with their proposal to set up a board which would have the sole power to determine the exact moment of the sighting. As must have been expected, a number of the ulema bitterly disagreed with the decision and five of the most notable, including Maudoodi, were imprisoned.

It should be emphasized that the Ayub Government had to ward off religious agitation on a number of occasions. The Muslim Family Laws, which the President insisted on implementing through special ordinance in 1961, infuriated many conservative elements. Few ulema supported the family planning program, the controls on Waqf, or the expansion of the banking system with all its so-called anti-Islamic features (particularly the Islamic tenet which enjoins Muslims not to accept interest or usury). But despite the opposition of the traditionalists and conservative orthodoxy, the government pressed its programs.

Example after example can be provided but the conclusion would not be different; Ayub's policies were conservative in structure but less so in function. Some issues clearly were more ideological in Ayub's conflict with the intelligentsia—foreign policy, the growth and concentration of private capital, etc.—but even these tend toward ambiguity when placed on a conservative-radical continuum.

The Democratic Issues

It follows that there is little in the argument that the forces of democracy were with the opposition in their fight with the Ayub administration. S. R. Ghauri, writing in the *Morning News* of Dacca, offered his impressions of a session of the National Assembly. "In the National Assembly, yesterday," he wrote, "every one was waxing eloquent about 'democracy.' . . . For what was clearly an act of 'democracy' to the Treasury Benches, to the Opposition Benches it was an act of 'dictatorship.' . . . For politicians, democracy is an affair of the heart—and belly." One opposition member, Hasan A. Shaikh, said the country was living through a period of tyranny; and the leader of the opposition, Nurul Amin, while acknowledging that the government-proposed Seventh Amendment Bill to the Constitution was democratic, chose to describe it as an act of "democratic niggardliness." The Seventh Amendment, passed on December 14, 1966, empowered members of the Assembly to move amendments to ordinances without prior consent of the President. Before this amendment to the Constitution, ordinances issued by the President could only be approved or disapproved—the Assembly had no power to amend them.

The former Muslim League Chief Minister likened the government to one giving ashes to a beggar as alms. When the beggar was asked why he was pleased with this gift he replied: "I know the ashes are worthless, but this is a good beginning for this would accustom the miser to give something—by and by." Another opposition member, Arif Iftikhar, picked up where Nurul Amin left off. He accused the government of scattering "crumbs" in front of the opposition. Indirectly attacking the President, he added that he would not insult the intelligence of the Law Minister who was present in the House by indicating he had thought up the Seventh Amendment. "It was of course thought up for him," he sarcastically concluded. In reply to the opposition barbs a government member reminded the Assembly that no matter the occasion, the opposition "starts shouting about autonomy and democracy—their red medicine." [10]

Of course the speeches and debates in the National Assembly were not the only means employed by the intelligentsia. Many used their professional associations to press their demands. Others applied pressure through their respective political parties. No approach was particularly effective, however. In sanctioning the play of political parties in 1962–63, the President made it clear he would not tolerate an act which in his judgment disrupted the public peace. When Mujibur Rahman presented his Six Point Program in 1966 the Government did not stand idly by. Mujib was imprisoned along with his followers while one of East Pakistan's leading vernacular newspapers was closed down and its editor incarcerated.

Later in a speech in the eastern province, President Ayub again said he would stifle all "disruptionists who were out to destroy national solidarity and unity in the country." [11] Most people were inclined to take the President seriously when he warned of "civil war" if it meant mantaining the territorial integrity of the state. However, with such comments Ayub could not expect to win many converts. It also tended to sully his democratic objectives.

AYUB: A SUMMATION PROFILE

Ayub frankly admitted his inadequacies and shortcomings but never questioned his own patriotism. But he was deeply suspicious of the motives of others. He had passed through Pakistan's turbulent years without ever being a mere observer of unfolding events. He used the Army time and again as an instrument of crisis-control to maintain civil order or ward off international threats. When Ayub seized power in 1958 it was with the conviction that no other course was open to him but to run the country himself. Hence his utter contempt for the politicians whose malpractices he perceived as responsible for his assuming authority.

Ayub perhaps dreamed of the development of a loyal political opposition in Pakistan. Had the politicians dropped their idea of restoring the parliamentary system and liquidating the Basic Democracies and agreed to support the Constitution of 1962, he might possibly have relaxed his grip and provided them with a larger voice in the country's affairs. But so long as they persisted in demanding an absolute change in the political structure of Pakistan's government, he felt he was duty-bound to meet their challenge with a stern response.

Speaking in Dacca in the President's behalf, Law Minister S.M. Zafar, after the passage of the Seventh Amendment to the Constitution, warned the East Pakistani "regionalists" that no quarter would be given should they persist in their agitation. No previous government had done more for regional autonomy. The continuing demand for more provincial power was interpreted as an old demagogic ploy, its only objective being to excite the emotions of a sensitive population and turn it against the President. The Law Minister intimated that statements calling for greater provincial autonomy would henceforth be considered a treasonous act and the government felt justified in using countermeasures. He reported "they [the opposition] would be identified, hunted, crushed and destroyed. This country is one and united and will remain one and united!" [12]

With such threats it was not suprising to find the opposition reconsidering the options. Pakistanis take their politics seriously but no one is really supposed to get hurt for playing the game too strenuously. President Ayub governed Pakistan for more than ten years but he never once called for or allowed the execution of a political prisoner. Countless persons were seized and imprisoned, parties severely restrained, and newspapers closed, but no one paid the supreme penalty for his acts. The same cannot be said for many other countries where the infractions are no more serious. Undoubtedly this is to Ayub's credit. It may also explain his forced retirement in March 1969.

It might be going too far to suggest that Ayub's humaneness gave the East Pakistani opposition an opportunity to announce they intended to engage in an all-out struggle against "Ayubshahi" (King Ayub). But the record speaks for itself. In an ultimatum to the President, Nurul Amin, head of the National Democratic Front and leader of the opposition in the National Assembly, Ataur Rahman Khan, who returned to the political wars after the expiration of EBDO, Abdul Haq, standing in for the ailing Maulana Bhashani (leader of the National Awami Party), Farid Ahmad of the Nizam-i-Islam Party, Alam Azam of the Jamaat-i-Islami, and Shah Azizur Rahman of the Awami League, all demanded that East Pakistan be granted more autonomy by March 22, 1967, or they would be compelled to launch a non-cooperation movement. Ultimatums like this one had been hurled at the government before and, as in the past, it registered little impact. Thus the dissidents were not silenced. At least not this time. Ayub was an ardent believer in democracy but it obviously was of a unique variety. Westerners would have difficulty in analyzing it and sophisticated Pakistanis could never accept it.

The Opposition in Retreat

The Pakistan Observer of Dacca summed up the ineptness of the political opposition as the inability to evolve a unified organization and platform. It can be suggested that their problems were more complex. Attempts at joining together were more symbolic than real, and no party commanded a following of sizable proportions outside the urban areas. The epithets hurled at the government were in keeping with conventional political techniques, but barely created more than "ripples" of enthusiasm among persons "long be-numbed by the dizzying merry-go-round of opportunistic politics." [13]

The general population seldom appeared more apathetic. Two of the leading exponents of opposition unity were Choudhri Mohammad Ali and Maulvi Farid Ahmad, both representing the Nizam-i-Islam. Together they pressed for a minimum program to which the various parties could agree. They cautioned the opposition not to lose sight of the example set by the combined opposition in the India elections of February 1967. The once unassailable Congress Party suffered a series of ignominious defeats, not because any one party rivaled the Congress in organization and influence, but because together the opposition could mobilize and exploit nationwide discontent.

The inability of the Pakistani opposition to merge their differences and contest Ayub's power must be partially attributed to the presidential system and the restrictions imposed by government. Time and again the President would say "the politicians would be permitted to participate in political activity within the four walls of law and not outside it." Commenting on the lifting of the EBDO restrictions, however, he warned them about the necessity of working within the political framework he had erected. Caustically, he noted: "if they thought they could again bring back the days of political anarchy and disruption, they were living in a fool's paradise." [14] Again on December 7, 1966, Ayub explained that there was only one version of a political party—the type that works for the solidarity and stability of the country. The essence of politics in Pakistan is survival.

Ayub's perception of the politicians was never really corrected. In his myopic vision they were agitators and demagogues, running amuck and inciting people to demonstrate and riot over issues which are not easily or quickly resolved. While he seemed prepared to allow the dissident political parties to oppose him in an election campaign he insisted that they follow unalterable guidelines. He also urged them to engage in non-political activities, i.e., contribute time to family planning programs, assist in the development of new agricultural techniques, provide education, and assist in the reclamation of land ravaged by nature and abused by man. The opposition was not about to let Ayub have his way, however, and refused to join in any of these activities. Agitational politics may have been a primitive medium but the opposition was determined to employ it.

Ayub emphasized the politics of stability. Stability was conducive to economic development but it also postponed political development. The emphasis on political stability in fact was a retreat to the vice-regal tradition and the dominant oriental mode.[15] Reference here is to total power, arbitrary decision-making, and the blind obedience of the masses. Given this set of conditions a leader can be compassionate and conciliatory, but also ruthless. The argument has been proffered that Ayub preached liberal cosmopolitanism but practiced authoritarianism.

THE STACKED SYSTEM

Even before his illness Ayub declared he did not want to be elected President for life.[16] The original idea for such an election is said to have come from a Basic Democrat of Nawabshah in West Pakistan. The President's critics, however, insisted the question was planted by Ayub; that it was the opening shot in a devious campaign to perpetuate his rule. In the hope of thwarting what it interpreted as a clandestine maneuver, the opposition in the National Assembly moved an amendment to

Article 9 of the Constitution which related to the presidency. The original clause simply said "there shall be a President of Pakistan." Makhlesuzzaman Khan, the opposition member pressing the matter, sought to have this changed so that only East Pakistani candidates would be considered in the 1970 elections.

The notion that Presidents should come alternately from West and East Pakistan was quickly defeated by the government majority, however. Later, an editorial in *The Pakistan Times* of Lahore (December 5, 1966) instead of clarifying the issue left it in doubt. After showing satisfaction with the President's reply, the paper analyzed Ayub's role and concluded that he should continue as long as his health permitted and age did not weaken his grip or impair his faculties. The editorial read in part:

> After all great national leaders have had life-Presidency conferred on them by grateful nations. (President Nasser is one notable example.)
>
> . . . life-Presidency . . . would be his for the picking. He has very aptly pointed out that by accepting life-Presidency he would be depriving the people of their constitutional rights to elect their President every five years; and since he is himself the author of the present constitution, he would be the last person to depart from any of its basic provisions.

Ayub Khan undoubtedly considered a life-presidency; he must have also weighed the possibility of constructing a one-party state. But both objectives were beyond his reach once viral pneumonia sapped his stamina. What Ayub demanded then was the acceptance of the 1962 Constitution, albeit in modified but not emasculated form. He was seriously wedded to a concept of democracy but he was just as strongly opposed to the transplantation of "foreign systems."

When Ayub denigrated Western philosophers and scholars, as he was prone to do, he was usually striking at those opposition members who justified their attacks by citing from Locke, Mill, and Bentham. Also, Muslim traditionalism was still a strong force and this was one way of currying its favor. Of course there is much in the argument that Ayub felt Western thought and experience had only token relevance for Pakistan. Nevertheless what does stand out is the opposition's use of Western dogma to intimidate his regime.

Ayub remarked that it is one thing to respect such things as the rules of procedure of the House of Commons or the American Congress; it was quite something else, however, to imagine that they were applicable in Pakistan. If the opposition was unable to make effective progress in the National Assembly, it was due to their failure to win the confidence of the people. The East Pakistan *Dacca Times* on March 26, 1965, presented a different explanation. "The people have, throughout the country, despised the National Assembly election results as a 'sham' and are convinced more than before that the system of indirect election has got to be done away with."

The opposition complained bitterly about the "brute majority" of the government party running roughshod over all opposition proposals. Nevertheless it did have a larger voice immediately after the promulgation of the 1962 Constitution.[17] In the 1965 elections, however, the Basic Democrats deserted the opposition en masse, and naturally there was talk of foul play. While accepting this latter argument, the *Dacca Times* admitted the division in the ranks of the opposition was also an important factor in their defeat.

> A scrutinizing reading of the polling table indicates that if the Combined Opposition would have acted in a more cohesive manner (without leaving some seats open and stopping any opposition men from contesting the election against their official nominations) and also if their decision to contest the election and the nominations that followed were not so delayed or haphazard as they were, the opposition would have won about half of the National Assembly seats in the province [East Pakistan] . . . in West Pakistan, it was more a story of suppression than election.[18]

While the government counseled the opposition to improve its image by behaving in a more constructive manner, the opposition emphasized that the political system was stacked against it. The indirect elections which gave the Basic Democrats the sole authority to elect the President and members of the legislatures ruined any chance of their achieving power. The Basic Democrats understood they would be disbanded if the opposition came to power and thus eagerly did the President's bidding. The President's response to this complaint was that every candidate had an equal chance to lay his case before the Basic Democrats. If the opposition accepted the B.D. system they might meet with less resistance and possibly more success.

While the opposition parties were disorganized and incapable of mounting a concerted offensive the government party tried to enlist the support of a wider following. The Pakistan Muslim League was reorganized at all levels in 1966 and its structure made to coincide with the various tiers of the Basic Democracies.[19] Moreover, a number of government study teams visited Yugoslavia and Communist China with the object of ascertaining the essential techniques for motivating self-help and community participation; social mobilization was the ultimate goal. Cultural and ecological characteristics in Yugoslavia and China in no way compared with those prevailing in Pakistan; but the country could build a national political organization which in collaboration with the bureaucracy could train, motivate, direct, and enforce the government's program. Hence the co-mingling of the Pakistan Muslim League with the Basic Democracies. Once again Pakistanis were to be told that the only party really representative of their interests was the government's own. Even those politicians who since the declaration of martial law had been prevented from participating in politics by the Elective Bodies Disqualification Order (EBDO) were now requested to sign up.[20] Needless to say, many did.

THE LAST CHAPTER

Ayub Khan earnestly desired to construct popular democratic institutions. Although his constitution endowed him with exceptional powers, it was not a rigid document. Amendments were in the direction of liberalization. In like measure he launched the Basic Democracies as a substitute for the more sophisticated parliamentary process. Ayub wanted to believe Basic Democracies could educate the peasants; that in time they would appreciate and be capable of operating an advanced system of representation. Hence the system was deliberately flexible. And as with the Constitution, modifications contributed to the slow devolution of responsibility on the elected members of the councils. Ayub also tried to revitalize the Muslim League party. Emphasis was on attracting a varied membership while significant steps were taken to connect it with the Basic Democracies. Thus the Constitution, the Basic Democracies, and Ayub's political party appeared to fit a national blueprint. In theory they meshed; in practice they not only did not harmonize but remained inchoate.

Without minimizing Ayub's accomplishments, one must conclude that political development in Pakistan was more myth than reality. Ayub, despite all his declarations, postponed political for economic development. Though interrelated they did not prove reinforcing. Hence the President's alienation of the city folk, his dependence on the permanent services, and the subsequent retardation of political goals. Here also is reason for the survival of the rural power structure. Perhaps the President was correct in saying the country was not ready for a full-blown experiment in self-government, but to persist in this argument was bound to conjure up images of the country's former white overlords. Traditional elites can help sustain the political status quo; they cannot mobilize or inspire a suspicious population. The maintenance of the traditional power structure actually reinforced the apathy of the masses.[21]

The result was a greater reliance on paternalism. But paternalism was no substitute for creative, selfless leadership. Dominant groups in the power structure were less than enthusiastic about implementing policies which aimed at transforming Pakistani society. They may have paid lip service to President Ayub's goals but it was unrealistic to expect their support for a program which endangered property, privilege, and position. This being the case, it mattered little how much time lesser administrators spent "educating" the peasantry or restraining the students. Social engineering, more so than economic development, required a forward-looking political process.

Pakistan's society is desperately in need of astute leadership to provide it with an effective political voice. If not forthcoming, the influence of special interests is destined to reach a precarious level; history already offers numerous illustrations of impoverished and submissive populations suddenly turning on their masters and subduing them with terrible fury. Of course, somewhere in the multitude is the artful manager of political revolution. National leaders know these stories in all their gory details. Undoubtedly they are cognizant of the consequences if they fail to respond at the crucial moment.

The problems Ayub faced were not so dissimilar from those puzzling his contemporaries in other countries; however, in his desire to avert a violent upheaval he still chose to place total confidence in the permanent services. Their patriotism was taken for granted; they were the most trustworthy in executing his programs. Moreover, he identified with them. In a real sense, the permanent services represented Ayub's political party. Although he tried not to see the inconsistencies of his dependence on bureaucratic decision-making, he must have been aware that he was avoiding a real test of his political experiment and hence jeopardizing the entire program of national reconstruction.

If Ayub was serious about changing Pakistani society, then another way might have been found. National unity, true integration, could not succeed by perpetuating the status quo. Easing the disparity between East and West Pakistan, closing the gap between bureaucrats, landlords, and peasants, and satisfying the urban sophisticates involved more than rhetoric. National unity implies more than political stability, economic progress for a few, and social stagnation. Yet, in all frankness, this is what President Ayub's performance personified. National unity therefore proved to be a mirage, always on the horizon, never within reach. And in the winter of 1968–69 the country was plunged into chaos. Once the turbulence swelled, all pretense at building a new society disappeared.

With the threat of widespread anarchy in the air the government was forced to react with even sterner measures. The last chance of legitimating Ayub's political system drowned in the blood of youthful martyrs. It was a forlorn personality who announced his retirement on March 25, 1969. Martial law is a byproduct of the permanent services. Their survival remains synonymous with national survival, but this too has little to do with national unity.

Epilogue

PRESIDENT AYUB KHAN'S priorities were misplaced, and future Pakistani governments cannot afford to repeat his errors. Martial law has again created a surface calm, but neither martial law nor the new tranquility are likely to last. Either the present regime will initiate radical innovations or it must eventually succumb to one that will. This is the legacy of the Ayub Era.

East–West Pakistan compatibility is essential to Pakistan's future. Sheikh Mujibur Rahman's derisive comment that the Yahya Khan regime "can't repair a building by just using whitewash" is informative. The new allocation of 53 percent of development funds for East Pakistan will not be sufficient to stem the tide of criticism, let alone guarantee Pakistani unity, and the country can no longer tolerate different political systems in its rural and urban regions. Moreover, special privilege has lost its functionality. Only when officialdom develops programs in cooperation with articulate interest groups can campaigns be mounted to mobilize the population for nation-building tasks. If a choice must be made between placing more restictions on the intelligentsia or on the prosperous classes and castes, the decision should be in favor of exerting more pressure on the latter. There is every reason to believe the wealthy and privileged can be "persuaded" to cooperate. The Monopolies and Restrictive Trade Practices (Control and Prevention) Ordinance (1970), which would provide measures against undue concentrations of economic power and other no longer tolerable trade practices, points to a concerted attack on heretofore sacrosanct family empires.[1]

Alfred Diamant suggests that political development is principally a matter of system capabilities. The key problem is how to confront new goals and demands without putting excessive strain on the political system. The question he raises centers less on maintaining old institutions than on how to develop new ones. By the same token, normative values need not be considered sacrosanct but should give way to innovative experimentation.[2]

Painless change is impossible, but change must proceed without throwing a society into chaos. Political development must allow for, but at the same time regulate social and economic change. Resistance to change in the name of political stability or systems maintenance fosters stagnation which can only lead to increased frustration and conflict. Lucian Pye cautions that political development cannot be gained at the expense of other forms of development. Similarly, economic development cannot progress at the cost of social change. What he refers to as the multi-dimensional process of social change involves all aspects and types of development.[3] Pye's development syndrome is a bit like Diamant's in that he too emphasizes the capacity of the political system to cope with demands made upon it. When a political system fails this test a state of disequilibrium exists; hence when political development ceases, political violence begins.

Pakistan has already experienced considerable political violence, but visible signs thus far are little more than the proverbial tip of the iceberg. Failure to understand this may ultimately mean the state's doom. Pakistan's single most important requirement still lies in the creation of a sense of national community. Islam alone cannot do the job. Disparate regions, classes, and castes must find a new integration denominator. This means dislocating the prevailing sociopolitical structure and necessarily reinforcing radical movements. A radical takeover does not imply a Communist victory, but it does involve a more popularly based innovative process. Moreover, this should be preferred to an armed struggle which might destroy any opportunity for constructive compromise. When freedom and necessity are opposed courses of action it is advisable to buffer the former, for it is always the weaker of the two. As Hannah Arendt notes: the "liberation from necessity, because of its urgency, will always take precedence over the building of freedom." [4]

Revolutions in freedom are not easy. No one can underestimate the difficulties involved in accelerating political change, or in permitting heretofore politically "irresponsible" elements to play a significant role in decision-making and plan implementation. Transformation is bound to prove costly and certainly will take time. Yet transformation must proceed with the consent and support of the intelligentsia or the consequences of a shattering revolution must be anticipated.[5]

To guard against a catastrophe the government of General Yahya Khan will have to win the confidence of the intelligentsia—and this group must be convinced that the attempt is not just a clever deception to neutralize its political activity. Political development, if it means policies leading to the evolution of self-governing institutions, also implies giving the intelligentsia political latitude. Only then is it likely to limit the use of such traditional instruments as agitation and violence.

Political parties organized by the intelligentsia should be encouraged to engage in constructive programs, but it is also necessary to provide opportunities for achieving political power. Only in an atmosphere of trust is it possible to strike a meaningful bargain. Only when persuasion begins to displace coercion is effective political bargaining possible.[6]

The 1962 presidential Constitution could be salvaged after significant modifications, and it is distressing to witness its total elimination. It would be preferable to resurrecting the 1956 parliamentary Constitution or even drafting an entirely new one along similar lines. Parliamentary experiments remain inconsistent with Pakistan's political culture. Direct elections of the national and provincial legislatures and, most important, the governors of East and West Pakistan are indispensable. But these can be conducted under a presidential system. Along with the direct election of the President, genuine popular participation could go far in reducing tension between the people and the government.

President Yahya Khan's decision to proceed with general elections in October 1970 is laudable. So is the emphasis on the principle of "one man, one vote." But these are hardly panaceas. The break up of the One Unit of West Pakistan is fraught with dangers. The over-all arrangement is likely to inflame rather than dampen regional passions. Moreover, the Legal Framework Order of 1970 calling for the following distribution of seats in the National Assembly can be expected to generate considerable controversy.

NATIONAL ASSEMBLY OF PAKISTAN

	GENERAL	WOMEN
East Pakistan	162	7
Punjab	82	3
Sind	27	1
Baluchistan	4	1
N.W.F.P.	18 ⎫	
Tribal	7 ⎭	1
	300	13

It is impossible to believe that the acrimonious exchanges in the legislatures, so prominent in the last twenty years, will suddenly disappear. On the contrary, the debates may be so heated as to negate the utility of the Assembly altogether. This can only mean that the bureaucracy will be in an even stronger position to perpetuate its influence. Similarly, the time limit of 120 days in which the newly elected National Assembly will have to draft an acceptable constitution is also somewhat unreasonable. No doubt the parliamentarians will produce the required document, but with martial law weighing on their deliberations the end-product will reflect the possible, not the desirable.

At this writing, President Yahya Khan's well-intentioned offering must be considered regressive, not forward-looking. It could be exceedingly divisive and may well lead to Pakistan's having to become a permanent garrison state. Moreover, there are no new faces on the political horizon. Thus President Yahya Khan is already considered a savior by some. It will indeed be a curious political marriage should Yahya Khan be compelled, for reasons of expediency, to take to his bosom Sheikh Mujibur Rahman. The Sheikh has long coveted high office. As Prime Minister he could for a time maintain the fiction of East–West Pakistan unity. Eventually, however, this alliance would probably wither, and the grand design become little more than a holding action. But by then it will be too late to correct Yahya's policies.

What are the alternatives? Although the country is in the process of playing out the present scenario (and it may well be too late even to suggest that there are other courses of action) the following can at least be stated for the record.

There is no need to play up the dramatic. While the Basic Democrats no longer act as an electoral college, there is no reason why the union councils cannot function as primary units of local self-government. They can certainly continue to organize socioeconomic programs. Arrangements must also be found to legitimate the presidency while strengthening the power of popular representatives at all levels. The direct election of national and provincial legislators might make political parties more responsive to popular aspirations; it can also help in drawing together urban and rural life-styles. The election of the governors would grant more autonomy to the provinces and should reduce some fundamental East-West Pakistan antagonisms.

In the urban centers, popularly elected individuals can assume the "political" positions now held by bureaucrats. Elected officials would govern the cities. For example, the police would come under their jurisdiction as would all other public administrators. The intelligentsia, especially its youthful members, must be made a part of the rural picture. After intensive training these young people could be assigned to wards and union councils in the modified village government system.

The student population represents a large, relatively untapped reservoir of enthusiastic, fairly well educated people.[7] They could be mobilized and formed into a Youth Corps. But such a corps, to perform constructively, will have to be developed from within the student and general intellectual community. The fact that General Yahya Khan has already announced his intention to recruit a National Literacy Corps of some 72,000 young people is intriguing. Pakistan's sophisticated youth want desperately to participate in the country's development, but past governments have made cynics of most. Like the political parties, they are more and more prone to stress socialistic procedures and objectives and are less and less comfortable with thoughts of personal privilege and power. Ahmad Iqbal Bukhari, writing in *The Pakistan Student* of March 1970, insists:

> The destiny of our country depends upon our ideals and our values. We will always remain backward if we do not care for the happiness of our people and do not address ourselves to the problems of alleviating suffering and exploitation.

As if to warn Pakistan's new leaders Bukhari adds:

> The glamor and the symbols of affluence of the West, which attract most of our attention, have resulted in dragging at the chariot wheels of the West by the elite of our country. In reality, we have no common grounds with the affluent countries of the West . . . our common bonds are with the struggling, the have-nots.

It is obvious that the Yahya Khan government will have to treat the students with the utmost tact and delicacy. A new generation of enlightened young people has surfaced. Eventually, it must take up the reins of leadership in all prominent sectors of society. It is impossible to say with any precision how they will perform but some things are certain: they will be conditioned by a different environment, will possess changed values, and will be motivated by distinctly collective philosophies. All the more reason why the present government must think with vision and act with determination. If coherent transition is to be made possible, new beginnings cannot wait for the conventional elite to pass from the scene.

Thus those who heretofore have been called Basic Democrats might now be identified as Councillors or People's Representatives. They should be given the political and administrative powers outlined in Chapter 7. It is absolutely necessary to dispense with the discredited term "Basic Democracies" while preserving the idea of rural government—albeit with the bureaucrats in a strictly service role. A more acceptable designation might be "Local Self-Government System." At the same time it is imperative that this change not be perceived as one of nomenclature alone. A formidable task! Every effort should be made to construct genuinely popular units of local government. Moreover, grassroots development should be permitted to set its own pace. In other words, immediate material progress may have to be sacrificed for limited psychological and attitudinal gains. Ronald C. Nairn would appear to support this thesis. He has written:

> This seems to be the critical element. . . . Neither the liberal West nor the totalitarian West display tolerance or, least of all, civility toward leisurely change based on its own worth and occurring at a rate those affected desire. Yet in the end, substantive change in a lasting and non-traumatic form comes about with measured tread.[8]

Perhaps this is what Pakistani students are also trying to say.

Because the major emphasis will be on responsible mobilization of all societal sectors, the politico-administrative legacy left by the British should be modified. It is therefore incumbent on President Yahya Khan to restudy the recommendations of the 1962 Pay and Services Commission. The public release of the Commission's report was an important first step. The new Commission, which is charged with the task of structural reorganization, is the second. Both are significant, but real proof of Yahya Khan's determination to revolutionize the bureaucracy will rest on what is done from now on. The establishment of twenty-one panels to review the Fourth Five Year Plan (1970–75) suggests that the elite services will once more be treated with exceptional circumspection, despite some purges. Fourteen of the panels are chaired by members of the "steel frame." Certainly the skeptics have a right to recall their heightened anticipation and final despair in 1958–59. Will history repeat itself once more?

Pakistan may well have survived because the old bureaucratic hierarchy was retained, but it is difficult to conceive of sustained progress if this edifice remains in its present form. An institution like the Civil Service of Pakistan (CSP) has made its contribution and like the Muslim League—which found itself philosophically, structurally, and operationally dysfunctional after independence—should be absorbed in a new, unified administrative system.

Just as some efforts are underway to break the monopolistic character of big business there should be no hesitancy in curbing the elite bureaucrats. If concentration of economic wealth is no longer tolerable, how can the concentration of politico-administrative power be justified? When the great industrial and financial families are being pressured to relinquish their holdings there should be no reluctance in restricting the elite services. Pakistan's new life-style should not only reflect a diffusion of ownership of enterprises but wider political opportunities for the country's growing middle class.

Appendix A

ALLOCATION OF MINISTERIAL PORTFOLIOS
(Central Government)

(October 28, 1958—March 25, 1969)

DIVISION	MINISTER
Cabinet	President F. M. Mohammad Ayub Khan
Commerce	Zulfikar Ali Bhutto
	Muhammad Hafizur Rahman
	Abdul Qadir
	Wahiduzzaman
	Ghulam Faruque
	Nawabzada Abdul Ghaffar Khan of Hoti
Communications	Khan F. M. Khan
	Khan Abdus Sobur Khan
Defense	President F. M. Mohammad Ayub Khan
	Vice Admiral A. R. Khan
Economic Affairs	Mohammad Shoaib
	President F. M. Mohammad Ayub Khan
Education	Habibur Rahman
	Akhter Husain
	Lt. Gen. W. A. Burki
	A. K. M. Fazlul Quader Chowdhury
	A.T.M. Mustafa
	Kazi Anwarul Haque
Establishment	President F. M. Mohammad Ayub Khan
	Lt. Gen. K. M. Sheikh
	President F. M. Mohammad Ayub Khan
Finance	Mohammad Shoaib
	Abdul Qadir
	Mohammad Shoaib
	N. M. Uquaili
Food and Agriculture	Muhammad Hafizur Rahman
	Lt. Gen. Mohammad Azam Khan
	Lt. Gen. K. M. Sheikh
	A. K. M. Fazlul Quader Chowdhury
	Rana Abdul Hamid
	A. H. M. Shams-ud-Doha

199

DIVISION	MINISTER
Foreign Affairs	Manzur Qadir
	Mohammad Ali
	Zulfikar Ali Bhutto
	S. Sharifuddin Pirzada
	Mian Arshad Husain
Health	Lt. Gen. W. A. Burki
	Abdul Monem Khan
	Wahiduzzaman
	Rana Abdul Hamid
	A. K. M. Fazlul Quader Chowdhury
	Wahiduzzaman
	Al-Haj Abd-Allah Zaheer-ud-Din (Lal Mia)
Home Affairs	Lt. Gen. K. M. Sheikh
	Zakir Husain
	Habibullah
Industries	Abul Kasem Khan
	Zulfikar Ali Bhutto
	Abdullah-al-Mahmood
	Altaf Husain
	Ajmal Ali Chowdhury
Information and Broad- casting	Habibur Rahman
	Zulfikar Ali Bhutto
	Akhter Husain
	Zulfikar Ali Bhutto
	Akhter Husain
	Habibur Rahman
	A. K. M. Fazlul Quader Chowdhury
	A. T. M. Mustafa
	Abdul Waheed Khan
	Khwaja Shahabuddin
Kashmir Affairs	Zulfikar Ali Bhutto
	Akhter Husain
	Lt. Gen. W. A. Burki
	Zulfikar Ali Bhutto
	Habibullah
	Ali Akbar Khan
	Vice Admiral A. R. Khan
Labour and Social Welfare	Lt. Gen. W. A. Burki
	Abdul Monem Khan
	Wahiduzzaman
	Rana Abdul Hamid

DIVISION	MINISTER
	A. K. M. Fazlul Quader Chowdhury
	Wahiduzzaman
	Al-Haj Abd-Allah Zaheer-ud-Din (Lal Mia)
Law	Mohammad Ibrahim
	Manzur Qadir
	Muhammad Munir
	Shaikh Khursheed Ahmad
	S. M. Zafar
Natural Resources	Zulfikar Ali Bhutto
	Abdullah-al-Mahmood
Parliamentary Affairs	Manzur Qadir
	Muhammad Munir
	Shaikh Khursheed Ahmad
Planning	President F. M. Mohammad Ayub Khan
Rehabilitation and Works	(This division underwent various organizational changes during the period. The different forms it took and their allocations are indicated below.)
Rehabilitation	Lt. Gen. Mohammad Azam Khan
	Lt. Gen. K. M. Sheikh
Works, Irrigation, and Power	Abul Kasem Khan
	Lt. Gen. Mohammad Azam Khan
Water and Water Resources	Lt. Gen. Mohammad Azam Khan
Works, Housing, and Water Resources	Lt. Gen. Mohammad Azam Khan
	Lt. Gen. K. M. Sheikh
Rehabilitation and Works	Lt. Gen. K. M. Sheikh
Rehabilitation	Lt. Gen. K. M. Sheikh
Works	Zulfikar Ali Bhutto
Rehabilitation and Works	A. K. M. Fazlul Quader Chowdhury
	Zulfikar Ali Bhutto
	Rana Abdul Hamid
States and Frontier Regions	Lt. Gen. K. M. Sheikh
	President F. M. Mohammad Ayub Khan

Appendix B—Basic Democracies Structure

IN RURAL AREAS

DIVISIONAL COUNCIL (16)
Chairman: Commissioner
Members: half or more elected, remainder officials

DISTRICT COUNCIL (78)
Chairman: Deputy Commissioner
Members: half or more elected, remainder officials

TEHSIL OR THANA COUNCIL (630)
Chairman: Subdivision Officer, Tehsildar or Circle Officer
Members: half or more chairmen of union councils, remainder officials

UNION COUNCIL (7, 614) OR TOWN COMMITTEE (220)
Chairman: elected
Members: 10 to 15 elected

IN URBAN AREAS

MUNICIPAL COMMITTEE (108)
Chairman: Official
Members: half chairmen of union committees, half officials

CANTONMENT BOARD (29)
Chairman: Official
Members: half chairmen of union committees, half officials

UNION COMMITTEE (888)
Chairman: elected
Members: elected

W A R D S

NOTE: The municipal corporations of Karachi and Lahore are also represented at the divisional level and are administratively subordinate to the West Pakistan Department of Basic Democracies and Local Government. These two corporations have component union committees.

SOURCE: Guthrie S. Birkhead, ed., *Administrative Problems in Pakistan* (Syracuse: Syracuse University Press, 1966), p. 32.

Notes

PART ONE
1. Ayub Khan: Genesis, Philosophy, and Reforms

1. Samuel Huntington, *Political Order in Changing Societies,* (New Haven: Yale University Press, 1968), p. 251.

2. See Appendix A for the allocation of Ministerial Portfolios.

3. Shoaib and Bhutto were considered the most successful members of the President's cabinet mainly because they survived so long. *Today* (Karachi), April 1965, p. 11.

4. For an intimate account of Ayub's early years see: Mohammad Ayub Khan, *Friends Not Masters: A Political Autobiography* (New York: Oxford University Press, 1967), pp. 1–8.

5. Col. Mohammad Ahmad, *My Chief* (Lahore: Longmans, Green and Co., 1960), p. 28.

6. Major General Fazal Muqueem Khan writes that his "appointment was universally acclaimed." This statement does not seem accurate on studying the historical record. See: *The Story of the Pakistan Army* (Karachi: Oxford University Press, 1963), p. 138, and Ayub's own account in *Friends Not Masters,* that "every officer felt that unless he was made Commander-in-Chief no one would believe that he had done well in life. . . . Perfectly sensible people, Brigadiers and Generals, would go about bemoaning their lot. Each one of them was a Bonaparte, albeit an unhappy one." Mohammad Ayub Khan, *op. cit.,* pp. 37–38.

7. M.H. Bhatti, *The Saviour of Pakistan* (Lahore: Star Book Depot, 1960), p. 42.

8. See: Government of Pakistan, *Correspondence Regarding No-War Declaration with Prime Minister's Statement* (Karachi, 1950).

9. See: Government of Pakistan, *Constituent Assembly Debates,* March 21, 1951.

10. Keith Callard, *Pakistan: A Political Study* (New York: The Macmillan Company, 1957), p. 279.

11. Col. Mohammad Ahmad, *op. cit.,* pp. 36–37.

12. Mohammad Ayub Khan, *op. cit.,* pp. 37–42.

13. Mohammad Ayub Khan, *ibid.,* p. 186.

14. See: Z.A. Suleri, *Pakistan's Lost Years* (Lahore: Progressive Papers Ltd., 1962).

15. *Ibid.,* pp. 125–148.

16. See: *Morning News* (Dacca), June 24, 1958; July 7, 1958; September 7, 1958; September 9, 1958. *The Pakistan Times* (Lahore), September 24, 1958; October 5, 1958. K.B. Sayeed, "Collapse of Parliamentary Democracy in Pakistan," *The Middle East Journal,* Vol. 13, No. 4 (1959), and Wayne A. Wilcox, *Pakistan: The Consolidation of a Nation* (New York: Columbia University Press, 1963).

17. See: Government of East Pakistan, *Report of the Enquiry into incidents that took place on the 20th and 23rd September, 1958, in the Chambers and Premises of the East Pakistan Assembly* (Dacca, 1959); *The Mail* (Dacca) May 13, 1959; John E. Owen, "Problems in Pakistan—The Background to Martial Law," *Internationale Spectator,* Jargang 13, No. 11 (8 Juni, 1959).

18. Fazal Muqueen Khan, *op. cit.,* pp. 202–203.

19. Mohammad Ayub Khan, *op. cit.,* p. 75.

20. *Chronology of Events in Pakistan, October 1958—June 1964* (Karachi: Pakistan Publications, 1965), p. 5.

21. Z.A. Suleri, *Politicians and Ayub* (Lahore: Lion Art Press, Ltd., 1965), pp. 210–12.

22. M.A. Khuhro, a former Chief Minister of Sind and Defense Minister in the Central Government at the time of the coup, was accused of selling a car on the black market. Later he was charged with forgery and cheating the government. Although he could have received at least fourteen years' imprisonment, Khuhro was later released as were the other politicians. *Muhammad Ayub Khuhro v. Pakistan,* P.L.D. 1960, SC 237. See also: Sharifuddin Pirzada, *Fundamental Rights and Constitutional Remedies in Pakistan* (Lahore: All Pakistan Legal Decisions, 1966), p. 476.

23. The author acknowledges the controversial nature of this subject. See: Ralph Braibanti, *Research on the Bureaucracy of Pakistan* (Durham, N.C.: Duke University Press, 1966), pp. 291–99.

24. Sher Hasan Khan, "A Short History of Corruption in the Country," (mimeographed, Lahore 1964), pp. 8–9, presented at the Symposium on Corruption (Lahore), May 25–26, 1964.

25. Malik Khuda Bakhsh Bucha addressed a distinguished gathering of officers and members of intelligentsia at the Pakistan Administrative Staff College in Lahore on June 4, 1966. Speaking on the subject of "the three main problems of administration," the West Pakistani Education Minister "points out that learned men with secular knowledge and those with religious knowledge should combine to evolve a system of education and institutions which would put the nation on the right path. He pointed out that the entire nation was in the transitional stage—still looking to the days past. Nostalgically, dissatisfied with the present and unaware of the future. It was only the combined efforts of the officers, the intelligentsia and the public which could help the nation to progress . . . it was not necessary to wait for the higher officers or leaders in order to become honest." *News and Views* (Pakistan Administrative Staff College, Lahore), January 1967, p. 63.

26. The Pay and Services Commission Report is examined in Chapter 6.

27. *The Gazette of Pakistan (Extraordinary),* 7 August 1959.

28. Sher Hasan Khan, *op. cit.,* p. 18. EBDO in effect replaced PODO which was considered inadequate because the former only affected persons who held public offices. Herbert Feldman, *Revolution in Pakistan* (London: Oxford University Press, 1967), pp. 80–81.

29. Karl Von Vorys insists that "approximately seven thousand persons were thus excluded from political life." Karl Von Vorys, *Political Development in Pakistan* (Princeton: Princeton University Press, 1965), p. 190. Feldman notes: "The exact number who became, in the cant of the times 'ebdoed' does not seem to have been published. In 1960, it was reported that in East Pakistan alone some

3,000 persons had been proceeded against under EBDO. However, the majority opted to retire or were disqualified. If this is so, then it seems that almost 6,000 persons laboured under the EBDO disqualification." Feldman, *op. cit.,* p. 81. The original EBDO ruling was repealed on December 31, 1966. See also: The National Assembly *Debates,* July 14, 1962.

30. *Iftikhar-ud-Din v. Muhammad Sarfraz,* P.L.D. 1961, LAH. 842, and *Iftikhar-ud-Din v. Muhammad Sarfraz,* P.L.D., 1961, SC 585.

31. *Press and Publications Ordinance, No. XV of 1960,* para. 23, cl. 1(i), pp. 9–10.

32. See: *The Gazette of Pakistan (Extraordinary)*, October 27, 1959; Lawrence Ziring, "The Administration of Basic Democracies: The Working of Democracy in a Muslim State," *Islamic Studies,* December 1965. Also the author's chapter in: G.S. Birkhead, ed., *Administrative Problems in Pakistan* (Syracuse: Syracuse University Press, 1966).

33. *Basic Democracies Manual No. 1* (Comilla, 1959), p. 4.

34. S.A. Saeed, *President without Precedent* (Lahore: Lahore Book Depot, 1960), p. 7.

35. Government of West Pakistan, *Democracy at the Doorstep* (Karachi, n.d.), pp. 14–19. It need only be reemphasized that a large percentage of eligible voters in the U.S., as in other Western countries, fail to exercise their voting privilege.

36. Khalid B. Sayeed, *The Political System of Pakistan* (Boston: Houghton, Mifflin Company, 1967), pp. 96–97.

37. Khalid bin Sayeed, like many others, felt the land reforms were mostly on paper, that little land had been taken from the landlords and distributed to the tenants, and that the land tenure problem was relatively unchanged. *Ibid.,* pp. 95–97.

38. *Chronology of Events in Pakistan, op. cit.,* p. 51.

2. POLITICAL RENAISSANCE: OLD ISSUES, NEW DIMENSIONS

1. See: *Report of the Constitution Commission, Pakistan* (Karachi: Government of Pakistan Press, 1961); *Constitution Commission, Pakistan: Questionnaire* (Karachi: Government of Pakistan Press, 1960); *Annexures to the Questionnaire Issued by the Constitution Commission* (Karachi: Government of Pakistan Press, 1960). G.W. Choudhury describes how the Ayub Government organized its review of the Constitution Commission's recommendations. *Democracy in Pakistan* (Dacca: Green Book House, 1963), pp. 176–77.

2. S.A. Saeed, *op. cit.,* p. 8.

3. Ralph Braibanti, "The Higher Bureaucracy of Pakistan," in Ralph Braibanti, ed., *Asian Bureaucratic Systems Emergent From the British Imperial Tradition* (Durham, N.C.: Duke University Press, 1966), pp. 221–22.

4. Mohammad Ayub Khan, *op. cit.,* pp. 207–26.

5. *Report of the Constitution Commission, op. cit.,* p. 70.

6. Von Vorys, *op. cit.,* p. 215.

7. *Report of the Constitution Commission, op. cit.,* pp. 68–77.

8. Mohammad Ayub Khan, *op. cit.,* p. 217.

9. *Report of the Constitution Commission, op. cit.,* pp. 79–80.

10. *The Constitution: The President Addresses the Nation* Government of Pakistan, The Bureau of National Reconstruction (Karachi, 1962), p. 12.

11. *Ibid.*, p. 10.

12. *Ibid.*, p. 14.

13. Government of Pakistan, *The Constitution: Question-Answer Meeting between F.M. Mohammad Ayub Khan and the Editors of Pakistan Newspapers* (Karachi, March 1, 1962), p. 2.

14. *Ibid.*, pp. 14–15.

15. *Ibid.*, pp. 14–15. Fundamental rights were made justiciable with the acceptance of the First Amendment to the Constitution.

16. *Ibid.*, p. 16.

17. *My Manifesto,* published broadcast by F.M. Mohammad Ayub Khan, March 23, 1962, Government of Pakistan (Karachi) p. 2.

18. *Ibid.*, p. 2.

19. *Ibid.*, p. 3.

20. On March 27, 1962, the presidential cabinet ruled that in the future there will be no nominations to any tier of the Basic Democracies, thereby removing one of the principal objections to the system. See Appendix B for the diagram explaining the arrangement.

21. My Manifesto, *op. cit.,* p. 6.

22. Karl Von Vorys gives some of these statistics. See: Von Vorys, *op. cit.,* pp. 236–37.

23. The government in 1964 contemplated organizing courses in parliamentary procedure, modern administrative practices, etc., for members of the National Assembly. Attendance was to be voluntary and the courses were to have been held at the Pakistan Administrative Staff College in Lahore. Because of the turbulence in the country, however, these expectations were never satisfied.

24. As Foreign Minister, Manzur Qadir probably did not have the full confidence of members of the Foreign Service. Many career officers believed he was ill equipped for the post, and the fact that he was better known for his domestic activities seems to add credence to this argument. Nonetheless, it was Manzur Qadir who launched Pakistan's "independent" foreign policy and it was not surprising that the President appointed him to head Pakistan's delegation to the Geneva Conference for the arbitration of the Rann of Kutch dispute with India in 1965–66.

25. The National Assembly was dominated by members supporting the President. Hence, legislative enactments were generally in the form of presidential ordinances. For an examination of the President's ordinance-making power, see: Braibanti, "The Higher Bureaucracy of Pakistan," *op. cit.,* pp. 230–42.

26. See the author's article: "Pakistan Then and Now: East and West" *Asia,* No. 7, Spring, 1967, pp. 4–6.

27. Questions and Answers, *op. cit.,* p. 11.

28. V.D. Mahajan, *The Constitution of Pakistan* (Lahore: Munawar Book Depot, 1965), p. 113.

29. *Ibid.*, p. 115.

30. *Ibid.*, p. 116.

31. *Ibid.*, p. 116.

32. G.W. Choudhury, *op. cit.,* p. 220.

33. *The London Times,* June 24, 1963.

34. *Report of Five Members of the Finance Commission* (Dacca: Government of East Pakistan, 1963), p. 11.

35. The Central Government has considerably increased its financial contribution to East Pakistan, as can be seen from these official figures. Combined financial contributions to the provinces rose from Rs. 714.2 million in 1958–59 to Rs. 2,305.1 million in the revised figures for 1962–63, an increase of 222.7 percent, rising further in 1963–64 to an estimated Rs. 3,000 million, showing an increase of 320 percent over the 1958–59 figures. East Pakistan was allocated Rs. 359.7 million in 1958–59. The allocation rose to Rs. 1,199 million in 1962–63 and to Rs. 1,550 million in 1963–64. East Pakistan is in effect getting slightly more in the way of development funds than West Pakistan. At the same time, it should be pointed out that money going into the Indus Water Basin scheme is not included in the development budget and if it were it would give West Pakistan a decided advantage over East Pakistan. *Ministry of Finance: Five Years of Revolutionary Government, 1958–63* (Karachi: Government of Pakistan Press, 1965), p. 8.

36. This subject is treated in slightly more detail in Chapters 4 and 5.

37. The Agartala Conspiracy is described in Chapter 5.

3. INTERNATIONAL EVENTS: THE DOMESTIC IMPACT

1. See: Wayne A. Wilcox, "China's Strategic Alternatives in Southern Asia" (unpublished manuscript), New York, 1967; and the accounts prior to the Chinese attack by Girilal Jain, *India Meets China in Nepal* (New Delhi: Asia Publishing House, 1959), and P.C. Chakravarti, *India's China Policy* (Bloomington: Indiana University Press, 1962).

2. Mohammad Ayub Khan, "The Pakistan-American Alliance: Stresses and Strains," *Foreign Affairs,* January 1964, p. 203.

3. Reference need only be made to Mohammad Ali's appointment as Prime Minister by the late Governor General Ghulam Mohammad in 1953 after the unceremonious dismissal of Khwaja Nazimuddin. Mohammad Ali (Bogra) was an ambitious individual, but he always knew his future was dependent on how he served those in high places. Principles were never permitted to interfere with personal need. Keith Callard, *op. cit.,* p. 23.

4. Bhutto's sentiments are amply portrayed in his most recent book *The Myth of Independence* (London: Oxford University Press, 1969).

5. Hasan Askari, "Problems of Leadership," *Today* (December, 1964), p. 11.

6. Z.A. Bhutto, *Foreign Policy of Pakistan* (Karachi: Pakistan Institute of International Affairs, 1964), p. 13.

7. Z.A. Bhutto, *The Quest for Peace* (Karachi: Pakistan Institute of International Affairs, 1966), p. 74.

8. This is not an easy subject to analyze. Even the President's more skillful critics acknowledge he was no demagogue. Favorable comments were forthcoming from this vocal group when he announced his new Cabinet of Talents after the January 1965 election victory. His previous cabinet gave representation to the politicians, but they were summarily dismissed as "pseudo-politicians" who though pretending to be "sincere" had only "their own selfish axe to grind." *Trend* (Karachi), August 1964, p. 11. The new cabinet was distinguished from the previous one by "the presence of men who are committed to definite stands." *Today* (Karachi), April 1965, p. 11. In other words, it appears the apolitical, almost bureaucratic composition of the 1965 cabinet was preferred because it

did represent clear-cut positions on vital issues. In this one can observe the sub-conscious preference for administrative as against political rule, despite the claims of the opposition for true representative government. The fact that neither Ayub nor his ruling bureaucrats were revered does not mean they were not respected. The overwhelming interest of young people in gaining a place in the bureaucracy is a case in point. The inability of the majority to secure these positions is what creates frustrations. This problem is studied in part in Chapters 4, 5, 6, and 7.

9. See: "Pakistan Can't Win," *The Economist* (London) September 11–17, 1965.

10. B.L. Sharma's polemic, if nothing else, highlights Indian suspicions concerning Pakistan-China collaboration. *The Pakistan-China Axis* (New Delhi: Asia Publishing House, 1968).

11. The text of the China-Pakistan Border Agreement will be found in Appendix I of Sharma, *ibid.,* pp. 183–86.

12. Wayne Wilcox notes: "When the U.S. protested a Karachi-Peking air link, Pakistan replied that BOAC had been seeking it for some time, but that the Chinese smiled on their application because of cordial diplomatic relations. When the Pakistan-China border agreement was signed, Pakistan said that surely the United States did not want to see Pakistan at war with China since the U.S. was pledged to come to Pakistan's aid." *India, Pakistan and the Rise of China* (New York: Walker and Company, 1964), p. 84.

13. *Morning News* (Karachi), December 30, 1964. See: *The Pakistan Times* (Lahore), December 8th and 9th 1964, and the article by Z. A. Suleri, "Ah, Our American Ally," in that same paper on December 11, 1964; *The New York Times,* June 16, 1967, 20:3.

14. During the campaign the Jamaat-i-Islami was suspected of taking United States funds for the publication *Risala Tarjumanul Quran,* but the organization and its leader Maulana Maudoodi have consistently displayed their displeasure with the U.S.

15. See: Bhutto's speech reprinted in *The Pakistan Times* (Lahore), December 13, 1964.

16. B.L. Sharma, *op. cit.,* pp. 115–20; Bhutto, *Myth of Independence, op. cit.,* pp. 131–34, 156–88.

17. See: L. Ziring, "The Establishment of the RCD Secretariat," *Pakistan Administrative Staff College Quarterly* (Lahore), December 1965.

18. Hasan Askari, "Attitudes to China," *Today,* August 1965 (Karachi), p. 15.

4. POST-TASHKENT POLITICS

1. *Muslimnews International* (Karachi), November 1965, p. 2.

2. See: *The Pakistan Times,* December 8, 9, 10, 11, 14, 17, 21, 1964. This student unrest led to the establishment of a Commission on Student Problems and Welfare which did not present its report until early in 1966.

3. *The Pakistan Times* (Lahore), February 9, 1966.

4. Douglas E. Ashford, *National Development and Local Reform: Political Participation in Morocco, Tunisia and Pakistan* (Princeton: Princeton University Press, 1967), p. 258.

5. *The Pakistan Student* (New York), March–April 1967, p. 5.

6. *Report of the Commission on Student Problems and Welfare,* Ministry of Education (Karachi: Government of Pakistan Press, 1966), p. 189.

7. "Students and Tolerance," *Today* (Karachi), December 1964, p. 7.

8. *Ibid.*, p. 7.

9. *Ibid.*, p. 7.

10. *The Pakistan Student, op. cit.*, p. 3.

11. *Ibid.*, p. 5.

12. *Ibid.*, p. 5. For an objective, highly intelligent analysis of educational problems in the developing countries see: Muhammad Shamsul Huq, *Education and Development Strategy in South and Southeast Asia* (Honolulu: East-West Center Press, 1965). That the Yahya Khan government recognizes the student dilemma can be seen in the May 1969 decisions to decentralize educational activities and provide more autonomy for the universities and colleges. For a summary of the new educational policy see: *Pakistan Affairs* (Washington, D.C.), Vol. XXII, No. 7, May 31, 1969.

13. *Peoples Age* (Bombay), June 8, 1947; See also: P.C. Joshi, *East Pakistan and the Unity of Bengal* (Bombay: People's Publishing House, n.d.).

14. *The Pakistan Times,* February 18, 1966.

15. *The Pakistan Times,* February 1, 1966.

16. The East Pakistani demands were included in Mujibur Rahman's Six Point Program which are enumerated in Chapter 2. See also: *Rezaual Malik v. Government of East Pakistan* P.L.D. 1968, Dacca 382; *Malik Ghulam Gilani v. The Government of West Pakistan,* P.L.D. 1967, SC 373.

17. See: *Emergency Laws in Pakistan,* Vol. XVII, No. 12 (Lahore: All Pakistan Legal Decisions, 1965).

18. *The Pakistan Times,* February 18, 1966.

19. *The Pakistan Times,* December 10, 1966.

5. RIOTS, REPRESSION, AND RETREAT

1. For a general survey of Pakistan's agricultural performance, see: Report of the Commission on International Development, *Partners in Development* (New York: Praeger, 1969), pp. 307–309.

2. See: E.H. Clark and M. Ghaffar, "An Analysis of Private Tubewell Costs," *Research Report No. 79,* Pakistan Institute of Development Economics (mimeographed), March 1969; H. Kaneda and M. Ghaffar, "Output Effects of Tubewells on the Agriculture of the Punjab: Some Empirical Results," *Research Report No. 80,* PIDE (mimeographed), March 1969.

3. Commission for International Development, *op. cit.,* p. 309.

4. Gustav F. Papanek, *Pakistan's Development: Social Goals and Private Incentives* (Cambridge, Mass.: Harvard University Press, 1967), p. 10.

5. *Ibid.,* p. 71.

6. *Ibid.,* p. 72.

7. *Ibid.,* p. 140.

8. Commission for International Development, *op. cit.,* p. 310.

9. Papanek, *op. cit.,* p. 67.

10. The text of the prosecution statement as read by the Chairman of the Special Tribunal was reprinted in *The Pakistan Times,* June 20, 1968.

11. *The New York Times,* November 29, 1968, 14:1.

12. President Ayub Khan in a broadcast to the nation December 1, 1968.

13. *Ibid.*

14. *The Statesman* (Calcutta), March 24, 1969.

15. Speech over Radio Pakistan by F.M. President Mohammad Ayub Khan, March 25, 1969.

16. *Pakistan Affairs*, Vol. XXII, No. 4, April 1, 1969, p. 3.

PART II

6. THE BUREAUCRATIC LEGACY

1. Rowland Egger, *The Improvement of Public Administration in Pakistan* (Karachi: The Inter Services Press, 1953), p. 5.

2. Keith Callard, *Political Forces in Pakistan* (Hong Kong: Hong Kong University Press, 1959), pp. 24–25.

3. *Ibid.*, p. 22. See also: *The Expanding Role of the Civil Servant in Pakistan's Democratic Structure* (Lahore: Social Science Research Center, 1960).

4. Masihuzzaman, *District Administration and other Essays* (unpublished manuscript), 1964, pp. 140–41.

5. Egger, *op. cit.*, p. 7. See also: Henry F. Goodnow, *The Civil Service of Pakistan: Bureaucracy in a New Nation* (New Haven: Yale University Press, 1964).

6. That the services are not entirely to blame for their aloofness from society, or for their unwillingness to accept the politicians, can be seen in this excerpt from a speech delivered by Mohammad Ali Jinnah, the father of the Pakistan nation, on April 14, 1948:
"The first thing I want to tell you is that you should not be influenced by any political pressure, by any political party or individual politician. . . . Services are the backbone of the State. Governments are formed, governments are defeated, prime ministers come and go, ministers come and go, but you stay on and, therefore, there is a very real responsibility placed on your shoulders. You should have no hand in supporting this political leader or that: this is not your business. . . . I wish also to take the opportunity of impressing upon our leaders and politicians in the same way that if they ever try to interfere with you and bring political pressure to bear on you—which leads to nothing but corruption, bribery and nepotism which is a horrible disease . . . if they try and interfere with you in this way, I say, they are doing nothing but a disservice to Pakistan." Quoted in: M.R. Inayat, ed., *Perspectives in Public Administration* (Lahore: Society for Public Administration: Civil Service Academy, 1962), pp. 1–2. See also: Inayatullah and A.T. Khan, *Administrator and the Citizen* (Lahore: The National Institute of Public Administration, 1964).

7. Muneer Ahmad in his penetrating study insists the bureaucratic "attitude" had hardened long before the arrival of the British who simply turned it to their own uses. Muneer Ahmad, *The Civil Servant in Pakistan* (Lahore: Oxford University Press, 1964), p. 5.

8. Egger, *op. cit.*, p. 8.

9. Muneer Ahmad, *op. cit.*, pp. 3–13.

10. Other observers have reached the identical conclusion. See: Inayatullah, ed., *District Administration in West Pakistan* (Peshawar: Pakistan Academy for Rural Development, 1964); Inayatullah, ed., *Bureaucracy and Development in Pakistan* (Peshawar: Pakistan Academy for Rural Development, 1962); Inayatullah, *Basic*

Democracies District Administration and Development (Peshawar: Pakistan Academy for Rural Development, 1964); Afzal Mahmood, *Law and Principles of Local Government: Basic Democracies* (Lahore: All Pakistan Legal Decisions, 1964).

11. Albert Gorvine, "Administrative Reform," in G.S. Birkhead, ed., *Administrative Problems in Pakistan* (Syracuse, Syracuse University Press, 1966), p. 189.

12. Bernard L. Gladieux, *Reorganization of Pakistan Government for National Development* (mimeographed version), May 1955, p. 73.

13. Ralph Braibanti has written at length on the importance of maintaining an independent judiciary capable of balancing the power of the bureaucracy. See his chapter in Joseph La Palombara, ed., *Bureaucracy and Political Development* (Princeton: Princeton University Press, 1963), and Braibanti, ed., *Asian Bureaucratic Systems Emergent from the British Imperial Tradition* (Durham, N.C.: Duke University Press, 1966).

14. Gladieux, *op. cit.,* p. 101.

15. See: Gorvine's analysis in Birkhead, *op. cit.*

16. F.M. Mohammad Ayub Khan, *My Manifesto* (Karachi: Government of Pakistan Press, March 23, 1961), pp. 2–3.

17. L.S.S. O'Malley, *The Indian Civil Service: 1601–1930,* Second Edition (London: Frank Cass and Company, Ltd., 1965), p. 168.

18. Quoted in O'Malley, *ibid.,* p. 173.

19. Amitai Etzioni, *Modern Organizations* (Englewood Cliffs, N.J.: Prentice-Hall, 1964), p. 19.

20. See for example: R.R. Kabeer, *Administrative Policy of the Government of Bengal (1870–1890)* (Dacca: National Institute of Public Administration, 1965), pp. 136–40.

21. *Trend* (Karachi), August 1964, p. 10.

22. *Today* (Karachi), December 1964, p. 5.

23. Hugh Tinker, *The Foundations of Local Self-Government in India, Pakistan and Burma* (London: The Athlone Press, 1954), p. 42.

24. Government of Pakistan, *Report of the Pay and Services Commission, 1959–1962* (Karachi: Government of Pakistan Press, 1962), p. 12.

25. The Pay and Services Commission comments on this matter. ". . . there shall be eliminated all machinery by which the powers and authority exclusively pertaining to the chosen representatives is being exercised, under antiquated or colonial conceptions of administration, by persons or groups inside the Services." *Ibid.,* p. 9.

26. Braibanti states that some fifty British officers remained to serve Pakistan. By 1954 there were only thirteen or about 6 percent of the elite CSP cadre as then constituted. By 1965 only three were still on the service list. Ralph Braibanti, "The Higher Bureaucracy of Pakistan," in *Asian Bureaucratic Systems Emergent from the British Imperial Tradition,* Braibanti, ed., (Durham, N.C.: Duke University Press, 1966), p. 245.

27. *Report of the Pay and Services Commission, 1959–1962, op. cit.,* p. 65.

28. In 1967, discounting the probationers undergoing training in the Civil Service Academy in Lahore, there were only 467 active members in the CSP. Government of Pakistan, *Gradation List of the Civil Service of Pakistan* (Rawalpindi: Government of Pakistan Press, 1967).

29. Braibanti, *op. cit.,* pp. 255–56.

30. *Report of the Pay and Services Commission, 1959–1962, op. cit.,* p. 67.

31. *Ibid.,* pp. 68–69.

32. *Ibid.,* p. 69.

33. The Report envisioned a "basic officer" class which they called the Junior Executive Grade (JEG). Entry into the CES would come through this body. *Ibid.,* pp. 48–52.

34. *Ibid.,* p. 55.

35. *Ibid.,* p. 56.

36. *Ibid.,* p. 57.

37. *Ibid.,* p. 57.

38. *Ibid.,* pp. 57–58.

39. *Ibid.,* pp. 23–37.

40. *Ibid.,* p. 31. It is only necessary to add that the CSP's "hold on all directory posts was maintained by the same system of reservation which was first enacted in 1793."

41. *Ibid.,* p. 74.

42. *Ibid.,* p. 74. Braibanti also comments: "In Imperial India the aspiration to transfer responsibility to local bodies was not always hailed with enthusiasm by the ICS and was foretold by the Montagu-Chelmsford Report as a problem; so the orthodox bureaucracy of Pakistan has not always appreciated the community-development idea." Ralph Braibanti, *Research on the Bureaucracy of Pakistan* (Durham, N.C.: Duke University Press, 1966), p. 201.

43. *Pay and Services Commission Report, op. cit.,* p. 77.

44. *Ibid.,* p. 78.

45. *Ibid.,* p. 81.

46. G. Mueenuddin succeeded J.D. Hardy as Secretary, Establishment Division, and was appointed to the Commission on June 27, 1961. Ali Asghar was an original member of the Commission.

47. *Report of the Pay and Services Commission, op. cit.,* p. 447.

48. *Ibid.,* p. 447.

49. *Ibid.,* p. 447.

50. *Ibid.,* p. 448.

51. *Ibid.,* p. 448.

52. *Ibid.,* p. 448.

53. *Ibid.,* p. 449.

54. *Ibid.,* p. 450.

55. *The Pakistan Student,* Vol. XIII, No. 3 (March–April 1967), p. 2

56. All quotations are from *The Pakistan Times,* December 2, 1966.

57. *The Pakistan Times,* December 3, 1966.

58. Begum Yazdani Malik said she had certain vital facts relevant to the matter which were known exclusively to her and which, for certain reasons, she had kept secret even from her husband. The Committee felt this would be extraneous to the matter under investigation (the alleged altercation in the Assembly), and therefore decided against accepting her request. *The Pakistan Times,* December 10, 1966.

59. *The Pakistan Times,* December 10, 1966.

60. *Ibid.,* December 10, 1966. It is also interesting to note that on the same day that the Committee's report was publicized charges were being brought against another CSP officer who had allegedly threatened an MPA. In this case the Deputy Commissioner of Jacobabad was the target. *Ibid.*

61. See: Government of Pakistan, *Decisions of the Cabinet on the Report of the Provincial Administration Commission* (Karachi: Government of Pakistan Press, 1962). In the Introduction the Pay and Services Commission voiced its displeasure with the Government policy creating a number of other commissions charged with studying administrative reform while it was still deliberating on the basis of its own mandate. It was even more annoyed that reforms should be introduced before the Commission's Report was ready for scrutiny. "This was done despite instructions issued by the Central Government at the instance of this Commission in May, 1960 . . . that no major changes were to be made in the structure and organisation of services and establishments, or in respect of their terms and conditions pending completion of our work." One explanation for countermanding the original order may have been to head off the recommendations of the Pay and Services Commission and institute needed reforms which could be more speedily and more realistically implemented. *Report of the Pay and Services Commission, op. cit.,* p. 3.

62. Government of Pakistan, *Report of the Provincial Re-organisation Committee, Part II—East Pakistan* (Dacca: Government of East Pakistan Press, April 1962), pp. 1–2.

63. Government of Pakistan, *Report of the Standing Organisation Committee on the Reorganisation of the Functions and Structure of the Central Government in the Light of the New Constitution* (Rawalpindi: Government of Pakistan Press, April 1962), p. 3.

64. *Ibid.,* p. 3.

65. *Ibid.,* p. 3.

66. Braibanti, *Asian Bureaucratic Systems, op. cit.,* p. 350.

67. This conclusion is also drawn in: Ralph H. Retzlaff, *Village Government in India* (London: Asian Publishing House, 1961).

7. POWER, POLITICS, AND THE RURAL SCENE

1. Akhter Hameed Khan, *Community and Agricultural Development in Pakistan* (East Lansing: Michigan State University Occasional Papers, January 1969), pp. 23–34.

2. S.A. Rahim, *Communication and Personal Influence in an East Pakistan Village* (Comilla: Academy for Rural Development, 1965), p. 7.

3. See: Government of Pakistan, *Census of Pakistan, 1961* (Karachi: Government of Pakistan Press, 1961); *Pakistan: Basic Facts* (Rawalpindi: Government of Pakistan Press, 1966); Government of Pakistan, *The Third Five Year Plan (1965–1970)* (Karachi: Government of Pakistan Press, 1965).

4. Government of Pakistan, *Population Census of 1961,* Census Bulletin No. 2, p. 14. See also: Kingsley Davis, *The Population of India and Pakistan* (Princeton: Princeton University Press, 1951), and H.N. Gardezi, *A Study of Pakistan Society,* Vol. I (mimeographed manuscript), 1964.

5. *Report of the Land Reforms Commission for West Pakistan* (Lahore: Government Printing, West Pakistan, 1959); *The East Bengal State Acquisition and Tenancy Act, 1950* (Dacca: East Pakistan Press, 1957); A.F.A. Hussain, *Human and Social Impact of Technological Change in Pakistan,* Vol. I (Dacca: Oxford University Press, 1956), p. 48.

6. Rahim, *op. cit.,* pp. 26–33.

7. A. Mannan and N. Ahsan, "Factors Associated with Limited Growth of Village Cooperatives and of Membership," *Research and Survey Bulletin No. 12* (Comilla: Academy for Rural Development, January 1965), p. 6.

8. For an interesting study of the historical antecedents of societal change in East Pakistan, see: Nazmul Karim, *Changing Society in India and Pakistan* (Dacca: Oxford University Press, 1956).

9. Barrington Moore writes: "Caste served, and still serves, to organize the life of the village community, the basic cell of Indian society and the fundamental unit into which it tended to disintegrate wherever and whenever a strong ruler was lacking." It can also be noted that caste, whether in Pakistan or India, reinforces the power of the dominant village landlord. Barrington Moore, Jr., *Social Origins of Dictatorship and Democracy* (Boston: Beacon Press, 1966), pp. 317–18.

10. Inayatullah, *Perspectives in the Rural Power Structure in West Pakistan* (Karachi: U.S.A.I.D. Mission to Pakistan, 1963), p. 5.

11. *Ibid.,* p. 32.

12. *Ibid.,* p. 33.

13. *Ibid.,* p. 34.

14. *Ibid.,* p. 46.

15. Moore, *op. cit.,* p. 316.

16. *Ibid.,* p. 317.

17. Lloyd I. Rudolph and Susanne Hoeber Rudolph, *The Modernity of Tradition* (Chicago: Chicago University Press, 1967), pp. 253–93.

18. *Basic Democracies Manual No. 1* (Comilla: Academy for Rural Development, 1959), p. 4.

19. Shahid Javed Burki, "West Pakistan's Rural Works Program: A Study in Political and Administrative Response," *The Middle East Journal,* Vol. 23, No. 3, Summer 1969, pp. 331–35.

20. See: Zuhra Waheed, *Contacts Between Villagers and Public Officials in Three Villages of Lyallpur Tehsil* (mimeographed, Lahore: Pakistan Administrative Staff College, 1964).

21. It is not to be implied that political patronage is involved. What is meant here is that votes are bought and sold for a few rupees.

22. *Personal Correspondence,* May 22, 1965.

23. Zuhra Waheed explains how desperately the villagers need astute, honest local leaders. She tells the story of a tax realization officer, perhaps a lambardar, going to villages to collect taxes on crops that higher authority had exempted that year. The officer demanded the tax on threat of punishment. But then another villager appeared who was familiar with the government ruling. He later reported: "But for my timely arrival on the scene he could have fleeced them thoroughly. Next day I came to know that he [the officer] had taken away more than 1000 rupees from the adjoining village by this ruse, since there was no educated person present in that village to stop him from doing so." Z. Waheed, *op. cit.,* p. 25.

24. Inayatullah, *op. cit.,* pp. 48–49.

25. Government of Pakistan, *Future Role of Basic Democracies* (Rawalpindi: Government of Pakistan Press, 1965), p. 27.

26. Inayatullah, *op. cit.,* pp. 50–51.

27. Huntington, *op. cit.,* pp. 412–17.

28. Inayatullah, *op. cit.,* p. 63.

29. Government of Pakistan, *Planners in the Making* (Karachi: Government of Pakistan Press, 1963), p. 10.

30. *Ibid.*, p. 16.

31. Government of East Pakistan, *A Retrospect on Basic Democracies in East Pakistan* (Dacca: East Pakistan Government Press, 1965), p. 7.

32. *Ibid.*

33. See: Felix Greene, *A Curtain of Ignorance* (Garden City, N.Y.: Doubleday and Co., 1963); Jiri Kolaja, *Workers Councils: The Yugoslav Experience* (London: Tavistock Publications, 1965); and Akhter Hameed Khan, *op. cit.*, p. 19.

34. See the author's chapter in: G.S. Birkhead, ed., *Administrative Problems in Pakistan* (Syracuse: Syracuse University Press, 1966), pp. 54–56.

35. *Ibid.*, p. 57.

36. *Ibid.*, p. 57.

37. The reports prepared by the Cooperative Institute of Management in West Pakistan reveal some of the special difficulties in building workable cooperatives in that province. A number of these reports are worthy of careful study. They are: Ejvind Sondgergaard, *Marketing of Agricultural Products through Cooperatives in West Pakistan* (mimeographed, Lahore, n.d.); Peder Elkjaer, *Problems of Cooperative Banking in West Pakistan* (mimeographed, Lahore, 1965); Peder Elkjaer, *Central Cooperative Banks* (mimeographed, Lahore, n.d.); Gunnar Bols Bundgaard, *Consumer's Supply Societies* (mimeographed, Lahore, 1964); Gunnar Bols Bundgaard, *Draft of Plan for the Establishment of a One-Unit Wholesale and Rental Cooperative Society in West Pakistan* (mimeographed, Lahore, 1965).

38. M. Nurul Huq, *Cooperation As a Remedy for Rural Poverty* (Comilla: Academy for Rural Development, 1963), p. 8.

39. Government of Pakistan, *The Third Five Year Plan, 1965–1970* (Karachi: Government of Pakistan Press, 1965), p. 533; Government of Pakistan, *The Outline of the Third Five Year Plan 1965–1970* (Karachi: Government of Pakistan Press, 1964), p. 236.

40. *The Comilla Project: An Experiment in Rural Administration* (mimeographed, Lahore: Pakistan Administrative Staff College, 1965), pp. 4–53.

41. Shahid Javed Burki, "West Pakistan's Rural Works Program: A Study in Political and Administrative Response," *The Middle East Journal*, Vol. 23, No. 3, Summer 1969, p. 337.

42. See: Government of East Pakistan, *Works Programme through Basic Democracies, 1963–64* (Dacca: Government of East Pakistan Press, 1964); and Government of West Pakistan, *West Pakistan Rural Works Programme Evaluation Report 1963–64,* Second Edition (Lahore: Government of West Pakistan Press, 1965).

43. Burki, *op. cit.*, p. 341.

44. Some regional institutes do exist, however. The operation at Nator in Rajshahi district in East Pakistan is a case in point. See: *Second Annual Report 1964–1965,* Nator Rural Development Project, 1965.

45. Qaiser Ali Khan, "Administration of Social Welfare in West Pakistan," in seminar papers for Session Eleven (mimeographed, Lahore: Pakistan Administrative Staff College, 1966), p. 148.

46. See: *Report of the Training Committee* (Lahore: Government of West

Pakistan Press, August 1964); *The Story of NIPA* (Karachi: U.S.A.I.D., 1966); *NIPA-Dacca, Development and Training Plan,* 1960–70 (Dacca: National Institute of Public Administration, May 1964); *The Pakistan Administrative Staff College* (Lahore: PASC, 1965).

47. *Muslim Family Laws Ordinance, 1961* (Lahore: Government of West Pakistan Press, 1961); *Conciliation Courts Ordinance, 1961* (Lahore: Government of West Pakistan Press, 1961).

48. Inayatullah and Q.M. Shafi, *Dynamics of Development in a Pakistani Village* (Peshawar: Academy for Rural Development, 1964), pp. 164, 167–68.

49. Inayatullah and Shafi, *ibid.,* p. 168.

50. Leonard Binder, *Religion and Politics in Pakistan* (Berkeley: University of California Press, 1961), pp. 3–6.

51. Dr. Fazlur Rahman, a director of the Central Institute of Islamic Research, and Akhter Hameed Khan, director of the Academy for Rural Development at Comilla, have been especially active in this regard. Both men have tried to convince the ulema and devout alike that there are no Islamic injunctions against family planning. A representative tract is: Akhter Hameed Khan, *Islamic Opinions on Contraception* (Dacca: Government of East Pakistan Press, 1963). See also: A. Majud Khan, "Family Planning in Three Villages," (mimeographed, Comilla: Academy for Rural Development, 1964).

52. M.I. Choudhury and M.A. Khan, *Pakistani Society: A Sociological Analysis* (Lahore: Noorsons, 1964), p. 236.

53. See: Masihuzzaman, *Community Development* (unpublished manuscript, 1964); Mir Naseem Mahmood, "The Revival of Village-AID, A Plan," (mimeographed, Lahore 1963); R.W. Jones, *Suggestions on Evaluation of Pakistan Village AID Program* (mimeographed, The Ford Foundation, n.d.); H.B.M. Homji, "Community Development and Local Government," in S.M.Z. Rizvi, ed., *A Reader in Basic Democracies* (Peshawar: Academy for Rural Development, 1961), pp. 186–212; Government of Pakistan, *Village AID: Five Year Plan* (Karachi: Government of Pakistan Press, 1956); Masihuzzaman, *Community Development and its Audience* (Lahore: Government Printing, West Pakistan, 1960); J.D. Mezirow and Frank A. Santopolo, "Community Development in Pakistan: The First Five Years," *International Social Sciences Journal,* Vol. XII, No. 3, September 1960; Government of West Pakistan, *Community Development Information,* Vol. I, No. 8, May 1960; Government of Pakistan, *Physical Achievements of Village AID Development Areas in East Pakistan, West Pakistan, Azad Kashmir, Gilgit and Baltistan* (Karachi: Government of Pakistan Press, 1960); Government of Pakistan, *Hasnie Sub-Committee Report* (Karachi: Government of Pakistan Press, 1960).

54. S.M. Rizvi, M.A. Subzwari, C.M. Sharif, *Consolidation of Holdings* (Peshawar: Academy for Rural Development, 1965), pp. 2–4.

55. Restrictions were imposed on partition of joint holdings and alienation of holdings under paragraphs 23 and 25 of the Martial Law Regulation 64. The Department of Consolidation set up by the Ordinance has now been amalgamated with the Revenue Department and the Commissioners and Deputy Commissioners have been made directly responsible for the work carried out under the scheme. *Ibid.,* pp. 6–7.

56. For the plight of the Sind tenant farmers see the classic: *Report of the Government Hari Enquiry Committee, 1947–48* (Government of Sind, n.p., 1948).

57. Hassan Habib, "Some Thoughts of Village Community Projects for Pakistan," (mimeographed, Lahore, 1955), p. 3.

58. *Ibid.,* p. 4.

8. END OF AN ERA

1. This comment does not ignore the pre-independence rural development schemes which are identified with F.L. Brayne and Malcolm Darling. It would be edifying to read: F.L. Brayne, *Better Villages* (London: Oxford University Press, 1937); Sir Malcolm Darling, *The Punjab Peasant in Prosperity and Debt,* Fourth edition (London: Oxford University Press, 1947).

2. David E. Apter, *The Politics of Modernization* (Chicago: Chicago University Press, 1965), p. 66.

3. See: C.J.H. Hayes, *Nationalism: A Religion* (New York: Macmillan, 1960); R. Niebuhr and Paul E. Sigmund, *The Democratic Experience: Past and Prospects* (New York: Praeger, 1969).

4. "In common usage the term 'nationalism' is simply a synonym for 'anti-imperialism.' But in a more basic sense, nationalism denotes a specific form of cohesiveness and integration within society. It was the absence within Indian society of this kind of *national* cohesiveness that had made possible the establishment of British rule in the first place." Martin Deming Lewis, "Gandhi and the Historian," (mimeographed paper delivered at the Conference of the American Historical Association, New York, 1966).

5. The term "class" seems more appropriate when discussing urban groups, although "caste" is not to be discounted.

6. *The Pakistan Times,* October 3, 1964.

7. Ideology is employed here only in its secular political meaning. All Muslim Pakistanis in one way or another adhere to something which they call "Islamic Ideology," but this has neither been defined by them nor is it discussed in this book. Although Pakistan is officially called an "Islamic Republic" by no stretch of the imagination should it be considered a theocratic state.

8. More than thirty-seven reform commissions and committees were set up by the Ayub Government between 1958 and 1966. These bodies reviewed virtually every aspect of Pakistani society and government but as has been noted not all the reports were released, let alone their recommendations implemented.

9. Some important members of the West Pakistan Bar Council were A.K. Brohi, Mahmood Ali Quasuri, Sardar Mohammad Zufrullah, Arbab Sikandar Khan, Dr. Nasim Hassan Shah, Abid Hasan Manto, and M. Anwar.

10. All quotations are from the *Morning News* (Dacca), December 15, 1966.

11. *Morning News* (Dacca), December 12, 1966.

12. *The Pakistan Times* (Lahore), December 15, 1966.

13. *The Pakistan Observer* (Dacca), April 10, 1966.

14. *The Pakistan Times* (Lahore), October 31, 1966.

15. See: Karl Wittfogel's somewhat uneven study, *Oriental Despotism* (New Haven: Yale University Press, 1956).

16. *The Pakistan Times* (Lahore), December 3, 1966.

17. For a complete list of National Assembly Members and affiliations in March 1966 see: *Morning News* (Dacca), May 7, 1966. At the time the govern-

ment Muslim League had 127 members, the official opposition 13, the independent group 6, and the unattached independents 6.

18. *Dacca Times,* March 26, 1965.

19. The President's true intentions are questioned in: "B.D.'s Muslim League," *Today* (Karachi), June 1965, p. 11.

20. Rafiq Rahbar, "When Spring Comes in Winter," *The Concept of Pakistan* (Karachi, November 1966), p. 49.

21. That this is not necessarily uncharacteristic can be viewed in Martin Deming Lewis' suggestion that Gandhi may have employed the identical tactics for similar reasons. He intimates that Gandhi wished to arouse the peasants against the British but at the same time keep them "safely under middle class control" in order to prevent them from launching a violent revolution. "Gandhi and the Historians," *op. cit.,* p. 11.

EPILOGUE

1. *The Gazette of Pakistan (Extraordinary),* February 26, 1970.

2. Alfred Diamant, "The Nature of Political Development," J.L. Finkle and R.W. Gable, eds., *Political Development and Social Change* (New York: John Wiley and Sons, 1966), p. 92.

3. Lucian W. Pye, "The Concept of Political Development," *ibid.,* p. 89.

4. Hannah Arendt, *On Revolution* (New York: The Viking Press, 1963), p. 108.

5. See: Manfred Halpern, "Conflict, Violence and the Dialectics of Modernization," paper presented at the 64th Annual Meeting, American Political Science Association, Washington, D.C., September 6, 1968.

6. See: Richard E. Neustadt, *Presidential Power* (New York: John Wiley and Sons, 1960), p. 10.

7. Atiquzzaman Khan, "Pakistani Youth and the National Front," *The Concept of Pakistan* (Karachi, November 1966), pp. 9–15.

8. Ronald C. Nairn, "Patterns of Social and Cultural Evolution—Needed: A Reordering of the Western Imagination on Asia," *Asia,* No. 15, Summer 1969, pp. 56–57.

BIBLIOGRAPHY

GOVERNMENT PUBLICATIONS

Central Government

Annexures to the Questionnaire Issued by the Constitution Commission. Karachi: Government of Pakistan Press, 1960.

Census of Pakistan, 1961. Karachi: Government of Pakistan Press, 1961.

Correspondence Regarding No-War Declaration with Prime Minister's Statement. Karachi: Government of Pakistan Press, 1950.

Constituent Assembly, *Debates.* Karachi: Government of Pakistan Press, 1951.

Constitution Commission Questionnaire. Karachi: Government of Pakistan Press, 1960.

Decisions of the Cabinet on the Report of the Provincial Administration Commission. Karachi: Government of Pakistan Press, 1962.

Democracy at the Doorstep. Karachi: Government of Pakistan Press, n.d.

Egger, Rowland. *The Improvement of Public Administration in Pakistan.* Karachi: The Inter Services Press, 1953.

Emergency Laws in Pakistan, Volume XVII, No. 12. Lahore: All Pakistan Legal Decisions, 1965.

Future Role of Basic Democracies. Rawalpindi: Government of Pakistan Press, 1965.

Gladieux, Bernard L. *Reorganization of Pakistan Government for National Development.* Mimeographed, May 1955.

Gradation List of the Civil Service of Pakistan. Rawalpindi: Government of Pakistan Press, 1967.

Ministry of Finance. *Five Years of Revolutionary Government 1958–63.* Karachi: Government of Pakistan Press, 1965.

National and Provincial Assemblies (Elections) Act, 1964. Lahore: All Pakistan Legal Decisions, 1964.

National and Provincial Assemblies (Elections) Rules, 1965. Lahore: All Pakistan Legal Decisions, 1965.

Pakistan: Basic Facts. Karachi: Government of Pakistan Press, 1966.

Report of the Commission on National Education. Karachi: Government of Pakistan Press, 1959.

Report of the Commission on Student Problems and Welfare. Karachi: Government of Pakistan Press, 1966.

Report of the Constitution Commission. Karachi: Government of Pakistan Press, 1961.

Report of the Pay and Services Commission, 1959–1962. Karachi: Government of Pakistan Press, 1962.

Report of the Standing Organisation Committee on the Reorganisation of the Functions and Structure of the Central Government in the Light of the New Constitution. Rawalpindi: Government of Pakistan Press, 1962.

The Constitution of Islamic Republic of Pakistan (As modified up to the 28th February, 1965). Karachi: Government of Pakistan Press, 1965.

The Electoral College Act (IV of 1964). Lahore: All Pakistan Legal Decisions, 1964.

The Electoral College Rules, 1964. Lahore: All Pakistan Legal Decisions, 1964.

The Gazette of Pakistan (Extraordinary). Karachi: Government of Pakistan Press.

The Muslim Family Laws Ordinance, 1961 (VII of 1961). Lahore: All Pakistan Legal Decisions, 1965.

The National Assembly. *Debates.* July 14, 1962.

The Outline of the Third Five Year Plan, 1965–1970. Karachi: Government of Pakistan Press, 1964.

The Presidential Election Rules, 1964. Lahore: All Pakistan Legal Decisions, 1964.

The Presidential Elections Act, 1964 with the Referendum Act, 1964. Lahore: All Pakistan Legal Decisions, 1964.

The Press and Publications Ordinance (XV of 1960). Lahore: All Pakistan Legal Decisions, 1964.

The Second Five Year Plan, 1960–1965. Karachi: Government of Pakistan Press, 1960.

The Third Five Year Plan, 1965–1970. Karachi: Government of Pakistan Press, 1965.

Village AID: Five Year Plan. Karachi: Government of Pakistan Press, 1956.

East Pakistan Government

A Retrospect on Basic Democracies in East Pakistan. Dacca: East Pakistan Government Press, 1965.

Report of the Enquiry into Incidents that took place on the 20th and 23rd September, 1958, in the Chambers and Premises of the East Pakistan Assembly. Dacca: Government of East Pakistan Press, 1959.

Report of Five Members of the Finance Commission. Dacca: Government of East Pakistan Press, 1963.

Report of the Provincial Reorganisation Committee, Part II—East Pakistan. Dacca: Government of East Pakistan Press, 1962.

The East Pakistan State Acquisition and Tenancy Act, 1950. Dacca: East Pakistan Press, 1957.

West Pakistan Government

Consolidation of Holdings Ordinance, 1960 (VI of 1960). Lahore: All Pakistan Legal Decisions, 1964.

Masihuzzaman. *Community Development and Its Audience*. Lahore: Government Printing, West Pakistan, 1960.

Report of the Government Hari Enquiry Committee 1947–48. n.p.: Government of Sind, 1948.

Report of the Land Reform Commission of West Pakistan. Lahore: Government Printing, West Pakistan, 1959.

Report of the Training Committee. Lahore: Government of West Pakistan Press, 1964.

The Colonization of Government Lands (Punjab) Act, 1912 (V of 1912). Lahore: All Pakistan Legal Decisions, 1964.

West Pakistan Maintenance of Public Order Ordinance, 1960 (XXXI of 1960). Lahore: All Pakistan Legal Decisions, 1964.

OTHER MATERIALS

Ahmad, Colonel Mohammad. *My Chief*. Lahore: Longmans, Green and Company, 1960.

Ahmad, Muneer. *The Civil Servant in Pakistan*. Lahore: Oxford University Press, 1964.

Ahmed, Manzooruddin. *Pakistan: The Emerging Islamic State*. Karachi: Allies Book Corporation, 1966.

Ali, Syed Anwer. *Election Laws in Pakistan*. Karachi: Syed Publications, 1965.

Anwar, Muhammad Rafi. *Presidential Government in Pakistan*. Second Edition. Lahore: Caravan Book House, 1964.

Apter, David. *The Politics of Modernization*. Chicago: Chicago University Press, 1965.

Arendt, Hannah. *On Revolution*. New York: Viking Press, 1963.

Ashford, Douglas E. *National Development and Local Reform: Political Participation in Morocco, Tunisia and Pakistan*. Princeton: Princeton University Press, 1967.

Ayub Khan, Mohammad. *Friends Not Masters: A Political Autobiography*. London: Oxford University Press, 1967.

Ayub Khan, Mohammad. "The Pakistan-American Alliance: Stresses and Strains," *Foreign Affairs*. January, 1964.

Beg, Aziz. *The Quiet Revolution*. Karachi: Pakistan Patriotic Publications, 1959.

Bhatti, M.H. *The Saviour of Pakistan*. Lahore: Star Book Depot, 1960.

Bhutto, Zulfikar Ali. *Foreign Policy of Pakistan*. Karachi: Pakistan Institute of International Relations, 1964.

Bhutto, Zulfikar Ali. *The Myth of Independence.* London: Oxford University Press, 1969.

Bhutto, Zulfikar Ali. *The Quest for Peace.* Karachi: Pakistan Institute of International Relations, 1966.

Binder, Leonard. *Religion and Politics in Pakistan.* Berkeley: University of California Press, 1961.

Birkhead, Guthrie S. (ed.). *Administrative Problems in Pakistan.* Syracuse: Syracuse University Press, 1966.

Braibanti, Ralph. *Research on the Bureaucracy of Pakistan.* Durham, N.C.: Duke University Press, 1966.

Braibanti, Ralph (ed.). *Asian Bureaucratic Systems Emergent from the British Imperial Tradition.* Durham, N.C.: Duke University Press, 1966.

Brayne, F.L. *Better Villages.* London: Oxford University Press, 1937.

Burki, Shahid Javed. "West Pakistan's Rural Works Program: A Study in Political and Administrative Response." *The Middle East Journal.* Vol. 23, No. 3 (1969).

Callard, Keith. *Pakistan: A Political Study.* New York: The Macmillan Company, 1957.

Callard, Keith. *Political Forces in Pakistan, 1947–1959.* Hong Kong: Hong Kong University Press, 1959.

Chakravarti, P.C. *India's China Policy.* Bloomington, Ind.: Indiana University Press, 1962.

Choudhury, G.W. *Constitutional Development in Pakistan.* London: Longmans, Green and Company, 1959.

Choudhury, G.W. *Democracy in Pakistan.* Dacca: Green Book House, 1963.

Choudhury, M.I. and Khan, M.A. *Pakistani Society: A Sociological Analysis.* Lahore: Noorsons, 1964.

Commission on International Development. *Partners in Development.* New York: Praeger, 1969.

Darling, Sir Malcolm. *The Punjab Peasant in Prosperity and Debt.* Fourth Edition. London: Oxford University Press, 1947.

Davis, Kingsley. *The Population of India and Pakistan.* Princeton: Princeton University Press, 1951.

Etzioni, Amitai. *Modern Organizations.* Englewood Cliffs, N.J.: Prentice-Hall, 1964.

Feldman, Herbert. *Revolution in Pakistan.* London: Oxford University Press, 1967.

Finkle, J.L. and Gable, R.W. (eds.). *Political Development and Social Change.* New York: John Wiley and Sons, 1966.

Gardezi, H.N. *A Study of Pakistan Society.* Manuscript, Lahore: 1964.

Goodnow, Henry P. *The Civil Service of Pakistan: Bureaucracy in a New Nation.* New Haven: Yale University Press, 1964.

Hayes, C.J.H. *Nationalism: A Religion.* New York: Macmillan, 1960.

Hameed Khan, Akhter. *Community and Agricultural Development in Pakistan.* East Lansing, Mich.: Michigan State University, 1969.

Haq, Mahbub ul. *The Strategy of Economic Planning.* Karachi: Oxford University Press, 1963.

Huntington, Samuel. *Political Order in Changing Societies.* New Haven: Yale University Press, 1968.

Huq, M. Nurul. *Cooperation as a Remedy for Rural Poverty.* Comilla: Academy for Rural Development, 1963.

Huq, Muhammad Shamsul. *Education and Development Strategy in South and Southeast Asia.* Honolulu: East-West Center Press, 1965.

Hussain, A.F.A. *Human and Social Impact of Technological Change in Pakistan.* Two Volumes. Dacca: Oxford University Press, 1956.

Inayat, M.R. (ed.). *Perspectives in Public Administration.* Lahore: Civil Service Academy, 1962.

Inayatullah. *Basic Democracies, District Administration and Development.* Peshawar: Pakistan Academy for Rural Development, 1964.

Inayatullah (ed.). *Bureaucracy and Development in Pakistan.* Peshawar: Pakistan Academy for Rural Development, 1962.

Inayatullah (ed.). *District Administration in West Pakistan.* Peshawar: Pakistan Academy for Rural Development, 1964.

Inayatullah. *Perspectives in the Rural Power Structure in West Pakistan.* Karachi: U.S. AID Mission to Pakistan, 1963.

Inayatullah and Khan. A.T. (eds.). *Administrator and the Citizen.* Lahore: The National Institute of Public Administration, 1964.

Inayatullah and Shafi, Q.M. *Dynamics of Development in a Pakistani Village.* Peshawar: Academy for Rural Development, 1964.

Jain, Girilal. *India Meets China in Nepal.* New Delhi: Asia Publishing House, 1959.

Jennings, Sir Ivor. *Constitutional Problems in Pakistan.* London: Cambridge University Press, 1957.

Joshi, P.C. *East Pakistan and the Unity of Bengal.* Bombay: Peoples Publishing House, n.d.

Kabeer, R.R. *Administrative Policy of the Government of Bengal (1870–1890).* Dacca: National Institute of Public Administration, 1965.

Karim, Nazmul. *Changing Society in India and Pakistan.* Dacca: Oxford University Press, 1956.

La Palombara, John (ed.). *Bureaucracy and Political Development.* Princeton: Princeton University Press, 1963.

LaPorte, Robert. "Succession in Pakistan: Continuity and Change in a Garrison State," *Asian Survey,* IX, 11, November 1969.

Mahajan, Vidya Dhar. *The Constitution of Pakistan.* Lahore: Munawar Book Depot, 1965.

Mahmood, Afzal. *Law and Principles of Local Government: Basic Democracies.* Lahore: All Pakistan Legal Decisions, 1964.

Mahmood, Shaukat. *The Constitution of Pakistan*. Lahore: The Pakistan Times Publications, 1965.

Masihuzzaman. *District Administration and Other Essays*. Unpublished manuscript, 1964.

Minattur, Joseph. *Martial Law in India, Pakistan and Ceylon*. The Hague: Martinus Nijhoff, 1962.

Moore, Jr., Barrington. *Social Origins of Dictatorship and Democracy*. Boston: Beacon Press, 1966.

Muqueen Khan, Major General Fazal. *The Story of the Pakistan Army*. Karachi: Oxford University Press, 1963.

Neustadt, Richard. *Presidential Power*. New York: John Wiley and Sons, 1960.

Niebuhr, Reinhold and Sigmund, Paul E. *The Democratic Experience: Past and Prospects*. New York: Praeger, 1969.

O'Malley, L.S.S. *The Indian Civil Service: 1601–1930*. Second Edition. London: Frank Cass and Company, 1965.

Owen, John E. "Problems in Pakistan—The Background to Martial Law," *International Spectator*, Jargang 13, No. 11 (8 Juni 1959).

Papanek, Gustav F. *Pakistan's Development: Social Goals and Private Incentives*. Cambridge, Mass.: Harvard University Press, 1967.

Pirzada, Sharifuddin. *Fundamental Rights and Constitutional Remedies in Pakistan*. Lahore: All Pakistan Legal Decisions, 1966.

Qureshi, Anwar Iqbal. *Pakistan Marches on the Road to Prosperity*. Lahore: Ferozsons, 1965.

Qureshi, Ishtiaq Husain. *The Struggle for Pakistan*. Karachi: University of Karachi Press, 1965.

Rahim, S.A. *Communication and Personal Influence in an East Pakistan Village*. Comilla: Academy for Rural Development, 1965.

Rizvi, S.M.Z. (ed.). *A Reader in Basic Democracies*. Peshawar: Academy for Rural Development, 1961.

Rose, Saul (ed.). *Politics in Southern Asia*. London: Oxford University Press, 1962.

Rudolph, Lloyd and Rudolph, Susanne Hoeber. *The Modernity of Tradition*. Chicago: Chicago University Press, 1967.

Rushbrook-Williams, L.R. *The State of Pakistan*. London: Faber, 1962.

Sayeed, Khalid B. "Collapse of Parliamentary Democracy in Pakistan," *The Middle East Journal*, Vol. 13, No. 4 (1959).

Sayeed, Khalid Bin. *Pakistan: The Formative Phase*. Karachi: Pakistan Publishing House, 1960.

Sayeed, Khalid B. *The Political System of Pakistan*. Boston: Houghton Mifflin Company, 1967.

Sharma, B.L. *The Pakistan-China Axis*. New Delhi: Asia Publishing House, 1968.

Social Science Research Council. *The Expanding Role of the Civil Servant in Pakistan's Democratic Structure*. Lahore: SSRC, 1960.

Stephens, Ian. *Pakistan*. New York: Praeger, 1963.

Suleri, Z.A. *Pakistan's Lost Years*. Lahore: Progressive Papers Ltd., 1962.

Suleri, Z.A. *Politicians and Ayub*. Lahore: Lion Art Press, 1965.

Symonds, Richard. *The Making of Pakistan*. London: Faber, 1950.

Tinker, Hugh. *The Foundations of Local Self-Government in India, Pakistan and Burma*. London: Athlone Press, 1954.

Tinker, Hugh. *India and Pakistan: A Political Analysis*. Revised Edition. New York: Praeger, 1967.

Von Vorys, Karl. *Political Development in Pakistan*. Princeton: Princeton University Press, 1965.

Wilcox, Wayne A. *India, Pakistan and the Rise of China*. New York: Walker and Company, 1964.

Wilcox, Wayne A. *Pakistan: The Consolidation of a Nation*. New York: Columbia University Press, 1963.

Wriggins, W. Howard. *The Ruler's Imperative: Strategies for Political Survival in Asia and Africa*. New York: Columbia University Press, 1969.

Ziring, Lawrence. "The Administration of Basic Democracies: The Working of Democracy in a Muslim State," *Islamic Studies*. December 1965.

Ziring, Lawrence. "Pakistan Then and Now: East and West," *Asia*. Spring 1967.

INDEX